MISTAKES TO SUCCESS:
LEARNING AND ADAPTING WHEN THINGS GO WRONG

Robert Giloth and Colin Austin

iUniverse, Inc.
New York   Bloomington

Mistakes to Success:
Learning and Adapting When Things Go Wrong

iUniverse books may be ordered through booksellers or by contacting:

iUniverse
1663 Liberty Drive
Bloomington, IN 47403
www.iuniverse.com
1-800-Authors (1-800-288-4677)

ISBN: 978-1-4502-4683-5 (sc)
ISBN: 978-1-4502-4861-7 (ebk)

Printed in the United States of America

iUniverse rev. date: 08/18/2010

Contents

Acknowledgements

We would like to thank the Annie E. Casey Foundation for sponsoring this important work on mistakes and learning and the two gatherings on the subject, and for providing support for the authors. MDC has been an enthusiastic partner from the beginning and has supported the study of mistakes in the community economic development field.

Three anonymous reviewers improved the manuscript greatly, and The Hatcher Group, especially Tom Waldron, has edited the chapters and shepherded the book to publication. We would like to thank colleagues who joined our gatherings to discuss mistakes: Maureen Conway, Tom Dewar, Barbara Endel, Isao Fujimoto, Josh Hawley, Gloria Cross Mwase, John Padilla, Brandon Roberts, Charles Rutheiser, Bill Schweke, and Beadsie Woo. In addition, Jillien Dube, Sheryl Lewis, and Jordi Waggoner played important roles in this project, and we appreciate the help and support of David Matheson and Catherine Matheson.

Most of all, we want to thank the authors themselves for being brave enough to write about their mistakes and what they learned.

1

A Primer on Learning from Mistakes

Robert Giloth and Colin Austin

President Barack Obama and his administration are making unprecedented investments in identifying, cultivating, and replicating social innovations. This unique federal effort seeks to build on the strengths of the nonprofit sector to improve the lives of children, families, and communities. At the same time, foundations are designing *prize* strategies to encourage innovation, spurred by the success of the X PRIZE. An overarching consideration in both approaches is that hunting for successful social innovations may not be sufficient: it is only a part of the answer. A treasure trove of innovation mistakes and failures exists, mostly out of sight, that could inform the design and replication of a next generation of social innovations. We need to know more about what hasn't worked and why. We need to learn from our mistakes.

Mistakes to Success: Learning and Adapting When Things Go Wrong is a collection of essays about social innovation failures, showcasing a small portion of this untapped resource. Two key challenges motivate the book. First, the overall challenge of solving intractable social problems like poverty is exacerbated by our inability to design and implement solutions that are effective and stick. We must admit that our progress has not been sufficient and that more innovation is needed. Second, our propensity for ignoring and hiding, rather than disclosing and reflecting on, failed approaches limits our ability for real learning and improved investments. In other words, the learning crisis we face in the nonprofit sector impedes our ability to be more effective in reaching better outcomes for families and communities (Giloth, 2007). We must ask ourselves whether we have an innovation problem or a failure-recognition problem, and consider what capacities, tools, incentives, and supports are needed to reflect more usefully about success and failure.

This introductory chapter makes the case for more explicit recognition of failures as a part of ongoing learning and design for community economic development (CED), those investments, institutions, and policies seeking to improve the economic circumstances of families and communities. CED includes workforce development, asset building, business creation and expansion, affordable housing, economic development, and community organizing. CED innovations are prone to failure because they can pursue resource redistribution, market change, policy change, and political empowerment, all at the same time. In other words, CED initiatives, by definition, grapple with uncertainty about problems and approaches.

Background

Mistakes to Success is the product of a multiyear search for stories illuminating CED failures. We solicited two rounds of papers from practitioners, scholars, investors, and policymakers and convened two sessions at which authors presented and discussed draft papers. From those, we identified the chapters included in this book. In the end, our CED stories focus mostly on workforce development—getting, keeping, and advancing in jobs—but also touch on a range of related topics, such as social enterprise, asset building, performance measurement, partnerships, scale, replication, and links with economic development.

The book calls attention to the untapped resource of mistakes in the nonprofit field that can be used to improve the performance of social investments. Unfortunately, the nonprofit field is generally reluctant to expose mistakes to a public that is already skeptical about the role and effectiveness of nonprofits. In fact, philanthropy itself is guilty not only for not naming its own mistakes but also for blaming nonprofits for lack of capacity when things do not turn out as intended (Giloth & Gewirtz, 2009). Of course, the nonprofit sector is not alone in its reluctance to acknowledge and reflect on mistakes. But the good news is that in recent years more people in the nonprofit sector are paying attention to mistakes as a tool for learning (Isaacs & Colby, 2010).

Mistakes to Success builds on the untapped resource of mistakes in four ways. First, it situates the mistakes discussion squarely in the arena of social innovation and social learning. The book pivots on the important distinction between "constructive" and "nonconstructive" mistakes, as Cohen and Gooch (1991) articulate. Constructive mistakes are those mistakes that occur when we marshal the best of theory, evidence, practice, and savvy—yet still fail or fall short of our goals. Nonconstructive mistakes occur when we do not do our homework or fall prey to any number of human limitations. Constructive mistakes focus our attention on strategic assumptions, quality of evidence, shifts in the environment, and other building blocks of design and implementation. Of course, we should prevent nonconstructive mistakes from overwhelming our projects; however, confronting constructive mistakes holds the key to better policies, strategies, and project implementation. For both types of mistakes, catching them as early as possible promises the opportunity for mid-course correction.

Even constructive mistakes, however, are not all made of the same stuff. It's important to distinguish between mistakes related to broad strategies or the missions of organizations like foundations and the operational mistakes found in specific initiatives, demonstrations, projects, and investments. An example of a broad strategic mistake might be the overwhelming focus on building low-income housing in low-income neighborhoods for the past 50 years. An operational-level mistake might relate to a specific housing development's failure to hire local residents during construction. *Mistakes to Success* focuses, for the most part, on the second type of constructive mistake, those that occur as a part of operational investments.

Acknowledging and reflecting on mistakes has implications for academics, policymakers, investors, and practitioners, primarily by generating useful knowledge for improving theory and practice. Academic interest relates to theory building in specific policy domains, interventions, and evaluative knowledge, and for training researchers, policymakers, and practitioners. Policymakers and investors are interested in improving the processes of replication, scaling up, and building the capacity of current and future implementers. Practitioners focus primarily on improving implementation, mid-course corrections, and leadership training for the nonprofit sector. This sector has not done a good job of documenting these areas and often fails to provide organized opportunities for sharing mistakes and lessons.

Mistakes to Success brings together authors anchored in community economic development practice. Many served as designers, investors, implementers, or evaluators in the stories and cases compiled here. Personal involvement presents its own challenges for objective writing and interpretation, but, in the end, it provides a more nuanced understanding of how mistakes and adaptations occur on the ground. In this sense, the book provides nonprofit leaders an opportunity to examine their own practice and formulate insights about projects—and mistakes—in which they were intertwined. This is no easy task. But we developed a process that allowed the authors to reflect on their experiences by bringing them together to listen, probe, and reflect on each other's stories.

The third way of building on this compilation is to use these stories to generate hypotheses about CED. The decision to gather stories from the nonprofit CED field allowed us to obtain a variety of perspectives on the same set of objectives—increasing economic opportunities for low- and moderate-income families and communities.

The stories in this book collectively suggest hypotheses that the CED field should address. Without our attention, the challenges these hypotheses identify will continue to disrupt practice and generate what eventually may become nonconstructive mistakes. A few examples of such hypotheses include the questions: What standard of knowledge should we use in designating an approach as a "best practice"? What site or organizational characteristics are most important for successful replication? What kinds of performance measures and accountability systems drive change? What are the criteria for building successful partnerships?

The best kind of mistake story is one in which adaptations take place during implementation and some level of success is ultimately attained—the proverbial happy ending. These mistake stories offer advice about how to increase the frequency of happy endings; this is the fourth way to build on our resource bank of mistakes. At the broadest level, implementing and investing organizations must be able to anticipate, learn, and adapt. This requires sufficient capacity, patience, and dedication to look unblinkingly at implementation, grapple with emerging evidence, and make tough choices and changes. Not all groups have the wherewithal to do this. Public and philanthropic investors can ease this process by making certain choices in investing, selecting groups for specific projects, supporting capacity building, and tolerating the bumps of implementation and adaptation.

Two related sets of mistakes and challenges arise in these failure stories. Many of the cases demonstrate overreach in complexity of design and drivers of change—nonprofits attempting something that is simply out of their reach. A majority of these same cases took the right steps by doing feasibility studies and business plans. But, no *ex ante* study can eliminate all risks and questions if an endeavor is truly innovative. Yet, the untested or poorly tested feasibility questions in many of these stories suggest that we need better standards for feasibility research and review panels that investors can turn to for second and third opinions. Failures will still occur, but they will be more productive failures.

The stories make clear that timing and environmental shifts can and will disrupt design and implementation assumptions, causing projects to stumble and sometimes fail. It's difficult to predict the unpredictable—that is the essence of the constructive mistake. The question is whether we can do anything about this unpredictability. These kinds of shifts call on us to make better up-front risk assessments of what could go wrong. Feasibility studies and business plans should include risk assessments, taking into account the ability of investors, partners, and implementers to intervene and adapt. How often do we acknowledge up front the risks that may sink our favorite projects? Providing training and feedback and building the capacity of implementers on the front end may help them survive as circumstances inevitably change and evolve.

Thinking about Mistakes

The literature about mistakes is growing. But within this literature, one is hard-pressed to find anything constructive about most of these mistakes. Thinking about mistakes in advance can enrich your reading of the mistakes stories to follow.

At the outset we need to make the obvious acknowledgement that mistakes and failures are inherent in the human condition. Obtaining good information is always difficult, and we face challenges in processing this information to produce useful theories and actions. Hallinan's 2009 review of the mistakes literature is sobering in its portrayal of our faulty premises and proclivities. The bottom line: we can't help but make mistakes.

Errors come through problems with knowledge, judgment, and action (Rescher, 2007). Moreover, trial-and-error experimentation is our way of life, whether improving on how we build bridges or how we deliver presentations (Petroski, 2006). There are lots of practical as well as philosophical distinctions one can make about how to think about mistakes. We can only offer a brief sampling.

Consider social innovations that change techniques, products, services, and approaches. Generating durable social innovations is hard enough because such innovations test the limits of existing theory and evidence. And even when innovations prove to be feasible, they must produce real results and be able to grow. If these challenges are not enough, the innovations of today may become irrelevant and even obstacles to future innovation if the environment changes in fundamental ways in terms of technology, markets, policy, or values. Unfortunately, some innovations developed before a major breakthrough are discarded at that point, so they are less easily tapped when the big breakthrough falters. In other words, the pathway to success builds in the potential for failure (Hatamura, 2003). With a little luck, someone else will come along with a better idea.

A good example of how a social innovation became an obstacle to progress involves public housing. Think about how long it has taken to undo the mistakes of public housing mismanagement and its contribution to concentrating poverty. Yet, in the 1930s, this social innovation was a major step forward in providing affordable and temporary housing for the employed going through tough times.

Do not think that distinguishing between success and failure is easy. Some failures are clear to most observers, such as products not selling, battles lost, or bridges falling down, but such clarity does not always exist in the social policy realm, where there is contentious debate about social values and cause-and-effect relationships concerning specific behaviors or interventions. Mark Wooster (2006) highlights a good example in *Great Philanthropic Mistakes*, bemoaning the launching of public television in the 1960s. For him, and other conservatives, this public investment substituted government action for the private market and, hence, failed to take advantage of the powers of competitive capitalism. Similar differences of opinion exist about the directions of welfare reform, sentencing guidelines, climate change, and many other issues.

Distinguishing between success and failure can depend on one's relationship to a particular mistake. Indeed, a mistake for one stakeholder may not be a mistake for someone else, especially someone downstream from the original idea. For example, foundations often blame the failure of specific initiatives on their nonprofit grant recipients rather than taking responsibility for faulty ideas, lack of capacity-building assistance, or their own short attention spans. Acknowledging shared ownership of mistakes is perhaps the most important first step in building a community of learning around mistakes.

We must also consider the timing of mistakes—whether, for example, a mistake is found mid-course, or failure is only disclosed after the fact in the final evaluation report. The timing of mistakes shapes our ability to respond and adapt to them. Is there enough time left in the project to make a mid-course correction, or is the project done? Of course, identifying mistakes during implementation is no easy task; sometimes we need a little time for the dust to clear so that we can see our mistakes.

How long did it take Robert McNamara and McGeorge Bundy to admit their mistakes about the Vietnam War? For them, it was decades, far too long a time to allow for mid-course corrections (McNamara, 1995; Goldstein, 2008).

Comparing mistakes of commission and mistakes of omission complicates our thinking by adding a consideration of intentions. We usually study mistakes that derive from planned actions that have been taken to achieve specific purposes. We establish targets for success that reflect our outcome definitions. But what do we know about mistakes that grow out of actions we decided not to take or those that are related to options for action that never surfaced? Who keeps track of these mistakes? Can we be held accountable for options we didn't pursue?

A common act of omission for many nonprofits and foundations is failing to join with others in partnership or coalition because of the fear of losing identity or brand. Not joining such efforts can lead to fragmentation and diminish overall accomplishments.

We should also consider mistakes that lead to what we might call collateral damage or unintended consequences. These are mistakes that we may not readily see and that our evaluation and documentation tools may miss. They occur because of our actions, but the fallout from them is not within our field of vision. The old joke captures it well:

"The operation was a success, but the patient died." An example is how the seemingly good diversion of our corn harvest for environmentally friendly biofuel production inadvertently contributed to the food crisis in developing countries.

All kinds of mistakes may ultimately derive from our cognitive and behavioral limitations as human beings. In *How Doctors Think* (2008), Jerome Groopman tells a wide range of medical diagnostic stories that involve mistakes. He argues that many physicians, including himself at times, have missed diagnoses because of a tendency to "seize on first symptoms and make snap judgments," what he calls anchoring errors; stereotyping patients to explain away their symptoms or behaviors based on the experience of other patients, or attribution error; or generalizing from the pattern that nobody else with these symptoms had a different condition or disease, what he calls availability error. These cognitive shortcuts can blind the practitioner to situations that don't fit. But it seems we are wired to find suitable answers that fit quickly, reinforcing the "satisfaction of search" or confirmation bias, as opposed to nudging our curiosity or skepticism. Dr. Groopman's antidote to these thinking errors is "constructive questioning" that opens up the uniqueness and special attributes of different situations.

So, what does this discussion of mistakes have to do with community economic development? A lot more than we think. How often do we promote answers or innovative solutions without really getting to know the specific situations in which they are to be implemented? Some have called this the "garbage can theory"—in which we try to fit a preselected set of answers to problems that we encounter (Cohen, 1972). A fundamental problem in community economic development is the mismatch between specific interventions and specific contexts in terms of relevance, conditions, and timing. We need to get to know specific contexts—the constraints and opportunities. Yet, we jump at success, wanting to latch onto models that have exhibited some success. We believe that we already have most of the answers and that we shouldn't waste time re-inventing the wheel—or taking the time to make sure we have the *right* wheel. And the pressures of reaching scale often push us to jam a round peg of innovation into a square environmental hole.

But cognitive limitations represent only one aspect of mistakes that are relevant for CED. To be sure, inadequate ability to implement a program generates its own share of mistakes. And many implementation mistakes occur because we are not being mindful, according to Karl Wieck and Kathleen Sutcliffe in *Managing the Unexpected* (2001). This sounds like a version of Zen, and it is. Mindfulness is the ability to pay attention to lots of moving parts while being acutely aware, moment to moment, of critical success factors and of what can go wrong. It's not simply focusing more acutely, but it's also a kind of cognitive peripheral vision that allows one to see implementation activity within a wider context. In doing so, one may become more aware of the unexpected that inevitably will happen in some form. Basic planning and feasibility studies should be improved, but battle—even on CED playing fields— inevitably involves a certain amount of chaos. Failure is likely unless you are paying attention.

But what should we pay attention to if we want to avoid mistakes? Gary Klein, in *The Power of Intuition* (2003), argues that we need to train our "gut instincts" and hunches. He developed the *pre-mortem* tool in which implementers articulate before implementation all the things that could go wrong in getting a project or innovation off the ground, not that one can foresee everything, of course. If we are more oriented toward those factors that can go wrong at the outset, our antennae will pick up signs and patterns that something needs fixing.

Even when acknowledging cognitive and implementation challenges, we tend to accept the notion that we can and should learn from mistakes. We hear sayings like, "Never make the same mistake twice." Or "Make only new mistakes." At a commonsense level in everyday life, we see people adjust behaviors after making mistakes, whether learning how to ride a bike, playing tennis, or cooking a meal. Adjustment or adaptation may differ in timing and quality, but most people and organizations learn. Of course, there are some who never seem to learn.

Unfortunately, no database exists for the nonprofit and social innovation fields about the frequencies of success and failure and whether learning actually occurs. And some peculiar features mask nonprofit failures and learning, such as the deep pockets of foundations, rigid public policy, or the deep-seated belief that some social problems are just too hard to solve.

Organization and Overview of Chapters

Mistakes to Success contains 14 chapters, including 12 about specific mistakes stories. The chapters are organized according to the broad categories of design, implementation, and learning. The six sections are: getting ready/design; best practices; investment approaches; managing change; complexity; and sustainability. Most of the mistakes stories contain multiple dimensions, but this organizational framework helps identify at least one core message from each chapter.

This chapter, *A Primer on Learning from Mistakes*, situates the mistakes discussion within the broader context of social learning about innovation and provides a number of helpful frameworks and distinctions in thinking about mistakes.

Two chapters in the getting ready/design section address key challenges in demonstration planning and implementation: picking the right ideas and the right sites. Chapter 2, *Replicating Model Program: A Fatal Attraction?*, reflects on replication mistakes in the design and operation of the Annie E. Casey Foundation's Jobs Initiative (JI). The major problem concerns the poor long-term evaluation results of the national replication of the Center for Employment Training (CET) and whether these results cast doubt on the underlying efficacy of the dual-customer, short-term, occupational training model for low-skilled adults. Was it a mistake to hitch the JI wagon to the CET bandwagon?

Chapter 3, *The Perils of Site Selection: Reflections on Picking Demonstration Places*, explores site selection mistakes in two foundation initiatives. Picking sites for community building is more art than science: while mistakes are inevitable, they are sometimes preventable.

The importance of site selection is conveyed in the folk wisdom that, no matter the design or aspiration of a demonstration, site selection is the decisive factor in determining ultimate success. Success or failure may depend on the sites selected.

Three chapters on best practices explore the sometimes murky question of what counts as a best practice. Chapter 4, *Salvaging Success from Failure: Chicago's Mercado Marketplace*, tells the story of an ambitious community development project that failed and then succeeded. El Mercado anchors a reviving commercial strip in a low- to moderate-income area and thrives today as a clear example of its sponsor's creativity and commitment to locally controlled development and benefits for community residents. Those who recall its original purpose when it opened in 1992 know, too, that the project never realized its goal of creating a successful "public market" consisting of dozens of stalls operated by local micro-businesses.

Chapter 5, *Are Best Practices Really Better? Stories from the Workforce Development Frontier*, tells the story of two experimental workforce development programs that, despite incorporating elements of these best practices, failed to link workforce and economic development in powerful ways. Replicating best practices in workforce development is problematic, not just because of issues of scale and context but also because of the ongoing failure to reconcile contradictory goals in workforce and economic development. Yet, despite the failure to replicate, the programs had unanticipated positive outcomes that might be considered promising practices in their own right.

Chapter 6, *Does "What Works" Work? A Case Study in Job Retention and Advancement for Low-Wage Workers*, describes how a well-established employment program in Boston pursued a strategy of providing follow-up, "post-employment" services to help its participants advance from entry-level to "living wage" jobs. After documenting the disappointing results that followed, the chapter examines how post-employment services came to be registered on the list of strategies that "work," and delves into the evaluation and other, relevant literature to discover to what extent empirical evidence supports assertions that this strategy "works."

The section on investment approaches contains two chapters on assumptions about how we invest and the outcomes we hope to achieve. Chapter 7, *In Pursuit of Scale for Nonprofit Organizations: Learning from Constructive Failures*, discusses preliminary research findings that even relatively well-implemented pilots do not lead to larger or more permanent changes in the field. A group of pilot Earned Income Tax Credit campaigns (EITC) offers a case in point. Lessons identify the need for greater infrastructure and operational capacity; the challenge of partnerships with both government and the private sector; the lack of understanding of what the market wants; and the dual problem of hidden costs and high per-unit costs in this work. Most important, however, the pilots revealed a critical error in the premise of the grants: the size of the solution must match the size of the problem, and small pilots, by their very nature, may never be able to point the way to scale.

Chapter 8, *Seedco's Community Childcare Assistance Initiative*, discusses the feasibility of nonprofits' generating income through social enterprises. Federal welfare policies that led to increased need for childcare in the low-wage workforce encouraged Seedco, a national workforce intermediary, to launch a childcare social enterprise. Unfortunately, the childcare venture failed on several counts. Few employers adopted it; it was not well received by employees and parents; and it was undercapitalized and unable to perform and adapt in a changing marketplace.

The managing change section contains three chapters that address the daunting management challenges that inevitably arise during implementation. The need for innovative thinking does not stop with coming up with a good design. Chapter 9, *The Dangers of Outcome Measures in Workforce Development*, discusses the constructive mistake of not anticipating the unintended consequences of establishing "robust" indicators of program success.

Chapter 10, *Learning the Limits of Project Partnerships*, discusses how public and philanthropic investors often require partnerships to leverage needed resources and produce a more coordinated, efficient effort. This chapter examines the experiences of two recent partnership-based projects: Connecting People to Jobs and Latino Pathways. The overall finding is that the process of organizing and engaging partners can produce significant results, but it can also cause unanticipated and sometimes terminal consequences.

Chapter 11, *Mistakes in Place: The Premature Termination of Illinois Workforce Advantage*, describes a multi-faceted effort by the Illinois Governor's Office in 2000–2002 to create a place-based community revitalization program. Illinois Workforce Advantage (IWA) engaged 18 state agencies in continuous deliberations aimed at supporting community economic development and family-strengthening efforts in nine low-income, rural and urban communities. The project succeeded in engaging community collaboratives and seeding innovative projects, but failed to develop a government constituency that might have helped the program weather government transition.

The complexity section has two chapters about navigating complicated markets and communities. Chapter 12, *Drive to Succeed*, describes an initiative that promised to take advantage of the thousands of used cars rotating back through Ford Motor Company's redistribution system. The project ultimately failed because of changed market conditions that sharply spiked the cost of used cars, lack of flexibility to shift over to other car makes and models, and the disconnect that so often occurs between the nonprofit and private sector in partnerships.

One chapter focuses on sustainability and addresses the institutional and financing aspects of long-term change—how to create durable innovations for future generations. Chapter 13, *CDC Management Lessons: Insights from the Demise of Eastside Community Investments, Inc.*, discusses the sustainability and effectiveness of community development corporations (CDCs). The Eastside Community Investments (ECI) failure in Indianapolis, Indiana, provides lessons in managing growth and assessing performance in the CED field.

The concluding chapter, *Mistakes to Success: Learning and Adapting When Things Go Wrong*, reflects on the lessons of the chapters and discusses the value of sharing failure stories to improve practice and investments.

We salute the authors who have shared these stories and encourage others to be inspired by their openness to learning and field building.

References

Cohen, E., & Gooch, J. (1991). *Military misfortune: The anatomy of failure in war*. New York: Vintage.

Cohen, M, March, J., & Olsen, J. (1972). A Garbage Can Model of Organizational Choice. *Administrative Science Quarterly, 17*(1) , 1–25.

Giloth, R. (2007). *Nonprofit leadership: Life lessons from an enterprising practitioner*. New York: iUniverse, Inc.

Giloth, R., & Gewirtz, S. (2009, Winter). Philanthropy and mistakes: An untapped resource. *The Foundation Review, 1*(1), 115–124.

Goldstein, G. M. (2008). *Lessons in disaster: McGeorge Bundy and the path to war in Vietnam*. New York: Henry Holt.

Groopman, J. (2008). *How doctors think*. Boston: Houghton Mifflin.

Hallinan, J. (2009). *Why we make mistakes*. New York: Broadway Books.

Hatamura, Y. (2003). *Learning from failure*. San Jose, CA: Syndrose LP.

Isaacs, S., & Colby, D. (Eds.). (2010). *To improve health and health care*. (Vol. X111). San Francisco: Jossey-Bass.

Klein, G. (2003). *The power of intuition*. New York: Random House.

McNamara, R. (1995). *In retrospect: The tragedy and lessons of Vietnam*. New York: Random House.

Petroski, H. (2006). *Success through failure: The paradox of design*. Princeton, NJ: Princeton University Press.

Rescher, N. (2007). *Error (On Our Predicament When Things Go Wrong)*. Pittsburgh, PA: University of Pittsburgh Press.

Wieck, K., & Sutcliffe, K. (2001). *Managing the unexpected.* San Francisco: Jossey-Bass.

Wooster, M. M. (2006). *Great philanthropic mistakes.* Washington, DC: Hudson Institute.

2

Replicating Model Programs: A Fatal Attraction?

Robert Giloth

Introduction

Social investing and social policy aspire to replicate and expand tested interventions in other community contexts (Schorr, 1997). Replication is both a way of evaluating the "traveling power" of specific models and of contributing to the achievement of "scale" impacts that address the magnitude of problems like poverty or unemployment. It is also a way of changing the design, investment strategies, and performance metrics of public systems and funding streams. Yet, despite the recognized importance of replication, we have a mixed record of success in achieving its goals.

This chapter tells a two-decade story about workforce model development, replication, evaluation, mistakes, policy adaptation, and new evidence. In some sense the animating question is "when is a mistake really a mistake?" This seemingly simplistic question is more complicated than you might think.

Background

The community economic development (CED) field, including workforce development, offers many examples of replication successes and failures. On the one hand, we have successes like the spread of community development corporations (CDCs), Individual Development Account (IDA) and microenterprise programs, the STRIVE job-readiness program, Habitat for Humanity, Project QUEST's workforce development replication in Texas, and the proliferation of volunteer-based Earned Income Tax Credit (EITC) campaigns. On the other hand, the workforce development field has experienced replication mistakes with the Bidwell Training Center, Cooperative Home Care Associations, PhAME, and the Asian Neighborhood Design Center.

We actually know a lot about what it takes to achieve successful replications (Bradach, 2003; Replication and Program Services, 1993). First, the more programmatic, product-like, or standardized the initial innovations are, the easier it is to reproduce in different situations with similar results. Local conditions are not critical factors and many organizations can successfully replicate products like IDAs. Second, more complicated programs or partnerships require a fundamental understanding of what makes the intervention effective—its *secret sauce*. This involves much more than understanding key program elements: it involves matters of context, relationships, leadership, and ways of doing business. In the end, this type of replication requires a "design replication" of key ingredients rather than a narrow "program" replication in a blueprint or cookie cutter fashion. The key task is identifying the best conditions for planning and implementing design replications—the "Petri dish" problem. That is, what threshold environmental conditions are prerequisites to program success?

Unfortunately, in some cases we cannot identify easily the determinative elements of project success before we engage in replication. Different contexts illuminate what design elements are variable or optional and which elements are necessary if replicators hope to achieve similar outcomes. Moreover, the power of a program model in one context may diminish in another, making the initial effort seem, in retrospect, to be dependent upon special circumstances, a specific population, environmental factor, or a misleading set of results. And replicating program elements may itself be a misleading approach for describing programs that are "responsive and adaptive" (Kato, 1999). Finally, the popularization of an approach or program almost always dilutes its effectiveness as key ideas are adopted by a variety of programs.

At the heart of the replication challenge is the question of evidence. How do we identify "best practices" in a field in which we have mostly "promising practices"? What types of evaluation knowledge are appropriate for different stages, from initial start-up through documentation and impact assessment? What are the kinds of knowledge we need to support adaptive models in changing markets as well as competing approaches to changing systems and influencing policy? Not surprisingly, many mistakes have been made, not only in replication but in how we draw upon different types of evidence to guide our work.

This chapter reflects on constructive mistakes concerning replication in the design and operation of the Casey Foundation's Jobs Initiative (JI). These mistakes concern the poor long-term evaluation results of the national replication of the Center for Employment Training (CET). A key question is whether these results for developing youth employment cast doubt on the underlying efficacy of the model and its key elements for adult populations as well. Consequently, for the JI, what were the implications of adopting CET principles for design replication? Was it a mistake to hitch the JI wagon to the CET bandwagon?

The Center for Employment Training (CET)

In a 1994 Casey Foundation site visit to the home office of CET in San Jose, California, Russ Tershy, the executive director of CET at the time, and involved since the founding of the program, was exuberant about "launching a thousand CETs across America" and maybe beyond. Two "gold standard," random assignment evaluations in the 1980s, JOBSTART and the Minority-Female Single-Parent Demonstration Project (MFSP), in addition to the more recent JTPA evaluation, had demonstrated CET's impact and effectiveness, in particular, a substantial income gain of an average of about $7,000 per year. What made this finding so startling was that we knew that obtaining a year of education leads to about $2,200 in additional income for a participant, and many employment and training programs, which have a shorter duration, produce, at best, income growth of $1,000 to $1,500 (King, 2004). Not surprisingly, CET was anointed a "silver bullet." It worked.

CET's effectiveness had evolved over decades since its founding in 1967 as the Opportunities Industrialization Center (OIC) of Santa Clara County, OICs being the network of organizations founded by the Reverend Leon Sullivan of Philadelphia (Melendez, 1996). Breaking off from OIC in 1972, CET had already begun to replicate in the 1970s and 1980s in California and along the west coast. By 1992, CET had 34 sites, most of which they operated directly rather than as affiliated programs run by other organizations. Through the process of replication and expansion, CET developed a corporate infrastructure and a cadre of staff that had learned the ropes of replication. Or, so they thought.

The CET model, on the surface, is relatively straightforward. It is a short-term (that is, six-month) classroom, occupational training model that offers open entry and open exit to participants and is occupationally focused. It provides contextualized learning, integrated services, and engagement with employers. Its funding is a mix of public workforce funding and Pell Grant student aid. CET focused on between four and six occupations (e.g., medical assistant or logistics worker) and the model defined participant success as having participants not just complete the program but also get a job. Beyond these features, sympathetic analysts contend that CET's positive results were tied to its deep connections to the community and business world. CET is not identified as a sector-based model but shares many core features, including a focus on good jobs and links to employers.

Starting in 1992, the federal Department of Labor (DOL) invested significant resources to replicate CET in such cities as Chicago, Newark, Camden, and Baltimore. This replication would focus on youth ages 16 to 21, rather than the overall adult population. DOL commissioned MDRC to evaluate CET's results with youth in 14 replication sites using a random assignment design (Miller, Bos, Porter, Tseng, & Abe, 2005). Researchers tracked the income and labor force participation of the experimental and control groups, consisting of 1,400 youth enrolled between 1995 and 1999, for 30 and 54 months, and spent considerable time documenting the implementation of the CET replication in different sites.

This national CET replication for youth employment, unfortunately, produced bad news. Replication sites were difficult to launch and a number of sites—especially on the East coast—closed their doors within three years. Within the MDRC evaluation of 14 sites there was further bad and somewhat inexplicable news. First, MDRC only qualified four of the 14 sites as "true" replications of the CET model. In other words, most of the replication sites could not implement key features of the CET model within a reasonable amount of time. Second, the sites that did implement the model fully had, in general, no long-term positive impacts on clients compared to the control group, although program participants had higher rates of training and credential attainment. Moreover, the control group had higher levels of training than in the earlier CET evaluations. In the end, this evaluation of CET did not show discernable improvements in income and earnings.

CET's lack of impact after passing the muster of multiple rigorous evaluations is puzzling and disheartening. Perhaps we want to believe that evaluation-vetted program impacts are replicable, at least over the short term. MDRC, not surprisingly, was equally puzzled by these evaluation outcomes and offered several hypotheses for why this divergence of evaluation impacts occurred, at least in regard to youth employment. The CET case raises uncomfortable questions about the "flip-flop rhythm of science," in which promising practices or interventions are eventually found to be less effective than previously thought. We seem to *know* much less than our actions and investments would suggest; yet, *knowing* based upon random assignment research is expensive and has its own limitations (Taubes, 2007).

Putting aside the major organizational challenges of replicating key elements of the CET design, which was no small problem itself, MDRC's hypotheses focused on the relationship of the CET model to environmental factors and to participant characteristics. Their overall explanation was that CET only worked for certain kinds of people under certain kinds of conditions. Change these parameters and CET outcomes would vary quite considerably, as the DOL evaluation demonstrated.

Two environmental factors stand out. The late 1990s was a time of economic growth and tight labor markets. What this meant for job seekers, even those with little or modest training, was that they could find better jobs than they had been able to. Employers desired job seekers who could show up and work; in many cases they were willing to provide the technical training, as needed, on the job. In short, they wanted job readiness or "soft skills," not more education and training, and sometimes even dropped or modified stated job skill requirements if a candidate had the job-readiness skills. A second changed environmental factor in the 1990s was the shift of the workforce paradigm to one that focused on the needs of both employers and workers—a "dual customer" approach. CET was an early exemplar; its success, and that of similar model programs, spread dramatically in the 1990s and was at least rhetorically institutionalized in the Workforce Investment Act (WIA) of 1998. What this meant for job seekers and incumbent workers was that many more opportunities existed for education and training in the field that connected to employer needs. For the CET evaluation, this meant that "control group" members were able to take advantage of similar employment and training opportunities, which diminished the distinctive impact of CET.

The CET replication sites served youth population that had somewhat higher literacy and education levels than the population served by CET previously. In the past, CET provided needed credentials to low-skilled workers, frequently dislocated from other industries, entering industries that were growing, such as high-tech manufacturing.

In the DOL replication context, higher-skilled participants, who might have been able to succeed anyway, were given training that employers may not have valued under the market conditions of the late 1990s. Moreover, the evaluation showed that many CET graduates ultimately chose occupations different from those for which they were trained or didn't consider the CET training and certificate as being valuable for their labor market experience. For example, a large percentage of placements were in the retail sector, not an industry known for good wages or career advancement opportunities. Again, these factors may reflect environmental conditions and participant characteristics.

It was obviously attractive to blame the poor implementation of the CET model for the lack of positive results. And, in fact, MDRC identified only four out of 14 sites as having fully implemented the model after several years, the most successful being CET sites in California that had been around much longer than the newer replication sites in the Midwest and East coast. But, those four high-fidelity sites showed no more positive results overall, taking away the argument that the rigors of CET replication might explain the poor evaluation results. Old hands didn't even get it right. Nevertheless, it is worth pondering why places had such difficulty putting the CET core elements in place.

The CET national replication made several constructive mistakes that are valuable for advancing knowledge and practice about replicating effective workforce interventions. A glaring observation is that perhaps the notion of "best practice" is a misnomer. Economic and educational contexts inevitably change, sometimes quickly. Maybe we would be better off talking about "promising practices" and that even "gold standard" evaluations require regular re-examination. Maybe we need to be more careful about which social innovations are ready for replication, especially if we are evaluating the effects for different populations in different economic and policy contexts.

A second constructive mistake for model workforce programs like CET is underestimating how they may influence the offerings and behavior of competitors and colleagues in the workforce development field. It would, of course, be a positive development if a high proportion of employment and training organizations and community colleges adopt CET's innovations. But, if that were to be achieved, the distinctive contribution of CET would likely diminish because non-CET participants would have better access to comparable services.

A third mistake seems less constructive. Serving less disadvantaged populations, sometimes called creaming, was a change from the original CET model and may account for the lack of success in the replication effort. CET offered a bridge for those who, on the surface, did not meet mainstream job requirements, having fewer credentials, fewer skills, and less job readiness. Was this refocusing a matter of federal DOL policy, resources, or incentives? Or, was it a matter of local pushback from organizations that operated other programs and felt the need to "make their numbers." This mistake could have been avoided, assuming everyone shared the commitment to serving the disadvantaged, but we will never know how an increased focus on the disadvantaged might have changed the evaluation story.

A final mistake of the CET national replication concerns the unraveling of CET itself (Yewell, 1999). This is an all-too-familiar story in the nonprofit world. CET grew at an unsustainable pace, leading to leadership transition at the top, the selling off of property assets to cover the bills, financial problems, and a decline in community reputation. CET still exists, but in scaled-down form, with fewer sites and no longer serving as a beacon for what works in the employment and training field.

More broadly, the CET replication experience raises questions about the role and responsibilities of major investors (e.g., DOL) that were anxious to find "silver bullet" solutions but did not provide sufficient resources, time, flexibility, and authority. Long-time CET staffers suggest, for example, that they were handed sites with lukewarm interest and saddled with program and policy constraints that conflicted with the CET model (Moore, 2007). Lisbeth Schorr, in *Common Purpose: Strengthening Families and Neighborhoods to Rebuild America*, comments on this investor problem for replication: "If their gamble on multiplying effective programs on the cheap doesn't pay off, they not only fail to improve outcomes, they contribute to the prevailing cynicism that nothing works" (1997, p. 31).

The Jobs Initiative, Center for Employment Training and Replication
In June 1995, the Annie E. Casey Foundation convened a Jobs Initiative (JI) design conference in Chicago. The purpose of this eight-year, six-city, $30-million initiative was to create stronger and more durable employment connections between young adults in inner-city neighborhoods and regional economies. The aspiration of the JI was to invest in best-practice employment and training models; advocate for workforce outcomes, including helping people find better jobs, stay employed for 12 months, and have career advancement opportunities; and use the implementation lessons to change workforce systems. Replication was at the heart of the JI (Giloth, 1996).

At this JI meeting about designing effective workforce interventions, teams from the six sites visited promising workforce models in Chicago, listened to expert practitioners and policy advocates discuss what works and for whom, and shared information about what employment interventions seemed to be most effective in their communities. A centerpiece of these shared lessons was a presentation by economists from Abt Associates, the lead evaluator for the JI, about the findings from their recent evaluation of the federal Job Training Partnership Act (JTPA), the precursor of today's Workforce Investment Act (WIA). Evaluators shared the pessimistic news that few employment and training programs worked very well for adults and youth, and that the programs that did work produced only modest positive income effects (Orr et al., 1995). While subsequent discussions questioned the applicability of this pessimistic conclusion because "averages" masked high-performing programs, the consensus was that the only clear exception to the pessimistic news was the Center for Employment Training (CET), based in San Jose, California.

The JI, in part, aspired to be a "design replication" of CET, emphasizing its dual-customer approach for engaging employers and job seekers, with a focus on accessing better jobs and regional labor markets; adopting contextualized, industry-based training; striving to achieve long-run job retention (that is, 12 months) and job placement; and building strong community connections. These principles, it was hoped, would guide JI site investments.

As it turned out, however, no JI sites formally replicated CET, although many adopted features of the CET approach for new industries, occupations, and community contexts. Many reasons accounted for this lack of take-up by the JI sites. CET's own national replication was launching programs in many cities, community colleges resisted, and other nonprofit providers saw CET as duplicating a role they played or would like to play. At the same time, a "work first" model of labor force attachment under welfare reform de-emphasized education and training, and the full employment economy, as noted before, created many work opportunities in the late 1990s that did not require training.

CET and the Jobs Initiative (JI)

The story of CET, JI, replicators, and evidence-based practice is not simple or straightforward. It raises questions about how we generate knowledge about effective practices, how we generate durable innovations, what kinds of evaluations are useful, and the connections between policy development and evidence. A paradoxical question remains: Did the failure of the second CET evaluation matter in the long run for the spread of this promising workforce development model?

JI sites did not adopt CET for both good and bad reasons. But many did implement training programs that embodied key CET principles— deep connections to industry and community, contextualized learning, and a focus on getting and keeping jobs. The JI evaluation by Abt Associates, although not a random assignment design, concluded that 26 of the 43 jobs projects started by the JI could be described as short- and medium-term, sector-based training models, one project being long-term training. The median length of these skills-building programs was 10 weeks. Programs focused in manufacturing, health care, construction and business services.

Abt Associates analyzed the job records of 12,570 enrollees as of March 31, 2001. JI participants were low-income young adults, typically in their late 20s, with a wide range of employability. The analysis found that access to some job supports and human services helped explain job placement; having job-readiness training was correlated with being able to stay on the job for more than three months; and investing in human capital, such as through education and training, was significantly correlated with one-year retention on the job. These results held for all participant groups. Easier to employ participants with skills training experience a 68 percent one-year retention rate compared to 51 percent for the harder to employ. Based upon follow-up surveys, JI participants made approximately $4,000 more per year after receiving JI services, a function of better jobs and increased hours of work (Abt Associates & New School University, 2003). Although not anchored in an experimental design, the JI's evaluation results were suggestive of the promising CET-like approach.

Next Generation Replication

Successful social policy change influences institutions, rules and guidelines, and financing. This is not always a straightforward process. Two efforts leading out of the JI pick up the thread of spreading the CET model, bolstered by the JI evidence but undercut by the negative national CET replication results. They are "workforce partnerships" and the SkillWorks funding collaborative in Boston. Ultimately, these paths converged in the formation of the new National Fund for Workforce Solutions, a funding mechanism initiated to spread the workforce partnership model and advocate broader policy change.

Workforce partnerships (or intermediaries) serve to knit together the resources, relationships, information, policies, and institutions needed to bridge labor markets on behalf of workers and businesses. The JI showcased and built a number of workforce partnerships and, not surprisingly, CET is a good example of this partnering role. Other conceptual frameworks like sector-based workforce development, employer-linked training, or "dual customer" strategies have described this distinctive approach, each conveying a similar role and strategy but from a slightly different vantage point. The word "partnerships" underscores the need for high-performing organizations to integrate financial and institutional resources while remaining adaptive and results-oriented.

Several foundations pulled together a nonpartisan dialogue called the American Assembly in winter 2003 to discuss workforce partnerships and how they could be better supported. Too often they grew up in spite of public workforce systems, in response to crises, or because of the inventiveness of individual social entrepreneurs. As a part of this effort, foundations compiled *Workforce Intermediaries for the Twenty-First Century,* which contained chapters on theory, practice, and evaluation. Drawing largely from non-experimental evidence across a number of initiatives, including a multi-method evaluation of Project Quest in San Antonio, the book concluded that there was strong emerging evidence that workforce partnerships represented a promising approach for achieving career advancement for low-income, low-skilled workers (Giloth, 2004; McGahey, 2004).

On a different but related track, the JI knowledge conference in September 2001 brought together foundations from Boston to learn how they might apply the lessons of the JI in their community. They had come together under the leadership of the Boston Foundation to investigate how they could promote career advancement practices in Boston by combining and focusing philanthropic and public sector resources. After several years of planning, aided by Abt Associates and Jobs for the Future, SkillWorks was born—a five-year, $15-million fund to support sector-based workforce partnerships and state workforce policy change. The fund included local and national foundations as well as the City of Boston.

SkillWorks' first five years led to strong results, by increasing support for workforce partnerships and employer engagement, improvements in career advancement programs, progress, the leveraging of local resources, and, eventually, policy change. Six workforce partnerships received support in health care, auto repair, and building services. About 3,000 workers received services, 500 workers were placed in jobs, and 250 incumbent workers received upgrade training and were promoted. The public policy coalition supported by SkillWorks achieved a major victory with the passage of economic stimulus bills that totaled $30.5 million. SkillWorks has refined its funding collaborative model for a second five-year investment in career advancement (SkillWorks, 2008).

In 2007, the trajectories of workforce partnerships and SkillWorks merged in the formation of the National Fund for Workforce Solutions (NFWS). Foundations formed this funder collaborative to invest in local and regional collaboratives that, in turn, would invest in the growth and development of workforce partnerships. Eight foundations and the federal Department of Labor assembled $23 million, chose 22 sites to invest in, began partnering with an additional 100 local and regional foundations, and leveraged $100 million in public and private resources. Overall, the NFWS sites are starting or supporting more than 40 workforce partnerships, predominantly in health care and construction, while, at the same time, advocating for federal, state, and local policy change (Baran et al., 2009)

The aspiration of the NFWS is to influence the next generation of workforce development policy by demonstrating the power of an integrated investment approach for career advancement. Many of the principles of the NFWS have already been adopted by the Obama administration as it developed and implemented the American Recovery and Reinvestment Act of 2009. Overall, the sector and career pathways approach to workforce development is becoming a dominant approach in the workforce field.

Just as the NFWS was coming into its own and sector-based workforce development was being embraced by nonprofits and states and within federal policy, Public Private Ventures (P/PV), a national intermediary and research organization, released the results of a new evaluation. This study, initiated in 2003, examined three model sector workforce programs, the Wisconsin Regional Training Partnership (WRTP), Jewish Vocational Services in Boston, and Per Scholas, a New York-based training program. Supported by the Charles Stewart Mott Foundation, the evaluation addressed the barrage of criticisms that workforce development did not work and that only "gold standard" random assignment evaluations could validate promising programs. The evaluation found that program participants experienced a $4,500 bump in incomes over two years, not just from working more hours but because of better jobs with better employers. Program participants were more likely to get and keep jobs. As with much policy development, however, the evaluation arrived after major policy adoption, helping to reinforce rather than jumpstart the credibility of this approach (Maguire, Freely, Clymer, Conway & Schwartz, 2010).

An important aspect of the P/PV evaluation is that one of its model programs, WRTP, grew largely from participating in the JI, expanding from incumbent worker training origins to a focus on training the unemployed. WRTP is now a key partner in Milwaukee's NFWS funder collaborative. Its initial focus was manufacturing but now it also has a strong focus in the construction industry. WRTP works closely with unions, community-based organizations, and local education and training organizations.

We come full circle from the JI adoption of CET design principles, the failure of the CET national replication, non-experimental positive results for the JI, new philanthropic investments in workforce partnerships, policy adoption of the sector partnership approach—and then robust, gold standard results. Indeed, the occupational training of Per Scholas and Jewish Vocational Services is more like CET than the robust sectoral approach of WRTP. What is clear but also troubling is that sometimes advocates of promising approaches have to be informed by evaluations of different types but also not be sidetracked by related evaluations.

Conclusion

This chapter has considered the challenges of social replication through the lenses of the national program replication of CET and the Casey Foundation's JI. Although embracing different approaches for moving from "pilots to scale," both of these efforts built upon the "successful" elements of CET. Both cases demonstrate constructive failures related to replicating model programs, picking the right workforce goals, evaluation, and engaging and changing workforce systems. Reflecting upon these mistakes raises several big challenges for workforce development and the broader realm of social policy, with the overarching challenge related to the proper definition of evidence and best practice.

These cases show that the mechanics of program and design replication are difficult. While design replications must address the problems of context and flexibility, one ever-present concern is the dilution of the most powerful elements of successful models. This is especially likely in the context of economic and policy changes that may alter the performance impacts of the model on target populations and hence replication validity.

The CET story raises questions about the conduct of national replications by programs, investors, and evaluators. Many of the features of CET have defined the new "common sense" of workforce development, including the dual-customer, industry-focused approach. Unfortunately, the CET national evaluation now reinforces the notion that even our best models may not work or may have a more accidental than predictable impact. Perhaps the potential implications of this entire effort should have been thought through more carefully before it was undertaken: replications and evaluations can harm an emerging field if not done carefully.

Above all, these constructive mistakes point to the challenges of new innovations reaching scale in the field of workforce development. It is fair to say that many of the design principles of CET and the JI are now widespread in terms of accepted ideas if not fully realized practices. In the opinion of many, there has been real progress.

What's striking, more broadly, is the lack of explicit discussion about constructive mistakes in the workforce field. A fear exists that talking openly about replication failures will reinforce the perception that nothing works in workforce development and that the "anointed" models of the field may have clay feet. This is an unfortunate state of affairs but not uncommon in the wider social policy realm. The problem is that it's almost impossible to come up with ways to change the workforce field, scale up innovations, and develop policy champions without digesting thoroughly what has worked and what hasn't worked. Somehow the field needs to develop a learning approach that is effective and safe, builds the capacity of relevant organizations, and allows for honest exchanges without penalty.

This inquiry began with the hopefulness inspired by CET and its positive evaluations in the 1980s and 1990s. Subsequently, workforce development adopted many CET design principles and practices and many of these projects produced solid outcomes. In light of the failed national CET replication, at least for youth employment, one has to wonder whether adopting these approaches was based upon a faulty premise—a rather big constructive failure. New evidence suggests otherwise.

References

Abt Associates & New School University. (2003). *Breaking through: Overcoming barriers to family-sustaining employment.* Cambridge, MA: Abt Associates.

Baran, B., Teegarden, S., Giordono, Lodewick, L. K., Benner, C., & Pastor, M. (2009, April 6). *Implementing the National Fund for Workforce Solutions: The baseline evaluation report.* Boston: National Fund for Workforce Solutions.

Bradach, J. L. (2003, April 1). Going to scale: The challenge of replicating social programs. *Stanford Social Innovation Review,* 19-25.

Giloth, R. (1996). *Mapping social interventions. Theory of change and the Jobs Initiative.* Baltimore, MD: Annie E. Casey Foundation.

Giloth, R. (2004). *Workforce intermediaries for the twenty-first century.* Philadelphia, PA: Temple University Press.

Kato, L. Y. (1999, April 30). *Diffusing responsive social programs by building learning organizations: The case of the Center for Employment Training (CET) National Replication Project* (Unpublished doctoral dissertation). Cambridge, MA: Massachusetts Institute of Technology.

King, C. T. (2004, July). *The effectiveness of publicly financed training in the U.S.: Implications for WIA and related programs.* Austin, TX: Ray Marshall Center for the Study of Human Resources, The University of Texas at Austin.

Maguire, S., Freely, J., Clymer, C., Conway, M., and Schwartz, D. (2010, July). *Tuning in to local labor markets: Findings from the Sector Employment Impact Study.* Available on www.PPV.org.

McGahey, R. (2004). Workforce intermediaries: Recent experience and implications for workforce development. In R. P. Giloth (Ed.), *Workforce intermediaries for the twenty-first century* (pp. 124–155). Philadelphia, PA: Temple University Press.

Melendez, E. (1996). *Working on jobs: The Center for Employment Training.* Boston: Mauricio Gaston Institute for Latino Community Development and Public Policy, University of Massachusetts.

Miller, C., Bos, J., Porter, K., Tseng, F., & Abe, Y. (2005). *The challenge of repeating success in a changing world: Final report on the Center for Employment Training replication sites.* New York: MDRC.

Moore, J. (2007, July/August). *Failure to copy right: Why a successful job training program couldn't be replicated. Youth Today,* 28.

Orr, L., Bloom, H., Bell, S., Lin, W., Cave, G. & Doolittle, F. (1995). *The National JTPA Study: Impacts, benefits, and costs of Title 11-A.* Bethesda, MD: Abt Associates.

Replication and Program Services, Inc. (1993). *Building from strength: Replication as a strategy for expanding social programs that work.* Philadelphia, PA: Author.

Schorr, L. B. (1997). *Common purpose: Strengthening families and neighborhoods to rebuild America.* New York: Doubleday, 31.

SkillWorks. (2008). *SkillWorks: Partners for a productive workforce.* Boston, MA: Author.

Taubes, G. (2007, September 23). Do we really know what makes us healthy? *New York Times Magazine.*

Yewell, J. (1999, August 26). Too big too fast. *Metro.*

3

The Perils of Site Selection: Reflections on Picking Demonstration Places

Robert Giloth

Introduction

Picking sites for community-building demonstrations is more art than science: mistakes are inevitable. Demonstrations test whether good ideas for changing social conditions work individually or in conjunction with other ideas and can be replicated in a variety of contexts. One foundation colleague advised me many years ago to expect only one of five demonstration sites to be successful. That always seemed a very low threshold of success; my hope was that half of our demonstration sites would produce good results. The challenge of site selection is of renewed importance as the Obama administration establishes a Social Innovation Fund and seeks to replicate social innovations like the Harlem Children's Zone.

This chapter explores some of the mistakes related to site selection by examining two Annie E. Casey Foundation demonstrations—the Jobs Initiative and Making Connections. Although these demonstrations were more complicated in design and implementation than many such initiatives, they still have valuable lessons for other investors about site selection.

The importance of site selection for social demonstrations is conveyed in the folk wisdom that, no matter the demonstration design or aspiration, site selection is the decisive factor in determining ultimate success. Success or failure hinges on the sites selected because new capacities are difficult to build as implementation unfolds. Many MDRC evaluations, for example, only look in depth at those sites that fully adopted a specific demonstration design, a much smaller number in some cases than one would have expected, as in the case of the Center for Employment Training (CET) and Jobs Plus evaluations (Miller, Bos, Porter, Tseng, & Abe, 2005). Gary Walker, former chief executive of Public/Private Ventures (P/PV), argues that, in most demonstrations, the model being tested never gets implemented fully (Walker, 2008). While there are many intervening and unpredictable factors in the life of a demonstration site, at root a site either has or does not have the right capacity and fit for a specific demonstration.

The basic challenges for demonstration site selection are threefold: 1) selecting sites with leadership, capacities, and relationships with intermediary organizations that are aligned and commensurate with the needs of the demonstration, including intermediaries and leaders; 2) selecting sites with these capacities that are also hungry to take on a specific initiative at the right time; and 3) selecting sites with diverse capacities and strengths so they can adapt to gaps in design and unforeseen environmental factors.

The Casey Foundation's Jobs Initiative (JI) was an eight-year, $30-million effort to connect low-income adults and communities to better jobs and regional economies. Potential sites required some experience implementing "dual-customer model" jobs projects that engaged both employers and workers; had candidates for an investment mechanism we called "development intermediaries"; and had a set of civic relationships, institutions, and resources, what we called *civic infrastructure,* that had supported anti-poverty efforts in the past. The JI required a threshold of capacity but not too much capacity or "traffic"; cities needed to be open to embracing and integrating a complex initiative. Through referrals by trusted experts and site visiting, 11 sites were asked to apply for the JI. Ten ultimately applied, six were chosen, and four were relatively successful in the long run. The core projects and organizations of three sites continue today. Once chosen, JI sites had to choose, in turn, their own development intermediaries and a target set of neighborhoods.

Making Connections (MC) is the Casey Foundation's 10-year, place-based, family-strengthening initiative that sought in its final years to improve family and child well-being through fostering better connections to economic opportunities, trusted systems and supports, and social networks. Simply stated, many families are disconnected or isolated from these supports. MC's initial investment approach called for leading with ideas, rather than money, and building a local infrastructure organically with partners, rather than handing off the initiative to any one organization at the outset. Casey identified cities that had previous large-scale Casey initiatives or strong relationships with the foundation and selected site team leaders from among its staff to guide start-up in each of the sites. An early on-the-ground decision was to choose specific neighborhoods for MC to focus on. MC started with 22 sites, but narrowed them down to 10 after three years. Now, in the final three years, six full-blown sites are in operation.

This chapter reflects on the mistakes and lessons about demonstration site selection based on my experience managing the JI and five MC sites at start-up. Mistakes and lessons to be discussed include:

- Identifying demonstration capacity requirements in advance helps to identify the right kind of sites.
- Reducing the costs of competition for sites encourages more honest site self-assessment.
- Minimizing internal and external politics in site selection requires clarity in defining required site capacities and preconditions for success.

- Performing well in one demonstration does not always predict high performance in another demonstration, even one that is broadly similar.
- Expanding our knowledge about site selection experiences would help the overall field of social policy demonstrations.

The other bit of folk wisdom that we should keep in mind at the outset is that successfully picking sites can be as random as a coin toss. Too many factors are involved to make this a straightforward, rational decision. Sites fool us at the outset, and sites change. Consequently, we may really be looking for good places to "get started and keep going" rather than places that are perfect at this moment. In this sense, local leaders, "spark plugs," and social entrepreneurs may be the most important site capacities to identify.

Background

Demonstrations are almost always complicated social interventions with multiple moving parts. Given the usual expectations that short-term progress is possible and desirable, picking sites with the appropriate capacities to implement a specific demonstration and produce successful outcomes seems like a straightforward task. But, in fact, it is much more difficult in practice to find the right sites, especially because other variables, like timing, leadership, competition, need, and site portfolio diversity, come into play, and because knowing a site sometimes only comes through acting together for a common purpose. In the worst cases, demonstration designers do not even go through the motions of identifying site capacities and preconditions.

The JI hoped to catalyze multiple jobs projects in places by linking low-income, low-skilled workers to good jobs in regions. The essential elements of this demonstration, launched in 1995, were a "development intermediary" that would make investments and guide the initiative; individual jobs projects; a lead community organization or partnership to create linkages to an impact community of 80,000 to 100,000 people;

and a jobs policy network that would lead advocacy and system change efforts in the final phase of the JI. A goal and measure of success for the JI investments was having participants stay in a job for at least one year; such retention indicated labor market attachment and served as a proxy for enhanced incomes.

The design principles of the JI derived from researching best and emerging practices, site visits, and consultative brainstorming and feedback sessions. Promising jobs projects focused on sectors, minority business development, human services, spatial mobility, and employment brokering. To achieve larger-scale impact in places required multiple jobs projects and, hence, a development intermediary that could play the investor role, staying with any one jobs project for only a short time before moving on to invest in other promising projects. The best of these jobs projects were "workforce partnerships" that brought together businesses, educational and training institutions, government agencies, and community-based organizations (CBOs). These partnerships were frequently regional in nature, as were labor markets, so the JI had to build preparation pipelines to low-income neighborhoods to demonstrate how residents could access these regional jobs. Finally, jobs policy networks recognized that workforce systems would have to be changed from the outside, not only or primarily by their own internal champions. Jobs policy networks would have to include advocates different from those who established jobs projects or ran the development intermediaries.

Looking back, these design assumptions seem overly optimistic and perhaps even implausible. Workforce partnerships take many years to develop and mature, making the expectation that the development intermediaries would revolve financial resources from one jobs project to another unrealistic. Funding could not be used as flexibly as had been expected. Moreover, the economy and policy environment of the 1990s reinforced the tendency of JI sites to stick with employment brokering and job matching rather than making investments in education and skills enhancement. Employers wanted employees right away, while public policy emphasized "work first." Most neighborhoods lacked the ability to build preparatory pipelines as many neighborhood organizations lacked the funds or the capacity to meet the increased demands the project had related to job retention and career advancement. Although most of the JI lead organizations existed outside of the conventional workforce systems, only one site established a formal jobs policy network.

JI designers were prescient enough to see that at least three aspects of site readiness, capacity, and fit were required for the JI to be successful. First, JI designers identified middle-size cities of moderate capacity that were open to new and complicated initiatives. That is, the JI, it was believed, wouldn't work in big, complicated cities, or in places that had already developed a nuanced or predetermined approach to workforce development that precluded new approaches and new actors. Second, JI designers identified the existence of a diverse and effective "civic infrastructure" of institutions, relationships, and experiences that could be mobilized to support an ambitious jobs effort. This was a version of the social capital argument that posited that social change depended on underlying social networks and norms. Third, sites had to have some experience with model jobs projects and have viable candidates for the development intermediary and other key initiative roles. The JI didn't have enough money or the faith that starting from scratch could be accomplished in the short term, so some capacity had to be in place already. JI designers identified sites where other investors had already started relevant jobs projects, such as spatial mobility investments to overcome geographic mismatches. Finally, there had to be an institutional convener in sites that could bring together diverse interests and stakeholders to fashion a JI application and start-up strategy, including making key decisions about neighborhoods and the development intermediary.

How could the Casey Foundation find such places? How would it know a promising place when it saw one? The JI opted for an invitation-only competition for an 18-month planning process, believing that a little bit of competition would be healthy and instructive about who really wanted the JI. Sites had to match financial resources for both the planning and implementation phases of the JI as well as leverage additional funding for specific jobs projects. The list of invitees derived from JI site visits, advisors, and foundation colleagues. Before the request for proposals was issued, however, the JI designers took two steps to hone their ability to recognize the capacities they were looking for, especially evidence of an adequate civic infrastructure. A consultative session convened by the Corporation for Enterprise Development (CFED) brought together a representative mix of likely site stakeholders in JI cities—public officials, CBOs, businesses, and city council members— that urged the foundation to make the JI more outcome-focused and more open to strategies to link residents and jobs. And the National Academy for Public Administration (NAPA) led JI designers on training site visits to Brooklyn and Kansas City to help develop a set of indicators about civic infrastructure as well as honing on-the-ground sensitivities to critical JI capacities.

In the end, 10 of the 11 sites submitted applications and initial plans. At the outset, the JI planned to pick five sites, but available resources and some internal politicking led to the addition of a sixth. Then, the JI was in the hands of the six sites to make some critical choices about development intermediary, target communities, and a first round of jobs projects. The JI launched.

By its conclusion, JI results produced substantial impact for large numbers of low-income job seekers, substantial coinvestment, the building or strengthening of key workforce partnerships, and myriad workforce system changes. In the end, however, no one site put together all aspects of the JI; rather, when sites are considered together, or as a portfolio of sites, they represented JI aspirations. This was a good outcome but was not the goal at the outset of the JI.

The Casey Foundation started Making Connections (MC) in 22 cities in 2000 as its third-generation effort in community building and designing comprehensive community initiatives. If the JI can be characterized as having had one overarching goal—long-term retention in good jobs—achievable through a variety of means, MC allowed for multiple goals at the outset and multiple means to achieve family strengthening. In short, MC was a more complicated and longer initiative that required more varied civic capacities.

The MC design started from the premise that kids do better in strong families and families do better when supported by their communities. MC's name itself derived from the belief that strong families require durable connections to economic opportunities, trusted services and supports, and social networks. Many low-income families are isolated and disconnected. Having these resources equips them to support and advocate for their children over the long term. The Casey Foundation developed the MC theory of change to attack the concentrated poverty found in tough urban neighborhoods around the country. Poor child outcomes proliferated in these neighborhoods.

The foundation started with 22 MC sites gleaned from a list of places that had hosted key Casey Foundation initiatives (related, for example, to jobs, community building, and teen pregnancy prevention) in the past, along with a few new sites. Familiarity and density of relationships defined readiness in the end, although many additional data were gathered on readiness factors for each of the cities through secondary data and trusted advisors. The foundation explicitly chose not to have a competitive site selection process, not wanting to "do harm" and engender negative reactions from rejected sites.

Nevertheless, after three years, the foundation reduced its list of sites by pulling out three civic or hometown sites for longer-term investments, nine family-strengthening sites received focused, three-year grants, and 10 full-blown MC sites became eligible for eight to 10 more years of funding. Several rationales informed this parsing of sites: the need for more flexible investments in civic sites and the lack of capacity in the family-strengthening sites to undertake the full MC agenda. More recently, six of the 10 MC sites were chosen for smaller, more focused investments, again because of capacity and leadership constraints.

The second MC site selection challenge was picking a target neighborhood or group of neighborhoods in each of the selected cities.

The foundation provided few meaningful criteria for making these choices except that the neighborhoods should have substantial poverty, an abundance of young families, and the capacity to take productive action, and be a good fit for the investment strategies of local stakeholders. Neighborhoods chosen for MC ranged in size from 8,000 to 150,000 and included single neighborhoods, contiguous neighborhoods, and a few examples of geographically distinct and separate neighborhoods.

A major difficulty in understanding MC site requirements and site selection is that the MC operational design was not completed at the outset and, once completed, evolved over time. At the outset, as site teams arrived in designated cities, the MC design might be characterized as getting traction and buy-in by making progress on five developmental outcomes related to messaging, champions, use of data, and seed projects. The subsequent four or five years focused on "closing the gap" strategies and results that fostered family economic success and children ready and prepared for school, The final three years focused on the tough challenges of scale and sustainability. To make things more complicated, MC core indicators narrowed from a dozen or more in the beginning to just a handful related to employment, asset building, school readiness, and resident engagement.

A simulation exercise was never used to delineate and test MC capacity-building requirements in cities and neighborhoods as was done for the JI, although consultative sessions explored various dimensions of the MC design. Simulations are not without problems and limitations, but at the very least they do elicit key assumptions and challenges. Looking back on MC, it's no surprise that a complicated initiative worked best in strong market cities with smaller pockets of poverty. And it's scarcely a surprise that MC did less well in neighborhoods with little organizational capacity or that were overwhelmed by poverty or gentrification.

Analysis of Mistakes
A variety of design mistakes in the JI and MC ultimately shaped their implementation and results. For the JI, mistakes included overestimation

of neighborhood-level workforce capacity and the openness of workforce systems to change; the unfinished and evolving design of the MC; and a prolonged start-up that undermined a results-focused discipline. This chapter focuses solely on mistakes related to site selection of these initiatives.

Too Much Capacity

The JI excluded from site consideration "high-capacity" cities and the largest cities, including New York, Los Angeles, and Chicago. In retrospect, no cities had really made enough progress to be considered as high-capacity, a designation that suggests nothing else was left to be done to improve the practice of workforce development. (In an odd turn of events, the JI excluded Boston as being high-capacity, but several years later, Boston gleaned a lot from the JI in designing the SkillWorks workforce funder collaborative, which in turn shaped the new National Fund for Workforce Solutions, a vehicle for disseminating JI lessons about workforce partnerships.)

The JI excluded the largest cities because of their geographic, organizational, and political complexity. This was a Casey-wide belief. JI designers, likewise, believed that it would be difficult to get the attention and investment of citywide stakeholders in the largest cities, given the requirement that each city pick one community to be the project's focus. And, important, Casey funding seemed inconsequential in large cities. In short, there did not seem to be enough room in these places for launching a complex new initiative. Nonetheless, the JI picked Philadelphia, the fourth largest U.S. city, to participate because of the interest of the Pew Foundation headquartered there. It is not surprising that Philadelphia had the toughest time building neighborhood connections and public sector investment.

Too Little Capacity

JI designers also believed that sites needed to have a threshold of capacity—civic infrastructure, jobs projects, and investment mechanisms and partners. That is, the JI wouldn't work if you had to start from scratch and build all the pieces. Yet, against its own instincts and assessments, the JI designers allowed a low-capacity site, New Orleans, to be part of the initiative after a higher-level foundation manager championed its inclusion. JI designers reframed this low-capacity site as being "high-risk, high-payoff" to justify the investment decision. It did not come as a surprise that the site failed to put together a comprehensive effort that won the support of local workforce systems. Ignoring the basic threshold capacity requirements for the JI produced few positive results in a community with great need.

It's the Intermediary, Stupid!

No matter the positive environmental capacities of sites, the development intermediary played the most significant role in achieving site success. The intermediary was the center of gravity of the JI for strategic planning, jobs project investments, leveraging coinvestments, building neighborhood pipelines, and advocating for workforce system changes. The JI chose not to work with conventional lead organizations that have been used in many demonstrations, such as community foundations or private industry councils (renamed Workforce Investment Boards), because it was on the hunt for "change agents."

The foundation did not pick the development intermediaries, however, at least not directly; it chose conveners that supposedly were objective, credible, and highly connected. It hoped to avoid the situation of an outside, national organization making the key decision about the development intermediary. Perhaps naively, we were surprised that the conveners most often chose themselves to be the development intermediary. That wasn't the plan.

This should have been no surprise in the case of Denver. The Piton Foundation was the model for the JI's development intermediary role, having incubated sector-based employment projects as well as small-business development and neighborhood projects. Could it really have chosen any other organization to play this important role? What was a surprise was that Piton came to define the Denver JI as an incubator for public system innovation, without much investment from the public systems. Unfortunately, its array of innovations failed to achieve many discernable results.

In Philadelphia, the Pew Charitable Trust chose The Reinvestment Fund (TRF) as the development intermediary, even though TRF had no workforce experience. Primarily a community development financial institution (CDFI), TRF stayed in the workforce world as long as there was money and alignment with its primary lending business. Yet, TRF achieved significant workforce impact for individuals and employers and developed policy advocacy strategies and tools that influenced Pennsylvania policymakers and beyond.

In Milwaukee, the Campaign for Sustainable Milwaukee chose itself as the development intermediary, but fell prey to a conservative attack in the *Wall Street Journal* just as it was completing its strategic investment plan. As a consequence of this attack on key members of the Campaign, local investors established a new entity, the Milwaukee Jobs Initiative (MJI) to oversee the initiative, with representatives from the community, labor, and business. While this move solved the immediate political problem, it left a governance quagmire because of the mismatch between formal and informal decision-making power.

MC had its own unique version of this problem; it didn't rely on lead organizations or intermediaries at the outset. Rather, it depended on the strength of Casey Foundation staff, who functioned as site team leaders for virtual site teams assembled over time. These staff members' knowledge, whether related to jobs or child welfare, and their skills and experience in on-the-ground design and strategy, distinguished these site team leaders and the shape and ultimate success of their sites. The fate of sites, regardless of site-specific capacities, rested in the hands of non-site capacities back at Casey headquarters in Baltimore.

More broadly, the MC reliance on the capacity of personal leaders underscores the reality that, no matter the site readiness or intermediary capacity in a place, it's the individual people who run projects that matter. Cities with more capacity in general may have a deeper bench of talent, and this is important because people inevitably leave and different skills are required for different stages of demonstrations. Even so, ignoring the critical importance of individual capacity at each site would miss a major part of the JI and MC stories.

JI Capacity for MC

All of the JI sites were automatically included on the list of invited sites for the MC initiative. Several rationales informed this decision. First, the foundation had been trying to integrate its various initiatives for some time, but the challenge was how to integrate. Second, jobs projects were bound to be a key part of MC neighborhood strategies, so why not take advantage of the good work already underway related to employment? Third, building on the JI enabled the foundation to take advantage of the relationships, partners, and local knowledge that had been accumulated over five years, a potential resource for navigating local policy environments on behalf of MC and ensuring a successful start-up. The Foundation concluded that the best way to take advantage of this knowledge, and to make sure the last years of the JI were not disrupted, was to have the JI program officer manage the start-up of the MC in these cities.

JI performance did not necessarily translate into MC success. Of the six JI sites, three made it into the final MC 10, including one failed JI site, and three sites were categorized as family-strengthening sites and slated for short-term, three-year investments. Of these family-strengthening sites, Philadelphia and St. Louis had other large-scale initiatives similar to MC that crowded out the potential for a separate MC start-up. In New Orleans, the MC start-up was small, slow in getting started, and lacked major stakeholder champions. Of the JI sites that made it into the MC top 10, two survived in the final six.

Looking more closely at the three JI sites that made it to the final list of 10 MC sites raises questions about the assumption that capacity and performance demonstrated during JI somehow predicted MC success in those sites. For Seattle, perhaps the most successful JI site in terms of results and leverage, MC did build on key relationships developed by the JI with an array of local and regional partners. Yet, the foundation ultimately established MC in an unincorporated area just outside the City of Seattle, named White Center, which had formerly been the site for the foundation's Plain Talk teen pregnancy prevention initiative. During the latter years of MC, a working relationship was developed with the Seattle Jobs Initiative, and Seattle's White Center has been a top-performing MC site.

The case of Denver is instructive. It withdrew from the JI because its development intermediary, the Piton Foundation, did not want to be accountable for more ambitious results and its existing strategies showed "no effect." As a site for another Casey initiative, Rebuilding Communities, Denver gained entrance to the MC. Its workforce strategies, however, ultimately showed the same high level of innovation but relatively few results.

Finally, Milwaukee made it into the MC list of top 10 sites but could not put together viable strategies in all MC results areas, build a solid staff and partner infrastructure, and attract long-term system investors and champions. Its final three-year plan will focus on prisoner reentry workforce strategies, including continued investment in the JI's workforce intermediary, the Wisconsin Regional Training Partnership (WRTP). Again, the Milwaukee JI experience showed capacity to build regional partnerships but not viable neighborhood networks. Moreover, the Milwaukee MC site showed how a Casey site team leader's knowledge and investment in a site can substitute in the short run for local capacity but cannot guarantee long-term sustainability.

Neighborhood Capacity

Picking a target neighborhood or group of neighborhoods was a common feature of both the JI and MC, but there were important differences. The center of gravity for the JI was the regional intermediary and its jobs projects, not the neighborhood. For MC, in contrast, the center of gravity was primarily the neighborhood or neighborhoods, even when city and regional stakeholders were engaged. Both initiatives experienced problems in choosing the right neighborhoods with the right size and capacity.

JI sites selected for the planning phase had to choose an "impact community" of 80,000 to 120,000 people as the focus for 50 percent of their job placements. In making these choices, most cities balanced political considerations, racial and ethnic demographics, and relevant public and philanthropic designations, including enterprise zones or community development block grants. Philadelphia chose the north side West Oak Lane and Logan neighborhoods, in part because they were already a part of Pew Foundation and TRF investments and the home base of an important political champion. Not only did the JI have difficulty in these neighborhoods because of their demographics and community capacity, but the lead organization dissolved as well. New Orleans, with low capacity, heroically chose to concentrate the JI in the public housing developments ringing the downtown, making a challenging initiative even more challenging by focusing on the hardest-to-employ.

In addition to having the right demographics, MC neighborhoods had to be smaller if saturation effects were to be achieved, and had to have some capacity to make change. Some site team leaders looked explicitly for neighborhoods with market potential that would kick in over the long run. In Seattle, MC started by exploring two neighborhoods, one in the city and White Center on Seattle's outskirts. The foundation ultimately chose the latter, even though it fell short on local capacity to design and implement projects. This tumultuous step of refocusing led to staff and partner turnover. Even so, White Center had challenges—namely, gentrification, escalating housing prices, and the imminent relocation of public housing tenants because of a new Hope VI project.

The Greater Milwaukee Foundation and the University of Wisconsin at Milwaukee assisted the Casey Foundation in picking a target neighborhood. Data were gathered on 10 potential neighborhoods and site visits focused on understanding neighborhood organizations and capacity. A collection of geographically contiguous neighborhoods was ultimately chosen. Within months, the potential lead community organization ran into major problems and no alternative organizations came forward to play the convening role, a problem that was ongoing. In retrospect, no neighborhood in Milwaukee met the capacity requirements for MC. The foundation probably should have recognized this fundamental lack of capacity and stakeholder interest in the first place.

Choosing Oakland's Lower San Antonio neighborhood represents another version of MC site selection that did not take full account of local conditions, in this case a hot housing market and a crowded nonprofit field. Like White Center on the edge of Seattle, Lower San Antonio was overwhelmed by escalating housing prices, making affordable housing out of reach for most families. Unlike White Center and Milwaukee, however, Lower San Antonio had an overabundance of high-capacity community development organizations within its boundaries, some of which served the city of Oakland and beyond. Many MC projects stalled because it was difficult to get these groups to collaborate on an ongoing basis.

Lessons from Site Selection Mistakes

Site selection is a key success factor in launching and implementing effective social policy demonstrations. Social investors can do better than throwing darts at a map—at least I think they can—and a higher success rate than one in five sites is possible. Yet, site selection is more art than science and thus imprecise and subject to mistakes. And, in the end, local leaders are key to getting initiatives started and to keeping them evolving. Nevertheless, several lessons for improving site selection derive from the JI and MC.

Anticipating Capacity Pays Off

A commonsense step not consistently taken to inform demonstration site selection is to identify key site capacities by analyzing design features and intended results. Too often social investors rely on good proposal writing, exemplary general site capacities, political balancing, and financial leverage rather than a more detailed analysis of how specific site capacities mesh with design requirements. Mismatches between demonstration designs and expected results and existing capacities are frequent.

Identifying relevant site capacities is not easy. Demonstrations that attempt to replicate promising model programs require certain capacities. Other community-building demonstrations or design replications require sites that can invent or adapt designs. In the first case, identifying capacities begins with analyzing a specific model or program, delving deeply into what made these programs a success—the secret sauce. In the second case, identifying, inventing, and adapting capacities may require demonstration simulations, charrettes, or the creation of prototypes that reveal the dynamic interconnections among places, designs, and results. And, finally, because some demonstrations represent a hodgepodge of good intentions and fashionable ideas stitched together in the name of innovation and community transformation, a lack of design clarity makes improving site selection extremely difficult.

Mitigating the Costs of Competition

The demonstration application process may reveal the strengths or weaknesses of key players. This is why forgoing the application step, whether or not it is competitively structured, is a bad idea. No matter how good and effective a place or organization has been in the past, it has to "show up" in the present with ideas, leaders, partners, and enthusiasm to take on the next initiative. And it is always important to ask: Who are the specific people or "spark plugs" who will get the work done? Motivation and readiness can be hard to find, a problem that runs through many aspects of social policy, and we need to be careful that the hoopla of wooing a new demonstration or initiative is not mistaken for an ability to implement a new project effectively. When a group of foundation program officers flew to St. Louis for a site visit about the

JI, for example, the airplane crew formally welcomed them to St. Louis over the intercom on the landing approach. In retrospect, this over-the-top welcome should have been recognized as window dressing, not a sign of capacity. At the same time, competitions have real financial and reputational costs for the sites as they expend political capital to attract partners and resources in the process of assembling applications. There are many ways to minimize these costs or to compensate sites when they do not meet initiative requirements. But, more broadly, places need to acknowledge that failing to win a demonstration competition is far better than failing at implementation.

One Initiative Is One Initiative
Every demonstration is different and moves at its own pace. Yet, we are forced to look for analogous efforts in places in which we work, hoping that factors behind one success will transfer to the incubation of subsequent investments. In the JI, for example, the imperfect metaphor of the "petri dish" was used to describe rich environments in which to grow new cultures, or in this case, new initiatives. We hope each petri dish contains the right ingredients and environment to support such incubation, and what better indicator of the presence of these nutrients than the successful growth of past innovative initiatives? But conditions change and environments evolve, so no one petri dish can grow all new investments.

JI success did not uniformly predict MC success, although two of the top JI sites made the final MC cohort. The Seattle site had many capacities that transferred to MC success, including a strong economy, government support, and a strong nonprofit community; Milwaukee had strong capacity in the workforce development arena. Ultimately, whether these sites had good local leadership made the most difference.

Why Do We Know So Little about Site Selection?
Given the importance of site selection to the success of demonstrations, replications, and most social investments, one would think that

a handbook of site selection "dos and don'ts" would have been compiled over the past decades. Think of all the federal, state, local, philanthropic, nonprofit, and private sector initiatives that have required some type of site selection. Where's the handbook? With new demonstrations and replications likely to occur under the Obama administration, and for many years beyond, this handbook is needed more than ever.

A lot more is known about site selection than we realize and certainly more than is shared publicly. Many demonstrations have been sponsored under the auspices of research intermediaries like P/PV and MDRC, which specialize in designing and implementing demonstrations that produce relevant social knowledge. These intermediaries must have created such a list or at least have a well-traveled folklore about picking sites. But if we take seriously Gary Walker's comments at the beginning of this chapter, then it may be wishful thinking that anyone has crafted the universal solution to site selection. Yet, a how-to guide for demonstration site selection would be a useful tool.

Conclusion

The critical thinking embodied in social policy demonstrations is frequently centered in the design. Too often implementation seems to be a matter of compliance or of heroically struggling to develop site capacities after the initiative has begun. Or there is certain fatalism that we can't rationally identify the right sites, so let's get on with it. And results come years later. Having the right capacities at the beginning of an initiative can have a decisive influence on the evolution and impact of a demonstration. A part of the challenge of site selection is cutting through the boosterism and discerning real site capacities. This chapter argues that productive steps can be taken early to improve site selection, which, in turn, will translate into better results, even as we acknowledge the inevitable uncertainty of site selection.

References

Miller, C., Bos, J. M., Porter, K. E., Tseng, F. M., & Abe, Y. (2005, September). *The challenge of repeating success in a changing world: Final report on the Center for Employment Training replication sites.* New York: MDRC.

Walker, G. (2008). *Reflections on the evaluation revolution.* Washington DC: Hudson Institute.

4

Salvaging Success from Failure: Chicago's El Mercado Marketplace

Bob Brehm

Community, political, and business leaders—particularly those with what are thought to be strong entrepreneurial skills—are often praised for their "visionary" leadership. This typically refers to their ability to see a future that is better than the present in ways that mere mortals cannot. This ability enables the leader to guide an enterprise in a direction where the benefits are not readily apparent to others, but which proves nonetheless to be the right course of action. With such track records, these leaders can steer their groups in significantly new or risky directions without the level of scrutiny typically applied to ideas that are generated by those with less of a reputation as a visionary.

As the executive director of a community development corporation (CDC) in Chicago in the early 1990s, I led our group in the development of El Mercado Public Marketplace, a risky community economic development project that represented a radical diversion from what was then commonly accepted practice in the field. Bickerdike Redevelopment had a well-deserved reputation as a bold, progressive CDC that was ready to challenge both conventional wisdom and the political power structure and that consistently developed and managed its projects well. The new economic development project, while ultimately turned around into a highly successful venture, failed in its initial format. Did it fail perhaps because my colleagues and I let my visionary leadership win over my eyes-wide-open management and risk-assessment track record?

Among the most significant mistakes on this project were:

- We tried to achieve too many project and community goals through this one development project.
- We assumed that our organizational skills and capacity in one area would readily transfer to a new economic development initiative.
- We designed a project that was totally dependent on our ability to help local individuals, of limited means, to open and successfully operate small businesses.
- We overestimated consumer interest in this type of market.
- We had an unwavering faith in our organization and its leadership's ability to pull off even a challenging, risky project like this.

A closer analysis of this project follows, from its history through early planning and its run through failure to ultimate success. And from that analysis several lessons can be learned and applied to work in this field:

- Develop a solid business model for economic development activities. Make active use of "What if?" considerations, backed by risk assessments, and adjust plans to respond to those analyses. In some cases the project should never get past the early planning stage; in others mid-course corrections can be effective and should be considered early and often.
- Groups trying to achieve multiple project goals should consider the extent to which those goals may come into

conflict with each other. For example, that meant trying to provide good-quality, dependable service and supporting the start-up of micro-businesses at the same time. Incorporate such considerations into project planning.

- Do not abandon community-organizing efforts in favor of development projects. Any one project cannot realize a broader vision of economic change.

Background and History

The Northwest Community Organization (NCO) established Bickerdike in 1967. Development in the community was stagnant after more than 40 years of neglect by the public and private sector development actors. In the late 1960s the racial composition of the area was changing from primarily first- and second-generation European immigrants to Latinos and African Americans. NCO was one of the original community organizations set up by fabled organizer Saul Alinsky in the 1950s and 1960s. He and his disciples promoted community empowerment through grassroots organizing and challenging the power structures on issues ranging from crime to education to affordable housing and jobs. Bickerdike was created to enable the community to act on its own behalf with regard to the development of the physical community and, in particular, affordable housing; its work has resulted in the development of several hundred units of affordable housing.

Bickerdike initially thought of itself as a catalyst for community development, spurring activity without getting mired in the role of owner and manager of property. That changed dramatically in the early 1980s as the group began to develop rental housing and commercial property. This set the stage for the Mercado project; being an owner and landlord were no longer anathema to its role in community development.

Transition from Housing to Economic Development

Bickerdike has long recognized the importance of putting local people to work on its development projects. Bickerdike believes that, for area residents to benefit from economic growth, there had to be access to both affordable housing *and* well-paying jobs. One example is its subsidiary, Humboldt Construction, which has been providing union construction jobs and contracting services for the organization and others for more than 25 years.

The group adopted a two-prong approach to expanding its work on economic development. It would continue to be active with others in the community on an organizing and advocacy level, working to stem the loss of jobs and to try to achieve the maximum benefit of new developments in the area for local residents. And when it undertook a development project designed to have a direct economic impact, it chose projects that had the potential to catalyze additional positive development and demonstrate the benefits of community control and action.

Planned as a variation on a traditional Latin American marketplace, El Mercado was the group's first project under those criteria. Neighborhood residents—who by the early 1990s were more than two-thirds Latino—would be able to purchase fresh produce, meats, and prepared foods; local entrepreneurs would be able to have successful small businesses as operators of booths in the marketplace; and local residents would be hired to work in the stalls. These guiding criteria determined much of the predevelopment planning for El Mercado and later became factors in the organization's reluctance to alter its direction, even when it became clear that it was foundering.

El Mercado represented a significant deviation from the type of economic development efforts typically sponsored by CDCs in Chicago and elsewhere. While there are many exceptions—and among those are some of the most interesting projects to consider—most CDC-sponsored economic development projects are essentially real estate ventures; the CDC develops the real property and the end users are businesses that are expected to provide an economic stimulus to the area by creating employment or business start-up opportunities. Less common are projects where the CDC operates the business activity and becomes itself the direct agent for job creation or business start-ups.

With real estate developments, success of a project depends on the income from the real estate. So if the best employers decline to rent the space, the CDC will ultimately have to recruit businesses with less potential for creating good jobs for area residents, just to ensure the real estate project's financial success.

At El Mercado, what Bickerdike set out to do was to put the local benefits first. Sure, there was a clear real estate development aspect to the project with capital to be raised and spent in rehabbing it, and a budget to be met to operate it. But the project would be a success—as initially envisioned—only if it met these non-real-estate goals:

- The overwhelming majority of economic opportunities within the project, including both micro-businesses and jobs, went to area residents.
- Neighbors benefited from the availability of ethnically oriented fresh and prepared foods, which at the time were hard to get in the community.
- The community achieved a sense of pride in its accomplishment, in the ability of a community-controlled project to do well and stand as a model, and from that sense came a renewed confidence in and commitment to the area.

El Mercado Public Marketplace was a great idea and represented an incredible creative and development effort. Nevertheless, as originally structured, it failed to achieve all three goals.

The Predevelopment Period

To achieve the project's goals and, in particular, its emphasis on *local* control and benefit, we undertook an extraordinary amount of community involvement in the planning and implementation of this project. Many, many CDC projects are initiated with similar goals, but without a working system of accountability, the projects often veer off, typically in the direction of practical, financial benefit decisions. Bickerdike wanted to ensure that, when faced with choices relating to the ease of development or financial benefits and risks to the organization on the one hand and maximizing community benefit on the other, it would always chose the latter. We believed that we would abandon a project rather than go ahead with one that could not meet the community benefit objectives.

To maximize local economic benefit, Bickerdike had to ensure that most of the booths and jobs went to area residents and, in particular, to low-income area residents. (The latter point was a key requirement for a federal grant.) This meant that when a business that was not from the community, or was not owned and/or operated by low-income residents, came to rent space, more often than not it had to be turned down. When not enough interested vendors who met the criteria could be found from among area residents, Bickerdike was faced with the option of compromising on that key goal or moving forward with either local vendors who were not really qualified or with empty space.

To achieve the goal of community control, Bickerdike committed itself to an ambitious level of community involvement in project planning and oversight and made key decisions based on that input. This process led to:

- the establishment of a steering committee comprising members of the Bickerdike Board of Directors, area merchants, supportive community organizations, and neighborhood residents;
- extensive conceptual planning work, including the use of project architects from both Chicago and Puerto Rico; and
- trips with members of the steering committee to tour markets and meet with businesses and management in Baltimore, Philadelphia, Hartford, and San Juan.

This process was immensely beneficial in informing the project planning on practical matters and in building support for the Mercado and a sense of teamwork among the committee members. Additionally, the process yielded some key decisions:

- There were limitations on the amount of space that could be leased by any one vendor, thereby maximizing the opportunity for small, independent micro-businesses to benefit.
- The governance and accountability structure was unique—recognizing that vendors, area consumers, and Bickerdike all had significant interests that should be represented.
- Vendors would not be allowed to sell alcohol, tobacco, or liquor—products that were in abundance in area stores.
- All local cultures (primarily Latino and African American) would be represented in both business owners and product offerings.
- The Mercado would be organized as a traditional public market, with opportunities for local organizations and artists to use the space for public events, and featuring frequent entertainment or special events.

The group's leadership was proud of these community planning efforts. Although the process was much more labor-intensive than simply planning a real estate development project with staff and architects, Bickerdike truly believed that it would lead to a committed community and a project that had the best chance of success on multiple levels—in practice, as a demonstration project, and in terms of community empowerment. As it turned out, the original structure failed on practical terms. Far too few vendors were able to run a small business and were interested in leasing space, and those who did experienced far less customer traffic and spending than projected. This suggests that, while significant, the community planning process did not set us up for success. Ironically, it may have succeeded in making us even more committed to an impractical vision by convincing us that it was, indeed, possible to replicate the model in a Chicago neighborhood.

During El Mercado's predevelopment phase, Bickerdike did little market research beyond obtaining data on supermarket gross sales and an estimate of the sales volume for the site's earlier occupant. Based on those figures, Bickerdike estimated sales projections for the stalls that, if achieved, could easily have supported 30 to 40 successful small businesses. Staff conducted extensive community outreach, which provided ample anecdotal evidence of community interest and support but did not more formally assess the interest and capability of area entrepreneurs.

El Mercado was funded through a mix of federal grants and equity Bickerdike had raised from successful multifamily housing developments. Had those resources not been available, Bickerdike would have had to obtain private bank financing, and the project would have been subjected to a more rigorous underwriting process. Lenders we approached asked for evidence of community interest in the project—to validate expectations of sales and marketability of the booths. Ironically, our ability to finance the project without debt let us get away without having to prove those expectations reasonable to anyone other than ourselves.

The Focus on Microenterprise

To enable start-ups to open booths in El Mercado, Bickerdike provided significant financial and technical assistance. We provided direct technical assistance to the businesses and a start-up loan fund. Because almost none of the potential vendors was bankable, Bickerdike capitalized the loan fund itself.

And Bickerdike helped each business build its stall. El Mercado was designed as an open market, with 48-inch-high partitions distinguishing the 37 booths. Each booth had its own utilities, and there were walk-in coolers for the fresh food stalls. Beyond that, vendors had to furnish counters, display cases or coolers, and workspace. Working with Bickerdike, and with some help from Humboldt Construction, vendors built out their booths, in many cases using plywood counters and displays made on site in a workshop in the back. It was during this process of building their physical space that the vendors and Bickerdike were able to plan together for the operations of the small businesses and forge a working relationship that was critical to moving forward with a shared common vision and respect for one another. It is interesting to note that the trust and respect developed during that period was in short supply when the market attracted far fewer vendors and customers than hoped. Still, it was a factor in enabling us to continue working together as long as we did. It was clear that most of the vendors respected and appreciated Bickerdike, even as their businesses were struggling.

Soon after opening we succeeded in luring a local bank to open a branch in El Mercado, which at the time was a unique concept. And we eventually turned over about half the space to a local mid-size business to operate a grocery. Other than from those two businesses, however, Bickerdike was unable to collect rent. What could we do, evict the very people we'd put so much effort into supporting? If we did evict them, where would that leave us, since there wasn't a line of entrepreneurs at the door waiting to lease space?

What Went Wrong?

El Mercado had a rousing opening week, complete with a full front-page color picture and story in the *Chicago Sun-Times* and crowds in the hundreds for four straight days of opening celebrations and entertainment. After that, sales were miniscule and flat.

Was it the site? Not likely. Located in the heart of the community, it was on a major commercial strip that, while run-down, had easy car, pedestrian, and bus access.

Was it the building? Doubtful. Bickerdike did a $2-million renovation, complete with exterior signage and murals that were real attention-grabbers.

Was it the booths? Most looked nice, if a little amateurish, with their painted wooden counters. But there was consistent, attractive signage—most of it hand-painted by local artists and hung on panels over the booths. The biggest problem was the lack of good product on display. Small businesses that weren't moving fresh produce, for example, were loath to throw out aging vegetables and fruit without the sales to support replacing the old product with new. Some vendors charged markups more typical of corner grocery stores than of larger markets. And most were unwilling or unable to stock much of a variety of products.

The community clearly knew about the project; there was no trouble attracting hundreds of people to El Mercado for entertainment or cultural events. And shoppers came, but ultimately they spent very little money. Some came for a jibarito sandwich for lunch or a tropical shake, enjoyed the sunlit atmosphere, and left without doing any shopping for fresh food. More successful were the small branch of a local bank with which Bickerdike had done business for years and the booth selling dairy and other goods subsidized through the Special Supplemental Nutrition Program for Women, Infants, and Children (WIC), both of which did well and attracted customer traffic.

Failure and Turnaround

With the project not generating customer traffic, none of the booths had enough sales to break even. This meant they could not make payments on either their monthly rent or their debt to Bickerdike for those who took start-up loans. Bickerdike itself began operating some of the booths, including a meat booth and a dairy booth that took part in the WIC program. (To qualify for a WIC license, the booth needed a nonprofit sponsor, so Bickerdike stepped in.) In both cases, Bickerdike managed the booths for maximum quality and good pricing and still lost money operating them.

Several of the small businesses failed, each one leaving Bickerdike with unpaid loans and rent and El Mercado with yet another gaping hole. Bickerdike took over a few of the booths and ultimately did a restructuring to bring in a local mid-size business to operate a dry goods business occupying about 40 percent of the space. The grocer paid rent to Bickerdike regularly, unlike many of the smaller businesses, and sales picked up a little. Still, the project was losing money every month for Bickerdike, and the group knew it could not sustain the losses indefinitely.

El Mercado opened in November 1992. By the time I left Bickerdike in February 1995, it was clear that something drastic had to be done with this failing project. It was no longer reasonable to continue the same strategies, hoping that eventually customers and small businesses would materialize and the project would become viable.

In October 1995, under the direction of its new executive director, Joy Aruguete, Bickerdike restructured the project. El Mercado would still provide fresh food for area residents and would commit to hiring local low-income residents for 75 percent of its workforce. And it would still be a major positive influence on the local retail economy. However, the group proposed moving away from the concept of having many booths operated by independent small businesses. Instead, the building would be leased to a mid-size grocer, who would pay Bickerdike rent under a net lease. Through this adaptation Bickerdike avoided a long-term failure and produced a successful project. This was possible for a number of reasons. The sponsor and its federal grant agency were both willing to pursue the modification. The underlying economics of the real estate project were sound, even if the public market use was not. And the CDC itself was strong enough to sustain the project through the lean years without being forced to abandon it.

Mistakes—Mostly Bad Assumptions
What were Bickerdike's mistakes on the El Mercado project? Among the most significant were these bad assumptions:

1. *Bickerdike could achieve multiple goals through one project.* From the outset, the organization wanted to develop a project that would have an impact beyond the tangible outcomes: jobs and economic opportunities for area residents on the one hand and choice and quality of products on the other. We were trying to make a statement—about

culture, economic opportunity, democratic economic structures, and community control—all the while expecting to generate significant economic activity and benefit to consumers. This was simply too much to ask of one project.

This unreasonable expectation played out in a number of decisions, small and large in impact:

- We decided to have no freezers, for example, because frozen food was anathema to *fresh* food. (We, of course, added freezers within the first year.) While relatively minor, this decision illustrates the kinds of tensions we faced and how we dealt with them.

- We stuck with the notion of having many small booths, rather than a mix of one or two larger businesses and a few small booths. And we maintained our support for local, low-income people to start small businesses for the first time. This turned out to be an enormously limiting factor in marketing the space. We were left with an unhealthy opening day mix of three experienced, fairly well capitalized entrepreneurs and a dozen others with no experience and no capital. Had we recognized this, and considered the possibility that low sales would leave those small vendors unable to pay rent, buy product, and keep their booths fully staffed, perhaps we would have taken a different approach. We also resisted leasing large amounts of space to one or more medium-size businesses. We worried that such a hybrid was likely to fail as a business model, but my sense is that the resistance was due more to an unwillingness to abandon the original concept.

- Despite being able to recruit only 15 vendors at the outset, we felt we needed to open the market, even though much of the space would be vacant. (In the early months we used panels adorned with colorful community artwork to cover the empty booths.) We did not seriously consider changing course prior to opening, but believed—vision over practicality at work here—that our "market of dreams" would work out much as the ball field did in the movie: If we build it, they will come. The expectation was that, once we opened, potential vendors would see the flock of customers coming through and would line up to lease space. And just like in the movie, we were asking people to join us in a vision based on fantasy.

- With the exception of the WIC/dairy booth, we were slow to see the need to operate booths ourselves. We recognized the need to have WIC to draw customers, and since the license was only available to a nonprofit and we could not find another nonprofit to do it, we made the wise decision to do it ourselves.

Why were we slow to apply that thinking to all of the empty space? We felt that it was a strategy of last resort, that we did not have the expertise or inclination to run small businesses.

2. *Bickerdike's competencies would easily transfer to success with El Mercado.* Bickerdike's current director, Joy Aruguete, the leader responsible for the project's successful turnaround, says:

> We see the same thing in our new mixed-use rental development. People think that just because we do residential property management—and we're good at that—that means we can do retail property management as well. And it just isn't that simple. There are different factors involved, you're dealing with different sorts of people, and they bring different issues to the table.

Bickerdike did not assemble a management team for El Mercado that was up to the task. We had turnover in the early years, including during predevelopment, when our carefully selected manager turned out to be dishonest and unskilled and had to be fired. This set us back several months in our early marketing of booths. We had staff people who were good at community planning and outreach, but they, too, were unprepared to negotiate with entrepreneurs. Because of my interest in the project, I took a leave of sorts from my desk job and worked full-time at the Mercado for about two years. I organized the build-out of the stalls with the vendors and participated in all of the lease negotiations and business decisions as we prepared to open and during the first year of operations. It was clear that with my total involvement, we brought more of Bickerdike's development and management skills than would have been possible with all new staff. What we did not have to offer was any experience in the food business and only limited experience in small business. We did not bring in anyone competent in those fields to work with us or even to advise us, other than a brief visit from a friendly consultant from Baltimore who offered his services pro bono.

When things were not going well—either in leasing or during the first year—we didn't have enough background and experience to make good decisions about changes in direction. This severely limited our abilities as *strategic* managers, something we prided ourselves on in all of our other work.

3. *Local residents of limited means would be willing and able to open and operate small businesses successfully.* The decision to favor small businesses owned and operated by low-income area residents meant that, in practice, most of the vendors would be novices. They had limited experience (ranging from none to some, with few who had operated actual businesses before); limited capital (ranging from none to a very small amount); limited technical knowledge of business planning and operation; and a limited customer base.

Local vendors were also reluctant to lease booths if rent was based on a percentage of sales. Some of the more savvy businesspeople Bickerdike approached thought it was fine, but the local start-up entrepreneurs had a visceral negative response: "If we make more money, then you'll make us give you all our profits! That's communism!" The organization felt that basing rents on a percentage of sales would improve marketing for booths, helping prospective vendors to get over the hurdle of their concern about sales projections. But in the face of opposition from small businesses on the steering committee and those already committed to the project, Bickerdike dropped the idea.

4. *Everyone would love to shop at a public market.* The failure to attract businesses cannot be seen as separate from its counterpart—the failure to attract shoppers and their money. The projections predicted economic viability if the entire marketplace achieved sales only comparable to that of the run-down, poorly maintained supermarket that was the site's previous occupant. We estimated that the earlier store had annual gross sales in the range of $4 million to $5 million. This seemed like a modest, conservative goal at the time; couldn't we do at least as well as the dumpy supermarket we were replacing? Apparently not. In its first three years of operation, El Mercado never had gross sales in excess of $1.5 million. At those sales levels, the project was not viable regardless of how it was structured.

Although there was no modern history of public markets in Chicago, Bickerdike expected El Mercado to catch on and succeed. That assumption was based on the apparent viability of the business model and on the notion that, with the cultural connection to this sort of shopping, the area's primarily Latino residents would readily give up the convenience of large supermarkets in favor of daily or weekly shopping at El Mercado. The reality was that the shopping was inconvenient. Customers had to pay at several locations and could not take carts outside, limiting the amount of purchases. In addition, most of the businesses did not accept checks or credit cards.

5. *The executive director will pull this off.* I brought to the role a good set of skills, drive, and a commitment to Bickerdike's values of community control, honesty, integrity, and doing things well. I had a track record as the organization's leader, and in spite of having my share of detractors, others tended to give me some credit when it came

to getting projects done successfully. Unfortunately, I also brought to El Mercado an unflinching commitment to El Mercado's multiple goals. When at first we couldn't attract vendors, and later when sales were not improving, my eyes were not entirely wide open. It took my departure, and the work of a new director with comparable values, skills, drive, and commitment—but not the emotional attachment to this particular vision—to guide the organization through a successful project restructuring.

All of these decisions, taken together, helped set the project on a course for failure. Ultimately, the project was turned around by making changes in ways that altered its character along those same lines. Had we been open to considering such changes prior to opening, or perhaps during the project's first year, we might have avoided the failure.

Bickerdike embarked on El Mercado largely because of its uniqueness and potential to benefit the community. When the project was restructured, which elements of its original qualitative metrics were retained? Jobs have been created for local residents; a mid-size minority entrepreneur flourishes there; fresh products appealing to the area's ethnic groups are readily available; and the community institution— Bickerdike—shares financial gains through space rental. That makes the project different from a typical CDC economic development project and it still benefits the local economy. Yet it lost the more substantive ways in which it was distinctive—the public market concept and the local economic empowerment through micro-business development.

No one at Bickerdike considers the project a failure, and it seems that the community at large feels the same way. The group should be commended for turning the project into a success, with the many community benefits it offers. Still, it raises the question of how many so-called successful CDC projects differ significantly in terms of concept or beneficiaries from their original plans. Is the CDC community—including government and private funders, associations, and the CDCs themselves—prepared to put a project into the "failure" column if it deviates from the group's purpose? My sense is that there are many such projects out there, and that those projects are not considered failures unless a loan goes unpaid or the property is abandoned to another use entirely.

How is it that Bickerdike was able to salvage success from a failing project? One reason is that the underlying real estate aspects of the project were sound. Another is that Bickerdike is, and was at the time, strong in two areas that are key to successful community development efforts: internal organizational capacity and active, effective community engagement. Groups with less capacity in those areas are more likely to see difficult projects fail or their organizations falter or go under because of risky undertakings.

What are the most important lessons from the El Mercado project? For me there are three:

- First, some of the best ideas in community economic development should not get beyond the early planning stages. We should continue to dream, plan, and get enough funding for feasibility studies, undergirded by a realistic assessment of the risks. And if the risk assessment doesn't lead to a reasonable expectation of success, the organization should drop the project. Why? There is just too much to lose.
- Second, if we apply rigorous planning to innovative new initiatives, maybe we'll do a better job of setting them up. For El Mercado, Bickerdike should have had an anchor tenant—maybe in meats and grocery. Produce, fresh fish, specialties, prepared food—those would have had a chance to succeed as small businesses surrounding a well-run grocery and meat store.

  We made several key mistakes in planning and operating El Mercado. On reflection I have come to believe that, even had we done a better job and avoided those mistakes, this project would still have failed in its original format. What we should have done was to take a closer, more critical look at the business model during the planning phase.

- Third, we shouldn't abandon our nondevelopment strategies for changing the local economic landscape, such as grassroots organizing and advocacy on policy changes. Whether the issue is protecting good jobs or better education and increased access to the jobs that are available, there is no shortage of activist organizing strategies that may have the potential for greater impact on the local economy than even our most successful development projects. For those of us who are committed to the notion that community *development* can play a critical role in the struggle for community *empowerment,* we need to chose our development strategies carefully and assess our success or failure based on whether our efforts have served that broader mission.

I am just as committed today as I was in 1990 to the notion that community development makes sense only if there is an agenda that entails using the development activity to support organizing for community empowerment. The experience of El Mercado has not changed my perspective on that notion. However, if the development project we undertake does not succeed, it can provide no community empowerment gains, and, in fact, the organizing agenda suffers for that failure.

Those familiar with the work of CDCs will recognize two familiar themes in this story that are widely accepted as true but often do not stand up to close scrutiny. There is the "double bottom line," implying that the sponsor can do good and make money simultaneously, and the notion that nonprofits have to learn to operate "more like businesses." Those concepts have been around for decades and still tend to influence the decisions we make about community development. When we follow those credos and continue to meet our mission, the CDC can do well. When we pursue our vision without adequate consideration of practical business factors, or when we adhere to the laws of business and the market at the expense of our community empowerment goals, that's when we fail.

5

Are Best Practices Really Better?
Stories from the Workforce Development Frontier

Karen Chapple

Introduction

The last 30 years have seen the emergence of numerous accepted best practices in workforce development. Based on dozens of evaluations of the Center for Employment Training (CET), Project QUEST, and other model programs by academics, policy think tanks, and government agencies, conventional wisdom has settled on a set of best practices, including building connections to regional employers, training in a mix of technical and soft skills, overcoming barriers (such as lack of transportation and childcare) to employment, linking workforce development to sectors and clusters, developing career ladders for low-skilled workers through sector strategies, and creating workforce development networks that link community-based organizations (CBOs), community colleges, and employers.

The success of these programs, as they have been implemented by CBOs and others, has led policymakers and others to posit a theory of change in labor markets: as employers shift to a more flexible labor force, workforce intermediaries closely tied to employers will be able to help workers enter and advance in the workforce (Benner, 2002; Giloth, 2004; Osterman, 1999). Various stakeholders have worked hard to disseminate knowledge about intermediaries and support their activities.[1] Moreover, a solid literature on networks and the embeddedness of the regional economy in social relationships (for example, Granovetter, 1995; Saxenian, 1994; Tilly & Tilly, 1994) suggests that improving connections is key to dealing with labor market shifts.

Yet, as new intermediaries try to adopt the best practices associated with success stories, they have met with mixed results. This is not a failure to replicate programs, as with CET (Giloth, 1998, and this volume; Kato, 1999). Rather than reproduce programs in exact detail, these intermediaries have embraced the best practices that are "in the air," or commonly held to be successful. Their premise is that if they can connect programs to employers, provide soft-skills training, and build workforce development networks (among other practices), they can be as successful as CET. But they often fail to translate these best practices in a way that makes sense in a particular new context. The essential mistake they make is to assume that they can manufacture intermediaries with the types of connections that characterize organic successes like QUEST and CET. As policymakers translate the descriptions of the best practices into prescriptions for new programs, they can lose sight of the key elements that make the exemplars work so well.

This chapter uses the case of a regional workforce development collaborative to illustrate the problems with adopting these prevalent best practices. This research draws from 40 semi-structured interviews with key informants and program staff conducted in 2003 and 2004.[2] The San Francisco Information Technology Consortium (SFITC) was a collaborative among CBOs and San Francisco City College that coordinated services to build a career ladder of training programs in information technology. This program was designed around three best practices: first, linking workforce development to key employers and sectors in the regional economy; second, networking among CBOs, community colleges, and employers; and, third, creating career ladders through training programs. The next section examines these three practices in more detail. Following is a description of the case and its successes and failures. A postscript examines what local workforce development officials and their funders have learned from these failures and are beginning to redesign in today's programs. The conclusion revisits the issue of how difficult it is to reform programs simply by adopting best practices.

The Emergence and Dissemination of Best Practices in Workforce Development

It is important to examine the origins of and assumptions behind three best practices that workforce development programs are following to become more effective: First, that linking workforce development to employers and sectors helps support the regional economy; second, that creating workforce development networks helps overcome barriers to employment; and, third, that training can build career ladders.

Practice Number 1: Link workforce development to employers and sectors so training will meet economic development goals. Over the last decade, scholars and practitioners have documented numerous workforce intermediaries that also meet some economic development goals, such as job and wealth creation (Giloth, 1998, 2004; Harrison & Weiss, 1998; Melendez, 1996). These intermediaries, most notably CET, Project QUEST, and the Wisconsin Regional Training Partnership (WRTP), credit their success to their close relationships with employers. An impressive set of evaluations (for example, Chapple, 2005b; Elliott, Roder, King, & Stillman, 2001; Zandniapour & Conway, 2003) has shown that these and other sectoral initiatives have a significant and positive impact on the employability, wages, and upward mobility of their participants.

Though evaluations are only just beginning to address the benefits for employers systematically (for example, Aspen Institute Workforce Strategies Initiative, 2005), these initiatives are seen as demand-responsive and linked to firms, sectors, and clusters in the regional economy, and thus able to facilitate economic development. For instance, WRTP arguably improves the productivity of its partner firms (Dresser & Rogers, 1998), and CET employers benefit from ready access to a trained workforce (Melendez, 1996).

Practitioners and policymakers have generally interpreted this success as stemming from two best practices: involving employers in the training and placement process and conducting training in key regional sectors or clusters. The notion of employer involvement is not new; it builds on several generations of attempts to improve the responsiveness of education and training to employers' needs, particularly in community colleges (Dougherty, 1994). When employers are directly involved in programs, curricula focus on the most appropriate skills, trainees become more familiar with workplace practices, and the intermediary may act as an employment broker, introducing workers to prospective employers. Yet, there are several potentially problematic assumptions here, for instance, that programs can adjust their curricula readily to meet employer needs and that employers have vacancies for which they will hire program graduates.

Sector initiatives are programs that target specific industry sectors, trying to create a win-win situation by restructuring employment practices in a way that is beneficial to both employers and low-wage workers (Marano & Tarr, 2004).[3] These "dual-customer" intermediaries, the most successful of which have been funded by the Charles Stewart Mott Foundation and the Annie E. Casey Foundation, not only attempt to improve wages and advancement potential for workers but also try to change internal labor market practices related to management, diversity, and mentoring (Giloth, 2000). Do they lead to economic development? Though evaluations have yet to measure employer outcomes effectively, critics point to several shortcomings (Fitzgerald, 2006; author interviews). Sector initiatives only work well with certain industries, with the most consistent successes occurring in health care and manufacturing. These sectors are unique in that they have problems with recruitment and retention (due to the difficulty of advancement), typically have union involvement, and tend to have a supportive corporate culture. And, in fact, from an economic development perspective, this type of industry targeting, which was popular in the 1980s and 1990s, is for the most part ineffective; in many cases it simply distorted resource allocation (Buss, 1999; Finckle, 1999; Wiewel, 1999).

Practice Number 2: Build networks among CBOs, community college providers, and employers for a more flexible workforce system. By the late 1990s, as the number of workforce intermediaries quickly expanded from the initial models, it had become conventional wisdom that, as firms reorganize into flexible networks and traditional internal labor markets disintegrate, workforce intermediaries would play a growing role in preparing and placing workers (Giloth, 2004; Harrison & Weiss, 1998; Osterman, 1999). To mediate effectively between workers and firms in the fast-changing labor market, these intermediaries would need to organize themselves into networks embedded in the regional economy (Dresser & Rogers, 1998; Harrison & Weiss, 1998). These workforce development networks would help overcome three labor market failures: the difficulty of transmitting information about job opportunities and requirements in a market of rapid turnover and specialized skill requirements; the development of trust as new firms and educational institutions replace well-established players; and the elimination of traditional boundaries or "silos" separating firms, educational institutions, job training providers, and other workforce intermediaries.

Harrison and Weiss (1998) discuss three kinds of networks: hub-spoke employment training networks with CBOs (such as CET or Project QUEST) at the hub; peer-to-peer employment training networks (networks of CBOs, such as the Chicago Jobs Council); and intermediary employment training networks with community colleges or other regional actors at the hub. Other forms of networks have emerged since, in part because of the advent of welfare reform (1996) and the Workforce Investment Act, or WIA (1998). For instance, employer-led consortia such as San Francisco Works appeared as downtown businesses, often pressured by city government, became engaged in implementing welfare reform. In these networks, employer partners commit to hiring graduates in either internship or full-time positions in exchange for customized training by CBOs.

These networks work by building ad hoc partnerships from the ground up that leverage resources from a variety of sources and take on difficult workforce problems (Giloth, 2004). Stakeholders perceive them as effective in part because such intermediaries have no "baggage." Yet, some networks never become effective in the labor market, perhaps because the following key assumptions underlying workforce development networks are not met: (1) greater familiarity among workforce development actors will result in more and better placements for workers; (2) networks are more nimble and informed about labor market trends than are isolated, stand-alone CBOs, and thus better able to respond to employer needs; and (3) connections among diverse network players will be able to overcome the restrictions of traditional funding streams.

Practice Number 3: Use training programs to construct career ladders. Career ladder initiatives originated relatively recently, and program experiments take several different forms (Fitzgerald, 2006). Simply increasing the pay of existing jobs (as Cooperative Home Care Associates has done in the Bronx), though not exactly a ladder, is a way to promote employees in their current positions. Another strategy is creating tiers within occupations that have a variety of job duties. This often takes the form of creating a bottom rung on the ladder, an entry-level occupation that can lead to employment in more advanced occupations that already exist (which is the idea behind the Building Essential Skills Training course work in bio-manufacturing in the Boston area). It can also facilitate an "upgrade and backfill" approach, in which training programs provide current workers with skill upgrades, thereby vacating their positions for entry-level workers; this was the idea behind the SFITC. A third strategy is to use education and training to advance workers into occupations with better pay—an approach adopted, though perhaps unsuccessfully, by the WRTP. Most of these initiatives focus on creating career ladders in sectors such as health care, biotechnology, manufacturing, and information technology (Alssid et al., 2002; Fitzgerald, 2006; Fitzgerald & Carlson, 2000; Prince & Mills, 2003).

The purpose of career ladder initiatives is to identify the skill sets that lead to workplace progression and thereby solve two labor market failures: the problem for employers of recruiting and retaining qualified workers, and the difficulty for workers of gaining more responsibility and wages within a given sector. Typically, these models are built around the community college system and begin with remedial education.

The career ladder approach means rethinking workforce development. Instead of training students for a particular job, workforce development focused on career ladders uses a series of training and educational programs to give entry-level workers new, related skills, enabling them to change jobs and increase earnings. By grouping related training programs together, training providers can show workers multiple avenues for upward mobility. Because of the potential for horizontal and diagonal movement across these channels, some call the ladder a "lattice"—for instance, a computer technician might move laterally into networking, vertically into programming, or, with some new business skills, diagonally into a business analyst position. At the same time, adopting a career ladder strategy requires stakeholders to leave their "silos" to think about the pipeline. Community colleges and community-based training providers, for example, have to think about a continuum of services, and the employers involved have to consider developing mechanisms for internal advancement.

The advantage for employers is not just more qualified employees, but also increased retention, particularly in high-turnover, low-wage industries like health care.

Yet, since only certain types of firms benefit from retention, there are limits to employers' interest in career ladder strategies. Moreover, there are serious concerns about the feasibility of these programs; they would have only limited effects on upward mobility and could depress wages as firms substitute less-educated workers for their traditional workforce recruited through the first-chance system (Mitnik & Zeidenberg, 2004).

Developing career ladders that lead to upward mobility is critical at a time when low-wage, dead-end jobs dominate the landscape of low-skill work. Clearly, because of all of the support systems and sectors that are involved in making upward mobility possible, the concept has helped to break down the silos. Yet, the most thorough evaluation of these programs (Fitzgerald 2006) cautions that they are unlikely to be replicated widely unless employers are willing to reorganize the workplace while the job training system undergoes a complete realignment. It seems that many initiatives fail to solve labor market failures related to retention and advancement. Perhaps they fail in part because they falsely assume that (1) the lack of career ladders is problematic for firms and workers, or (2) the missing rung in career ladders is job training. This then diverts resources from the real issue: the lack of jobs that pay family-supporting wages.

San Francisco Information Technology Consortium

The concept of the SFITC arose in 1999 as the San Francisco Department of Human Services began to think strategically about how to get its welfare-to-work clients into better-paying jobs with potential for advancement, focusing on the information technology (IT) and construction sectors. Initially funded by the James Irvine Foundation, and then through the California Labor and Workforce Development Agency and the U.S. Department of Labor's H-1B technology training program, a new collaborative emerged among six nonprofits and a community college experienced in providing IT, ranging from remedial to advanced.[4] Its mission: "The SFITC is a membership organization that provides training and promotes access to career pathways in IT for economically or educationally disadvantaged people."

The SFITC created an integrated set of short training programs, including basic computer literacy, hardware repair, Web design, networking, and Unix programming, that would help graduates to obtain a first job and be ready to move up an IT career ladder. The overall strategy was to "upgrade and backfill"—that is, train and promote incumbent workers so that entry-level slots become available for SFITC graduates. In this model, the CBOs at the beginning rungs of the career ladder serve a more disadvantaged clientele, while those providing advanced training tend to see clients with more education. Because the Bay Area Video Coalition (BAVC) had developed its curriculum through close collaboration with the many employers who used its multimedia facilities, the other CBOs borrowed liberally from it.

The focus of the collaboration was mostly on the supply side, to coordinate curricula, create skill standards, and facilitate transfers between training programs so that graduates could move quickly up the ladder of IT occupations. As one respondent said, "It becomes a seamless process. . . . Programs save slots for each other because they have transfer agreements.[5] Everyone understands the basic criteria for training." At the same time, trainees gained new awareness of career ladders; as one consortium participant described it, "There was a vision that we could help students see that opportunities are beyond initial training. We could keep introducing them to new technologies." The end educational goal was a college degree; toward that end, many of the classes offered college credit.

Although the IT training programs arose out of employer demand in the late 1990s, and consortium members generally felt that training should be responsive to business needs, their primary customers were disadvantaged job seekers. Thus the collaborative's primary economic development goals were redistributive, which was reflected in its approach to its clientele. For instance, the SFITC developed a model of joint case management to provide intensive support for disadvantaged trainees. As one member described it, "The strength of the collaborative is the passing of knowledge. It means that we have a community of people supporting a person. So there's much more effort and time put into one person's success."

The SFITC largely succeeded at recruiting its target population to IT training programs at the CBOs: 68 percent of the participants were low-income, 13 percent were ex-offenders, and only 20 percent had any post-secondary education. In all, 88 percent completed the programs. Placement rates, which include the "placement" of graduates in another training program, fluctuated widely, from a high of 80 percent when the regional economy was strong to only 40 percent at the trough of the "dot-bomb" cycle. However, for most of the program, one organization, the Bay Area Video Coalition (BAVC), essentially carried the collaborative in terms of placement, with a placement rate as high as 90 percent, compared to 20 percent to 30 percent for some of the other partners.[6] In 2005, the SFITC disbanded its career ladder training program due to lack of employer demand and shifted its focus to employer-based training, with CBOs and/or San Francisco City College conducting custom training for large employers (for instance, keyboarding for nurses at local hospitals). Within a few years, the SFITC ceased to exist.

Linking Workforce Development to Employers and Sectors

The SFITC altogether placed about 800 mostly low-income, often minority graduates in jobs or other training programs but was unable to survive after the business cycle peak. Most of the individual members discontinued or downsized their IT training programs, and only BAVC has continued to evolve (currently focusing on incumbent worker training).

The SFITC did not think of itself as a sector or cluster initiative, since IT occupations are dispersed across a wide variety of unrelated industries. Yet, the job losses in the IT industry showed the collaborative's vulnerability to one sector's fortunes, and it ultimately turned to custom training in hospitals. This suggests that training programs, at least in IT, might best focus on certain skills that are in high demand across occupations and industries, rather than trying to respond to sectors that are currently driving the regional economy.

The real mistake of the SFITC was to assume that it could parlay the strong employer connections of one CBO into connections for all the collaborative members, thus improving curriculum and placement rates across the board. BAVC brought by far the strongest employer relationships to the collaborative. However, the other CBOs were not able to benefit; years of interaction had helped employers trust BAVC enough to hire its graduates, but they were not inclined to trust its partners as well.

Beyond placement, another advantage of employer ties is the ability to keep curricula up to date. However, the SFITC was too unwieldy to adjust its curricula; having spent years to develop an articulated ladder of training programs that included all of its partner CBOs, it was not able to eliminate or reconfigure programs easily as the market for skills shifted.

Building Workforce Development Networks

The SFITC collaborated well because of its clear division of labor and services and strong personal relationships among its members, perhaps due to frequent meetings and a culture of collaboration in San Francisco. Yet, it failed to realize many of the advantages of the workforce development networks in the best practice models.

Most important, the trust among partners did not extend to sharing employer connections, and the network suffered by not including employers explicitly. More partners meant not more job opportunities, but the loss of potential opportunities as individual CBOs were supposed to share job leads with each other. As one partner asked, "How much do we want to dilute these employer relationships by sharing them?"

Though networks are supposed to engender more flexibility and responsiveness to changes in the labor market, the SFITC found itself hamstrung by a cumbersome process (involving approval from all the partners) to make curricular changes. But, apart from the initial H-1B grant, it was also unable to obtain funding from a range of sources by collaborating.

The SFITC's critics argued that the collaborative lacked purpose, particularly from the perspective of employers. Said one workforce development expert, "They knew they were supposed to collaborate and get some money. It's collaboration for collaboration's sake versus getting something done." Another suggested that the SFITC is only about skill standards on the supply side; unlike the best practice network models, which derive standards directly from employers, the CBOs negotiated standards among themselves. The mistake, then, was building a network without the responsiveness and flexibility that characterize the best workforce development networks.

Developing Career Ladders

The SFITC's major focus was the career ladder. By defining training niches for the different programs, it reduced overlap in curricula and encouraged the transition of graduates from one program to the next. Before, graduates of such basic programs as office technology or computer repair often would fail to acquire enough skills to enter the workforce—or even enough confidence to enter the community college system. The ladder gave them an alternative next step and helped more advanced programs diversify their enrollment with underprivileged but well-prepared students.

The idea that taking a sequence of short-term job training programs can help workers advance up a career ladder seemed appropriate at the peak of the dot-com boom, when there were new skill demands and IT labor shortages. However, in a slow economy, their new skills may not pay off immediately in a new job. As one participant said, "Careers were compressed during the boom, and we thought people could move up quickly. Now, we can place someone in an $11-an-hour job, but they're not going to be in a $15-an-hour job in six months." Moreover, ascending a rung or two in the career ladder is a process that takes years, especially for workers who have family obligations or no college degree. If a career ladder into a high-skilled job paying a family wage will take a decade to accomplish, businesses will not wait; instead, they will import skilled workers to become more competitive. Meanwhile, workers who enter a career ladder program build toward occupations for which there may be no market by the time they are prepared for them.

Problems with labor demand are compounded by issues on the supply side. Skill sets change quickly in IT, and training programs typically lag the emergence of new skills by months or years (Flynn, 1988). Thus, workers may acquire skills more quickly on the job than through external training programs. In this case, the primary issue of advancement is whether they are compensated adequately for their new skills. Finally, the disadvantaged workers who are entering IT for the first time through these training programs may not have ambitions to move up the career ladder, because they feel challenged by the job and satisfied with the relatively high starting wages (Chapple, 2006). Thus, the SFITC mistake in this instance was more one of translation—the assumption that the lack of a career ladder is an issue in the IT sector just as it is in other fields.

Lessons Learned?

Lessons from the SFITC case were slow to infiltrate the local workforce development world, perhaps because its completion and placement rates were respectable, but more likely because few took the time to reflect on the extent to which one CBO, rather than the entire collaborative, was responsible for the positive results. The James Irvine Foundation quickly went on to fund three other regional workforce development collaboratives, based explicitly again on the idea that collaboration could build a network and supply-side intervention could create career ladders. But, once again, collaboration was not enough to get employers to commit to hiring graduates, and where the initiatives were successful, it turned out again that just one dynamic CBO was behind outcomes for the entire network (Chapple, 2005a).

The consultant who had helped the SFITC conceptualize the articulated career ladder between programs successfully replicated the career ladder approach for a new biotechnology training program for the South San Francisco firm, Genentech, working with Skyline Community College. Though that program was considered a success (with a 90 percent graduation rate, 79 percent employment rate, and an average hourly wage of $16.89 as of early 2007), two attempts to replicate it in the Bay Area have essentially failed due to the lack of similar employer engagement (Love & Voth, 2009).

The newfound interest in workforce development for green jobs offers the latest opportunity to incorporate insights from the experience of the SFITC and similar workforce development collaboratives. In the Bay Area, new leaders have emerged, but they seem to have learned some lessons about sectors, networks, and careers. Perhaps the best example is the East Bay Green Corridor Partnership, a coalition of eight cities, two community college districts, California State University, the University of California, Berkeley, and the Lawrence Berkeley National Lab, founded in early 2008 to promote the region's green economy.

After some initial confusion about which "green sector" to do job training and placement in—eerily similar to the early confusion in the dot-com boom about where the most accessible IT jobs would be—the lack of demand for low-skilled workers in most energy-related sectors (such as solar installation and environmental consulting) is leading the partnership to focus on workforce development within a traditional sector with a green component: green building. This provides graduates with a safety net within the construction industry should the expected market demand not emerge. The partnership itself avoids the pitfalls of other workforce development networks by collaborating in a more sustainable way. Since a group of cities, rather than CBOs, forms its core, it can rely on existing staff funded with permanent revenue sources, leading to greater institutional memory and more stable relationships. Though networks with community colleges and CBOs often duplicate services, the partnership has found synergies instead. For instance, the model Richmond Build solar installation training program now trains students from Berkeley as well as Richmond. Likewise, its approach to green careers shows a growing sophistication; it recognizes that careers are not simple, short-term linear pathways from job training programs to work, but may involve exits to the labor market at multiple points. It acknowledges explicitly not only that outreach is necessary to build applicant pools, but also that community colleges, unions, and four-year colleges all play a role in the career pathway.

Conclusion

The community economic development field has only recently become familiar with success, after decades of failed experiments. When an organization makes significant progress in addressing a "wicked" problem like workforce development, as CET, Project QUEST, and WRTP have, practitioners, policymakers, and academics understandably trumpet those successes as "best practices." If an organization has succeeded in bringing about change, then its practices become conventional wisdom.

Why, then, do organizations fail at adopting these practices that are "in the air?" Perhaps the evaluations are inadequate, or these models do not constitute a theory of change that can be adopted generally. Or perhaps others fail to translate well-established lessons—such as developing programs for jobs in demand and collaborating with needed partners, not for collaboration's sake. The foundations that fund these initiatives are also part of the problem, since they not only gravitate toward trendy approaches, but they also like to shield themselves from failure by funding collaboratives, which makes finger-pointing difficult.

But it may well be that the problem lies in the nature of the economy itself. Having established that economic relationships are shaped by and depend on social relations, that we live in a network society driven by economic sectors that are embedded in regions, it may be somewhat of a leap to then prescribe the construction of connections and networks to produce a more inclusive economy. Even if these social relations can be established artificially, they may not be readily translated into economic interaction. Networks don't necessarily lead to transactions, but, rather, offer latent potential for economic action—when serendipity strikes (Chapple, 2006).

Asked about the failure of this case and others to produce viable workforce development networks, several of those involved argued that their goal (and that of the foundations involved) was not actually workforce development but, more modestly, to start a conversation across "silos." The conversation, indeed, started, at great expense. Continuing it, however, will require some more fundamental changes.

Writing about career ladders, Fitzgerald (2006) argues that "the presence or absence of complementary regulatory, macro-economic, and demand-side policies are [sic] a crucial determinant of the strategy's impact even at the local level" (p. 183). Similarly, these cases suggest the limitations of reform from the bottom up. Unless there is a skill shortage or market failure, employers and sectors have little incentive to hire from workforce development programs. If labor market programs such as WIA remain cumbersome and underfunded, there is no real benefit to building networks for collaboration. Perhaps more flexible mechanisms, such as subcontracting relationships, would be more effective.

Finally, without any push from the federal government to improve job quality, programs to build career ladders will simply be swimming against the tide. Though labor market policy reform would not have been able to remedy the larger failures in these programs (for example, the dot-com crash in San Francisco), it could create conditions more conducive for success. One hopes the next generation of investments will not be left to the third sector alone.

References

Alssid, J. L., Gruber, D., Jenkins, D., Mazzeo, C., Roberts, B., & Stanback-Stroud, R. (2002). *Building a career pathways system: Promising practices in community college-centered workforce development*. New York: Workforce Strategy Center. Retrieved from http://www.workforcestrategy.org/

Aspen Institute Workforce Strategies Initiative. (2005). *Business value assessment for workforce development organizations handbook.* Washington, DC: Aspen Institute.

Benner, C. (2002). *Work in the new economy: Flexible labor markets in Silicon Valley.* New York: Blackwell.

Buss, T. F. (1999). The case against targeted industry strategies. *Economic Development Quarterly, 13,* 339–356.

Chapple, K. (2005a). *Building institutions from the region up: Regional workforce development collaboratives in California.* Institute of Urban and Regional Development Working Paper 2005-01. Berkeley, CA: University of California, Berkeley.

Chapple, K. (2005b). *Promising futures: Workforce development and upward mobility in information technology.* Institute of Urban and Regional Development Monograph 2005-01. Berkeley, CA: University of California, Berkeley

Chapple, K. (2006). Networks to nerdistan. *International Journal of Urban and Regional Research, 30*(3), 548-563.

Dougherty, K. (1994). *The contradictory college: The conflicting origins, impacts, and futures of the community college.* Albany, NY: SUNY Press.

Dresser, L., & Rogers, J. (1998). *Networks, sectors, and workforce learning.* In R. Giloth (Ed.), *Jobs and economic development* (pp. 64–84). Thousand Oaks, CA: Sage.

Elliott, M., Roder, A., King, E., & Stillman, J. (2001). *Gearing up: An interim report on the Sectoral Employment Initiative.* Philadelphia, PA: Public/Private Ventures.

Finckle, J. A. (1999). The case against targeting might have been more . . . targeted. *Economic Development Quarterly, 13,* 361–364.

Fitzgerald, J. (2006). *Moving up in the new economy: Career ladders for U.S. workers.* Ithaca, NY: Cornell University Press.

Fitzgerald, J., & Carlson, V. (2000). Ladders to a better life. *American Prospect, 11*(15), 54–60.

Flynn, P. M. (1988). *Facilitating technological change: The human resource challenge.* Cambridge, MA: Ballinger Publishing Company.

Giloth, R. (Ed.). (1998). *Jobs and economic development.* Thousand Oaks, CA: Sage.

Giloth, R. (2000). Learning from the Field: Economic growth and workforce development in the 1990s. *Economic Development Quarterly, 14,* 340–359.

Giloth, R. (Ed.). (2004). *Workforce intermediaries for the twenty-first century.* Philadelphia, PA: Temple University Press.

Granovetter, M. (1995) *Getting a job: A study of contacts and careers* (2nd ed.). Chicago: University of Chicago Press.

Harrison, B., & Weiss, M. A. (1998). *Workforce development networks: Community-based organizations and regional alliances.* Thousand Oaks, CA: Sage Publications.

Kato, L. Y. (1999). *Diffusing responsive social programs by building learning organizations: The case of the Center for Employment Training (CET) National Replication Project* (Unpublished doctoral dissertation). Massachusetts Institute of Technology, Cambridge, MA.

Love, E., & Voth, R. (2009). Sectoral strategies for disadvantaged workers: Bay Area bridge programs and biotechnology (Unpublished paper). Berkeley, CA: University of California, Berkeley.

Marano, C., & Tarr, K. (2004). The workforce intermediary: Profiling the field of practice and its challenges. In R. Giloth (Ed.), *Workforce intermediaries for the twenty-first century* (pp. 93–123). Philadelphia, PA: Temple University Press.

Melendez, E. (1996). *Working on jobs: The Center for Employment Training.* Boston: University of Massachusetts, Boston, Gaston Institute.

Mitnik, P. A., & Zeidenberg, M. (2004). *Too many bad jobs: An analysis of the prospects for career ladder initiatives in the service economy.* Paper presented at the 56th Annual Meeting of the Industrial Relations Research Association, San Diego, CA.

Osterman, P. (1999). *Securing prosperity: The American labor market: How it has changed and what to do about it.* Princeton, NJ: Princeton University Press.

Prince, H., & Mills, J. (2003). *Career ladders: A guidebook for workforce intermediaries*. Boston, MA: Jobs for the Future. Retrieved from http://www.jff.org

Saxenian, A. (1994). *Regional advantage: Culture and competition in Silicon Valley and Route 128*. Cambridge, MA: Harvard University Press.

Tilly, C., & Tilly, C. (1994). Capitalist work and labor markets. In N. J. Smelser & R. Swedberg (Eds.), *The handbook of economic sociology* (pp. 283-312). Princeton, NJ/New York: Princeton University Press/ Russell Sage Foundation.

Wiewel, W. (1999). Policy research in an imperfect world: Response to Terry F. Buss, "The case against targeted industry strategies." *Economic Development Quarterly, 13*, 357–360.

Zandniapour, L., & Conway, M. (2003). *SEDLP Research Report No. 3: Gaining ground: The labor market progress of participants of sectoral employment development programs*. Washington, DC: Aspen Institute.

---

1   See, for instance, the work of the National Network of Sector Partners and Public/Private Ventures.

2   Research was funded by the James Irvine Foundation and the National Science Foundation.

3   According to Marano & Tarr (2004), an estimated 243 organizations, or 10 percent of the workforce development field, are full intermediaries; most are nonprofits less than10 years old.

4   The nonprofits included the Bay Area Video Coalition (BAVC), a media arts center; Glide Tech, a faith-based, community-based organization (CBO); Arriba Juntos, a CBO serving residents of the largely Latino Mission District; Opnet (a Web design training program for youth); and two national nonprofit training providers, Goodwill and Jewish Vocational Service. The community college partner was first Mission College and then San Francisco City College.

5   Actualizing this idea of transferring to build career ladders was only possible through H-1B funding, which allowed transfers to count as placements.

6   Since the SFITC focuses on careers rather than jobs, a better measure of success than placement might have been the acquisition of new skills or wage progression. As one participant argued, "We need to broaden how we think about placement—can it be "re-placement" into similar jobs?"

6

Does "What Works" Really Work?
A Case Study in Job Retention and
Advancement for Low-Wage Workers

Charles N. Goldberg

Introduction

This chapter describes how a Boston employment program pursued a strategy that has been widely accepted as effective: providing follow-up, "post-employment" services to help its participants retain their entry-level jobs and take steps to advance to better jobs. That the result was disappointing should not have been surprising since there is little evidence that such a strategy actually does improve retention and advancement outcomes. Yet, all too often, programs are constructed on a foundation of conventional wisdom about "what works" and on the mistaken assumption that because something is commonly believed to be true, it therefore must be true. All too often, the quest for the certainty of "what works" steals our attention away from mundane and practical questions about how things actually do work in real-life situations.[1] It is only by answering such questions, however, that we can reach a more nuanced understanding of the differences between successful and unsuccessful efforts to achieve desired social outcomes.

Project Background

Interest in post-employment services arose from efforts during the early and mid-1990s to move people from the welfare rolls to employment, culminating in the welfare reform law of 1996. Because many who left welfare for jobs did not remain employed for more than a few months, and eventually went back on welfare, there was much interest in determining whether providing services to former welfare recipients would help them retain and advance in their jobs. The first nationwide study of the effects of such services was launched in 1994 under the banner of the Postemployment Services Demonstration (PESD), a three-year, four-state initiative that was evaluated by researchers at Mathematica Policy Research (Rangarajan & Novak, 1999).

While the Mathematica report did *not*, in fact, validate post-employment services as an effective way to keep former welfare recipients employed, several policy papers that appeared around the same time highlighted the importance of such services, not only for welfare recipients, but also for other low-income, entry-level workers. Papers by Giloth (2000), Strawn and Martinson (2000), and Poppe, Strawn, and Martinson (2003) emphasized the need for post-employment support, especially case management services, to help people overcome the obstacles to employment retention and advancement. These papers, along with several more recent multiyear studies, have sustained interest in post-employment services as a means to help people stay employed and helped give rise to the common perception that the effectiveness of such services has been proven. It is not surprising, therefore, that organizations such as the one in this case study should seek to adopt such a strategy as a means to improve employment outcomes for those who participate in their programs.

Post-Employment Services in the New Careers Program[2]
The Boston New Careers Program (NCP) is a pseudonym for a program that has been in operation since 1984 to train unemployed and underemployed adults for jobs in high-demand occupations. It

maintains close relationships with employers to develop occupationally relevant curricula and place its graduates in training-related jobs. In recent years, NCP has focused its efforts on training in computerized office skills for jobs in the financial and health care sectors. Its 20-week program includes instruction in basic computer skills and applications, job readiness training, practice in a simulated office environment, internships at local companies, and help with job search and placement.

In 2006, NCP received grants from a local family foundation and the local United Way to implement a new component that would help employed program graduates remain employed and advance in their jobs. Participants would receive one-on-one case management and opportunities to attend workshops and other group activities. The grant would also enable NCP to follow up with program graduates to determine their current employment status.

The United Way approached Commonwealth Corporation, a quasi-public organization specializing in workforce development, to evaluate whether the new post-employment services were resulting in better job retention; more wage increases; higher promotion rates; and greater participation in education, training, and other career development opportunities. In their analysis of data through December 2007, the evaluators found that there were no clear differences in either the services received or retention or advancement outcomes between the program group, which was to receive the post-employment services, and a comparison group of NCP graduates whose members had completed their training several months before the program group. Further, the researchers learned that it had been difficult for the NCP post-employment specialist to maintain contact with members of the two groups, to collect follow-up employment information and, in the case of the program group, to offer post-employment services.

What went wrong? It seemed sensible to continue supporting program graduates to help them remain and advance in their jobs, and the policy literature seemed to give ample support to the idea as well. As it turned out, however, the program's graduates showed little interest in the post-employment services that were offered, and there was no evidence that those who did receive the services were achieving better outcomes than those who did not. While there was general acceptance of the notion that providing post-employment services is a strategy that "works," the NCP experience seemed to run counter to the perceived wisdom in this case. To find out what other, more successful, post-employment programs were doing that, perhaps, NCP was not, the researchers suggested to the United Way that it would be useful to review what other evaluators of such programs had learned about this subject.

Evaluations of Post-Employment Services: What Do the Data Tell Us?
The researchers identified five projects, including NCP, in which an important objective of the project evaluators was to determine the effectiveness of post-employment services. General information about each of these projects is presented in Table 6.1.

Table 6.1 Projects Reviewed in This Study

Project Name	Study	Population	Project Sites
1. ERA (Employment Retention & Advancement)	1999–2009	Current or former welfare recipients	CA, IL, MN, NY, OH, OR, SC, TX (15 local projects)
2. NCP (New Careers Program)	2006–2008	Low-income training program graduates	Boston
3. PASS (Practices for Advancement Success)	1998–2001	Low-income training program graduates	Chicago, Indianapolis
4. PESD (Postemployment Services Demonstration)	1994–1996	Newly employed welfare recipients	Chicago, Portland (OR), Riverside (CA), San Antonio (TX)
5. SWPI (State Workforce Policy Initiative on Employment Retention and	1998–2002	Low-income	CO, FL, OK, OR, WA (10 local projects)

Three of the projects (numbers 1, 4, and 5 in the table) were national in scope; while the other two had a narrower geographic focus—either one site (number 2) or two (number 3). Two projects (1 and 4) targeted current or former welfare recipients. The others served a more broadly defined "low-income" population but also included high percentages of welfare recipients.

Key information about the evaluations of these projects is presented in Table 6.2. Note that the Employment Retention and Advancement (ERA) project is represented by three different programs (Chicago, Riverside, and Texas), which, according to project evaluator MDRC, exemplified especially "promising models" (Bloom, 2007).

Table 6.2 Project Evaluation Studies

Project Name	Evaluator(s)	Key Studies	Evaluation Design	Sample Size	Are post-employment effects isolated?
1. ERA-Chicago	MDRC	Bloom, Hendra, & Page, 2006	Program + Control	808 prog. 808 cntrl.	Yes
2. ERA-Riverside	MDRC	Navarro, van Dork. & Hendra, 2007	Program + Control	1,627 prog. 1,143 cntrl.	Yes
3. ERA-Texas	MDRC	Martinson & Hendra 2006	Program + Control	1,757 prog. 1,757 cntrl.	Yes
4. NCP	Commonwealth Corporation	White, Nemon, & Goldberg, 2007; Goldberg, 2007	Program + Comparison	24 prog.* 38 comp.*	No
5.PASS	Corporation for a Skilled Workforce	Corp. for a Skilled Workforce, 2003	Program + Comparison	111 prog.**	No
6.PESD	Mathematica	Rangarajan & Novak, 1999	Program + Control	1,863 prog. 2,770 cntrl.	Yes
7. SWPI	Public/Private Ventures	Clymer, Roder, & Roberts. 2005	Program group only	477	Yes

NOTES: Abbreviations used in Table 6.2: *comp.* = comparison; *cntrl.* = control; *prog.* = program.
* Sample size reduced from original sample of 41 in the program group and 52 in the comparison group.
** PASS project participants in Indianapolis (N = 74) were compared to program graduates from the previous two years, but the number of comparison group members was not stated.

As Table 6.2 shows, the studies differ with respect to sample size and evaluation design. ERA (numbers 1–3) and PESD (number 6) were random-assignment studies, with both treatment and control groups. NCP and PASS (numbers 4 and 5) compared the outcomes of a program group with those of participants in previous training cycles. In the SWPI project (number 7), the evaluators studied data for all program participants, without reference to a control or comparison group.

The four random assignment studies were designed to determine whether there was a probable causal relationship between receiving post-employment services and achieving retention or advancement outcomes. This also seems to have been the case, though to a lesser extent, with the SWPI evaluation, in which participant outcomes were compared with regard to the intensity of the post-employment services they received. In the two other studies, it is not possible to determine whether the observed outcomes can be attributed specifically to post-employment.

Program Services

Table 6.3 lists the services the different programs provided. Except for ERA-Chicago and PESD, which offered only post-employment services, all of the other projects had a mix of both pre- and post-employment services, although the other two ERA projects (2 and 3) focused primarily on post-employment services.

Table 6.3 Program Services

Project Name	Pre-Employment Services								
	Case Management	Occupational Training	Soft Skills Training	Job Readiness Training	ABE/ESOL	Internships	Mentoring	Support Services	Job Search & Placement
1) ERA-Chicago									
2) ERA-Riverside									❖
3) ERA-Texas	❖							❖	❖
4) NCP	❖	❖	❖	❖		❖	❖	❖	❖
5) PASS	❖	❖	❖	❖		❖	❖	❖	❖
6) PESD									
7) SWPI	❖	❖	❖	❖	❖	❖	❖	❖	❖

Project Name	Post-Employment Services												
	Case Management	Support Services	Help with Subsidies/Benefits	Emergency Assistance	Help Finding New Jobs	Help with Further Education & Training	Group Activities	Employer Visits	Mentoring	Computer Skills Training	Newsletter	Retention Incentives	Participation Incentives
1) ERA-Chicago	❖	❖			❖					❖		❖	❖
2) ERA-Riverside	❖	❖	❖	❖	❖	❖	❖		❖				
3) ERA-Texas	❖	❖			❖	❖	❖	❖				❖	❖
4) NCP	❖	❖	❖	❖	❖	❖	❖	❖			❖	❖	❖
5) PASS	❖	❖	❖	❖	❖	❖	❖	❖	❖	❖	❖		❖
6) PESD	❖	❖			❖	❖							
7) SWPI	❖	❖	❖	❖	❖	❖	❖						

Among pre-employment services, case management, support services (such as referral to childcare and transportation), and job search and placement were the most common. NCP and PASS were similar in the range of pre-employment services they provided. Both included occupational training, mentoring, internships, and job-readiness workshops. SWPI varied across the 10 local program sites, but six of the 10 provided only post-employment services.

On the post-employment side, all programs offered case management, referral to support services, and help with finding new jobs. While the evaluation studies do not give details about the exact nature of case management, common features appear to be "checking in" with participants to offer support and encouragement, counseling them on work-related problems, and referring them to social services. As Table 6.3 shows, most programs also offered a broad range of other services: help with finding new jobs or gaining access to further education or training, assistance with benefits and subsidies, and group activities such as peer support groups and workshops on various topics (for example, life skills, financial literacy, and asset accumulation). Less commonly mentioned services included visits to employers to intercede on participants' behalf, mentoring, computer skills training, and the distribution of a program newsletter.

A final category of post-employment services—providing cash or in-kind incentives—is especially worthy of mention. Several studies highlight incentives as an effective way to engage participants and encourage them to achieve retention or advancement objectives (Bloom, Hendra, Martinson, & Scrivener, 2005; Martinson & Hendra, 2006; Strawn & Martinson, 2000).

Post-Employment Contact and Engagement

Most of the projects found it difficult to reach and engage participants. Only a few—PESD, some local sites in ERA-Riverside, and the PASS programs in Chicago and Indianapolis—were successful in contacting and securing the participation of more than two-thirds of program group members (see Table 6.4). As the MDRC evaluators noted about the ERA projects they studied, "almost all the programs have struggled to keep participants engaged and active over time" (Bloom et al., 2005). Many found it difficult to locate potential participants; and, even when they were successful in doing so, people were often reluctant or unwilling to participate. The evaluators observed that "typically, these are single parents struggling to balance low-wage work with family responsibilities, and they may have little time or energy for additional activities."

Table 6.4 Post-Employment Contact and Engagement

Project Name	Extent of Participant Contact	Type of Contact or Participation
1) ERA-Chicago	• 78% with some initial contact • 61% of program group with continued contact • 31% of control group in contact with a service provider	• Orientation and development of retention/advancement plan • Case management; help with services and benefits
2) ERA-Riverside	• 61% avg. contact rate across 5 sites over 6 months • Range across sites: 48%–92%	• 47% of program group received at least one service during 2-yr. period, vs. 8% of control group* • Range across sites: 32%–60%
3) ERA-Texas	• Mandatory contact during 1st 4 months (TANF earning disregard)	• 30% received stipend at 1 site • 20% received stipend at 2 other sites
4) NCP	• 44% of original program group • 38% of original comparison group	• Follow-up on employment status • Case management; help with services • Information on available services
5) PASS	• 90% of program group	• Follow-up on employment status • Case management; help with services • Group activities
6) PESD	• Range: 60%–80% across 4 sites	• Case management and counseling (59%–81%)** • Help with expenses (17%–64%)** • Help with benefits (24%–65%)** • Help with job search (38%–43%)**
7) SWPI	• No information	• 61% received services ≥6 months • 31% average ≥ 3 staff contacts per mo.

* Case managers contacted program group members regularly; control group members had to take the initiative to request services.
** Indicates range across 4 project sites.

The evaluation reports shed little light on why some projects were more successful than others in this regard. In PESD, the evaluators reported that most programs were successful in making contact with participants because of case managers' "extensive outreach and rapid follow-up," but they do not give further details (Rangarajan & Novak, 1999, p. 16). In ERA-Riverside, three of the five organizations involved contacted two-thirds or more of their assigned participants, a success rate the evaluators explained as resulting from frequent contact attempts, perseverance, and the willingness to "modify outreach and recruitment activities" by offering transportation assistance (Navarro et al., 2007, pp. 24–26). They also report, however, that few participants took advantage of the transportation assistance when it was offered, so it seems unlikely that this is what made the difference in the relatively high contact rates those programs achieved. In the case of PASS, the evaluators emphasize the strong personal relationships case managers had with their clients, but similar descriptions of the relationships between clients and case managers can be found in reports on other projects that were not as successful in contacting and engaging participants.

Over and above the quality and intensity of participants' relationships with their case managers, it seems plausible that higher rates of contact and engagement can be achieved by offering cash or in-kind incentives to participate. The data, however, do not support this line of reasoning. The ERA programs in Chicago and Texas both mandated participation by program group members and penalized those who did not participate by cutting their Temporary Assistance for Needy Families (TANF) benefits. It appears that this did have the effect of sustaining contact with a large majority of the participants for as long as they continued to receive TANF, but participation declined considerably when they reached the limit of their benefits. Once that point was reached, the Texas programs offered $200 monthly stipends to participants who worked at least 30 hours per week and attended at least one program workshop each month. Those who met these criteria could receive stipends for up to a year—a total of $2,400 over 12 months. Yet, despite this strong financial incentive and the "solid effort" that was made to "market" the stipends, the Texas programs had limited success in keeping participants engaged. Among the three project sites, the highest "take-up rate" for the stipends was 30 percent, in Corpus Christi, while the other two sites each had a take-up rate of 20 percent (Martinson & Hendra, 2006). Thus, even where there was a strong incentive to remain involved, the large majority of eligible program group members did not participate.[3]

Retention and Advancement Outcomes
Table 6.5 summarizes the evaluators' findings with respect to participant outcomes. The table shows that, in two of the projects—NCP and PASS—the evaluators did not know whether the observed retention and advancement outcomes were attributable to post-employment services. The NCP study was designed to compare two groups of program graduates, one that received post-employment services and one that did

not. But there was little difference in practice between the services the two groups received, so there is no basis for comparing their outcomes. Moreover, as the data suggest, retention and advancement data were similar for both groups.

Table 6.5 Retention and Advancement Outcomes

Project Name	Employment & Retention	Advancement	Impact of post-employment services
1. ERA-Chicago	*Prog:* 55% employed for 4 quarters *Ctrl:* 51% employed for 4 quarters	*Prog:* $6,596 avg. yearly earnings in 2nd year *Ctrl:* $6,032 avg. yearly earnings in 2nd year	*Retention:* modest impact *Advancement:* modest impact
2. ERA-Riverside	*Prog:* 60% employed for 4 quarters *Ctrl:* 57% employed for 4 quarters	*Prog:* $18,366 avg. yearly earnings after 2 years *Ctrl:* $16,578 avg. yearly earnings after 2 years	*Retention:* not significant** *Advancement:* large impact
3. ERA-Texas	*Prog. range:* 37%–49% employed for 4 quarters *Ctrl. range:* 36%–45% employed for 4 quarters	*Prog. range:* $8,269–$9,802 yearly earnings after 2 years *Ctrl. range:* $8,088–$9,206 yearly earnings after 2 years	*Retention:* not significant** *Advancement:* not significant**
4. NCP	*Prog:* 67% employed as of 12/07* *Comp:* 50% employed as of 12/07*	*Prog:* 38% with wage increase as of 12/07* *Comp:* 37% with wage increase as of 12/07*	Not known
5. PASS	*Tot. prog:* 80% for 6 mos. *IN prog:* 86% for 12 mo. *IN comp:* 73% for 12 mos.	24.5% wage increase after 18 mos.	Not known
6. PESD	*Prog. range:* employed 59%–78% of time over 2 yrs. *Ctrl. range:* employed 58%–80% of time over 2 yrs.	*Prog. range:* $5,724–$7,324 annual earnings *Ctrl. range:* $5,468–$7,308 annual earnings	*Retention:* not significant** *Advancement:* not significant**
7. SWPI	*Recv'd svcs ≥6 mos.:* 71% worked ≥9 mos. *Recv'd svcs <6 mos.:* 57% worked ≥9 mos.	*≥3 contacts/mo.:* 64% w/ ≥$1 hourly increase *<3 contacts/mo.:* 43% w/ ≥$1 hourly increase	Positive impact***

NOTES: Abbreviations: *Comp.* = comparison; *ctrl.* = control; *grp.* = group; IN = Indiana; recv'd = received; svcs. = services.
* Refers to percentage of those who were known to be employed 11 months earlier, in February 2007.
** Not statistically significant at 90% confidence level or higher.
*** Not based on a statistical measure of significance.

In the case of PASS, the evaluation report did not present complete data on the differences between the program group members and their counterparts from earlier training cycles. The one instance in which such data were reported shows that program group members in Indianapolis had a higher 12-month retention rate than did the graduates of the prior two cycles, but there is no information on the number of individuals in the comparison sample and no way of knowing, based on the report, whether this finding is significant.

In contrast, it is possible to judge the impact of post-employment services in the four random assignment studies (1, 2, 3, and 6) and in the SWPI study (7). As Table 6.5 shows, no significant differences were found between the program and control groups in the Texas ERA project, in spite of the large cash incentive that was offered to the program group. In the Chicago ERA project, the evaluators found "modest" impacts on both retention and earnings, but the results were low for both groups—less than 60 percent employed for four quarters or more, with annual earnings between $6,032 and $6,596—indicating that, in both groups, most people were still living in poverty after two years of participating in the project.

The Riverside ERA project is the only one in which the evaluators discovered a "large impact" from post-employment services. Evaluators found that the only significant difference between the program and control groups was in the total earnings of program group members, which were 11 percent higher than the earnings of control group members. Further analysis showed that this difference was due primarily to program group members who left their initial jobs (the ones they had when they enrolled in the program) became employed more quickly, and often with higher wages, than did control group members who left their jobs. No difference was found between the two groups with respect to retention or advancement in their first jobs. Thus, the principal effect of the project was to assist program group members in finding subsequent jobs. Because most people in both groups became unemployed at some point during their time in the program, the availability of case managers to help program group members find another job proved to be a useful service. The evaluators concluded that "it may be that employment and retention services . . . can be more effective when offered soon after sample members lose their jobs, perhaps because individuals are more receptive to services at that time" (Navarro et al., 2007, p. ES-8).

The only other random assignment study among those reviewed was the Post-Employment Services Demonstration project (PESD). After analyzing data from 10 programs across five states, the evaluators found no significant differences in outcomes between the program group, which received post-employment services, and the control group, which did not.

Finally, though not a controlled random-assignment study, the evaluation of the State Workforce Policy Initiative (SWPI) did seem to suggest that relatively long-term and high-frequency post-employment services could be beneficial. Comparing participants who received post-employment services for six months or more with those who received services for less time, the evaluators found that 71 percent of the long-term service group had worked at least nine of the previous 12 months, versus only 57 percent of the short-term service group. Further, evaluators determined that program participants who were in contact with their case managers relatively frequently—at least three times a month—were more likely than others to have increased their wages during the preceding year. As Table 6.5 shows, 64 percent of the high-contact group received a wage increase of at least $1 per hour, versus only 43 percent of the low-contact group.

In summary, although there is some evidence that post-employment services can help produce better retention and advancement outcomes for some participants, especially those who need help finding new jobs or are in frequent contact with their case managers, the results from most studies on this subject are inconclusive at best about the effectiveness of those services.[4]

Other Perspectives: Who Gets Ahead and Why?

Further insights about retention and advancement can be gained from studies of low-wage workers who have successfully advanced toward self-sufficiency and how they achieved that result. Do differences in services explain why some people advance and others do not? What does the literature say about this?

Harry Holzer and his colleagues present an economist's perspective on this question in their study of changes in income for an exceptionally large number of workers over a nine-year period (Andersson, Holzer, & Lane, 2005; Holzer, 2004). They found that workers who "escaped" from the low-earning category of $12,000 per year or less and advanced to a higher-earning category of more than $15,000 per year were much more likely than were non-advancers to have found better jobs with different employers.

These findings on the importance of finding better jobs with better employers are reinforced by the work of Katherine S. Newman, who followed a group of fast-food restaurant workers over a 10-year period, from 1993 to 2002, and gathered a wealth of information on how the lives of her subjects changed over time. "Switching jobs," she found, "is crucial to getting higher wages"; the majority of those who were employed had changed jobs three or more times (Newman, 2006, p. 77). It is not surprising, however, that the people she studied varied considerably in their labor market experiences. One group, whom she called the "high flyers," progressed to well-paying jobs with opportunities for further advancement; another, the "low riders," cycled in and out of the labor market; and a third, the "up but not out" group, continued to work and increased their earnings over time but still fell short of achieving "real economic security."

How, Newman asked, did the "high flyers" succeed in getting ahead? She found that there were three routes to upward mobility: (1) internal promotion in a growing firm that pays good wages; (2) acquiring more education and skills (the "human capital road"); and (3) "landing a union job." For the middle, "up but not out," group, Newman discovered a great deal of job changing in the search for "better versions" of similar jobs, but with firms that offered greater flexibility and better benefits. For those workers, "breaking out [of the middle group] requires a lucky break—a union connection, a jump to a high-paying firm—or new skills, like a completed degree." Those who chose to pursue more education or training, she found, often did so "in fits and starts." Advanced skills and credentials, if they achieved them, tended to be accomplished over a long period, and there was no indication that the availability of services had any effect on workers' ability to get ahead.

Newman concludes that "the most advantaged workers are those who find wives, husbands, or long-term cohabiting partners who can contribute additional income and be available to share the burden that work and family impose on all of us." Further, "Mobility through the labor market is largely contingent on household and family configurations that are obscured by an exclusive focus on skills or education. Human capital is a necessary but not sufficient prerequisite for upward mobility; if it is not backed up by support from a kin network it cannot easily be deployed, at least not in a society where the raising of children is largely a private matter" (2006, p. 152).

Newman's emphasis on family and kinship ties as an integral part of people's labor market experience is reinforced in the work of another ethnographer, Roberta R. Iversen, in her studies of participants in the Annie E. Casey Foundation Jobs Initiative programs. She concluded from her research that "family is paramount in advancement decisions and actions" (Iversen, 2004, p. 261), and that programs should "replace assessment of individuals with comprehensive assessment of families, understanding that mobility is embedded in families and social networks, not in atomistic job seekers" (Iversen & Armstrong, 2006, p. 118). On the issue of post-employment case management, Iversen's interviews with program participants led her to conclude that a supportive relationship with a case manager "often made the difference between staying at or leaving a job, particularly during tumultuous life or work periods" (Iversen, 2002, p. 12).

Another major theme in Iversen's analysis was the discovery of a "life-stage mismatch" between the life circumstances of the program participants she studied and the low-level jobs in which they found themselves. Those jobs, she says, tend to be better suited to people who are younger, healthier, and single, and have few responsibilities for children or other dependents. Moreover, while education and training are the "key" to advancement, "getting more education and training proved to be well beyond what most of the families could do even three or more years into their jobs" (Iversen, 2002, p. 39). Acquiring more education and skills, she found, is the "steepest barrier" to overcome, with "untenable opportunity costs" for those "who had children to raise and were saddled with debt and other life burdens" (p. 8).

The difficulty of completing education and training programs is also highlighted by the evaluators of the Project Match program in Chicago. Over a period of 10 years, only 57 percent of those who started a training program or college eventually finished the program and received a credential. The evaluators conclude that, "as much as the field needs to maintain or even increase access to education and training, we can't expect it to be the advancement silver bullet, since completion rates can be low, even among people who are motivated to enroll in the first place" (Wagner, Chang, & Herr, 2005).

What Have We Learned about Post-Employment Services?
What conclusions can we draw from this review of the literature and the analysis in the preceding pages? Three key points seem to emerge:

1. *There is no clear, compelling evidence that post-employment services are effective in promoting retention and advancement.* Well-controlled studies that isolate the effects of post-employment services show little or no difference between program and control groups. The ERA-Riverside evaluation produced the most interesting finding among these studies: that those who received post-employment services were more likely to find another job more quickly and, hence, to earn more than their control group counterparts who took longer to find another job.

This general conclusion about the lack of proven effectiveness of post-employment services is echoed by two other reviews of the literature on the subject: Harry Holzer and Karin Martinson's review of various efforts to improve job retention and advancement among low-income working parents (Holzer & Martinson, 2005), and a comparative review of studies on employment retention in the United States and the United Kingdom by Minoff, Greenberg, and Branosky (2006).

2. *Some post-employment service programs are more successful than others at making contact with people and keeping them engaged, but the literature is not sufficiently detailed to extract the critical ingredients for success.* The MDRC studies and other evaluation reports describe how difficult it was for many programs to maintain contact with participants and persuade them to take advantage of the services they were offering. In one MDRC report, the evaluators wrote that "creative marketing strategies" were needed to increase participation (Anderson & Martinson, 2003). This emphasis on the difficulty of marketing, or selling, post-employment services evokes the image of customers who need to be persuaded that a product is worth buying. It seems there is a trade-off between participating in post-employment activities and using one's time and energy for other things, such as being with one's family.

3. *Time and life circumstances are critical factors. It may take a long time before someone is ready to make use of post-employment services.* As explained in the ethnographic studies by Newman and Iversen, family circumstances and individual life issues are critical determinants in people's choices about employment and whether to pursue further education or training. The problem, therefore, is not simply whether services are available but whether people's life situations are such that they are ready to use those services. As Herr and Wagner (2007) suggest, a "human development approach," which responds to a more complex panorama of individual and family needs through time, requires that service providers commit themselves to long-term relationships with their clients, extending over a period of years. It seems doubtful, however, that most programs would have the capacity to do this.[5]

Analysis and Lessons Learned

One does not have to look very hard to find all sorts of prescriptive solutions, often in the form of nicely numbered lists, to just about any problem one might have. A Google search for the phrase "what works" yields nearly 13 million hits, from solutions to medical problems (back pain, obesity, hair loss) to a wide range of educational and social issues (improving student learning, crime prevention, working with troubled teens, reducing recidivism). The "what works" seal of approval gives an aura of authority to whatever appears under it, but the understandable desire to settle on a clear, authoritative solution needs to be balanced by a large dose of skepticism and questioning: Does "what works" really work? If so, under what circumstances? What is the evidence? How convincing is it?

In the case of the post-employment strategy adopted by the New Careers Program, practitioners and funders alike seemed to find assurance in "what works" assumptions that were grounded in conventional wisdom, which, in turn, seemed to be based on a kind of commonsense logic ("It stands to reason that . . .") but weak empirical evidence. The implication is clear that, as much as possible, it is important to question such assumptions carefully and examine whatever evidence exists to support them. Current emphases in policy and public administration circles on "data-driven" or "outcomes-driven" practice are a necessary corrective to less rigorous ways of thinking that give too much credence to conventional wisdom.

This is not to argue, however, that even "what works" solutions that are well supported by empirical evidence, with clear outcomes and strong corroborative data, provide a sufficient basis for action. In the realm of social action, even the most rigorously argued and substantiated "what works" solutions are shaped by the conditions and circumstances in which they were developed, making it necessary to qualify "what works" kinds of statements with that troublesome phrase, "all other things being equal." When it comes to human psychological and social phenomena, however, things are seldom, if ever, equal, thus making it difficult to replicate successful models or practices in different environments or even bring them "to scale" in the environments in which they were nurtured originally.

In a recent paper, Gary Walker (2008), former president of Public/Private Ventures, reflects on the difficulty of finding workable programmatic solutions to social problems, even as funders, both public and private, are calling more and more for well-measured outcomes and rigorous evaluation. But, says Walker,

> while the science of evaluation has been improving and growing in sophistication, size, and resources devoted to it, our ability to actually improve lives through social programs has been consistently unimpressive. . . . our impatience for results, the fact that new political administrations and new philanthropists want to be known for their innovations, means that [the lesson that it takes time for programs to begin to work] is not a lesson well learned. Instead these factors conspire to promote a sophisticated and maturing field of evaluation, thrust upon an ever-immature field of demonstration social programs (pp. 4–5).

Walker believes that "the challenge for philanthropy and the public sector over the coming decades relates less to measuring outcomes or impacts, or to churning out innovations, than to helping establish—and measure—quality in program performance." More attention, in short, needs to be paid to implementation—not only to "what works," but to how programs roll out on the ground, how they change over time, and how the people who run them and fund them reflect on and learn from their experience.

On a parallel track, the recent concern among a number of foundations to learn from "mistakes" is leading to a realization that more work needs to be done to understand how programs develop at ground level (Brest & Canales, 2007; Strom, 2007). A case in point is the study commissioned by the William and Flora Hewlett Foundation to examine a neighborhood improvement initiative that fell short of meeting expectations. Brown and Fiester (2007), the authors of the study, conclude their analysis with the suggestion that foundations strive to develop two new "core competencies" to do this work more effectively: "the ability to establish productive relationships with the diverse people and organizations with which a foundation must work to achieve community change, and the ability to take a learning stance throughout the entire enterprise" (p. 57).

Our case study of the New Careers Program suggests that a similar set of responses might be called for on the part of the United Way and others that fund such initiatives. Funding organizations should engage more closely with grantees to question assumptions and think through the practical implications of a proposed course of action. When funded programs are up and running, they should engage grantees in an ongoing dialogue to understand better how and why things work, or don't work, the way they do. And, to avoid the seduction of certainty offered by the "what works" view of the world, they should follow the advice of the great American philosopher John Dewey:

> We cannot permanently divest ourselves of the intellectual habits we take on and wear when we assimilate the culture of our own time and place. But intelligent furthering of culture demands that we take some of them off, that we inspect them critically to see what they are made of and what wearing them does to us. We cannot achieve recovery of primitive naïveté. But there is attainable a cultivated naïveté of eye, ear and thought. (Dewey, 1929a, p. 35)

What this means in practical terms is the adoption of a "working hypothesis" approach, also suggested by Dewey:

... that policies and proposals for social action be treated as working hypotheses, not as programs to be rigidly adhered to and executed. They will be experimental in the sense that they will be entertained subject to constant and well-equipped observation of the consequences they entail when acted upon, and subject to ready and flexible revision in the light of observed consequences. (Dewey, 1954, pp. 202–203)

In this formulation, every case is replete with experience and the potential for learning. Our purpose is not to discover "what works" in any definitive sense, but to deepen our understanding of how things really do work, and to apply that understanding, in incremental fashion, to future practice.

References

Anderson, J., & Martinson, K. (2003). *Service delivery and institutional linkages: Early implementation experiences of employment retention and advancement programs.* New York, NY: MDRC. Retrieved from http://www.mdrc.org/publications/356/full.pdf

Andersson F., Holzer H. J., & Lane J. I. (2005). *Moving up or moving on.* New York: Russell Sage Foundation.

Bloom, D. (2007, September 26). PowerPoint presentation on the ERA project presented at U.S. Department of Labor Workforce One "Webinar."

Bloom, D., Hendra, R., Martinson, K., & Scrivener, S. (2005). *The employment retention and advancement project: Early results from four sites.* New York: MDRC. Retrieved from http://www.mdrc.org/publications/413/full.pdf

Bloom, D., Hendra, R., & Page, J. (2006). *The employment retention and advancement project: Results from the Chicago ERA site.* New York: MDRC. Retrieved fromhttp://www.mdrc.org/publications/441/full.pdf

Brest, P., & Canales, J. E. (2007, August 9). Let's stop reinventing potholes. *Chronicle of Philanthropy*. Retrieved from http://philanthropy.com/free/articles/v19/i20/20003301.htm

Brown, P., & Fiester, L. (2007). *Hard lessons about philanthropy & community change from the Neighborhood Improvement Initiative*. Menlo Park, CA: The William and Flora Hewlett Foundation.

Clymer, C., Roder, A., & Roberts, B. (2005). *Promoting opportunity: Findings from the State Workforce Policy Initiative on Employment Retention and Advancement*. Philadelphia, PA: Public/Private Ventures.

Corporation for a Skilled Workforce (2003). *Enhancing job retention and advancement: The challenge of changing cultures*. Ann Arbor: MI: Corporation for a Skilled Workforce. Retrieved from http://www.traininginc.org/Files/PASS_2.pdf

Dewey, J. (1929a). *Experience and nature* (2nd ed.). LaSalle, IL: Open Court Publishing.

Dewey, J. (1929b). *The quest for certainty: A study of the relation of knowledge and action*. New York: Minton, Balch & Company.

Dewey, J. (1954). *The public and its problems*. Denver, CO: Alan Swallow.

Dresser, L. (2007). *Stronger ladders, stronger floors: The need for both supply and demand strategies to improve workers' opportunities*. Madison, WI: Center on Wisconsin Strategy. Retrieved from http://www.cows.org/pdf/rp-ladder_ld.pdf

Giloth, R. P. (2000). Learning from the field: Economic growth and workforce development in the 1990s. *Economic Development Quarterly, 14*(4), 340–359.

Goldberg, C. (2007, July 25). New careers retention & advancement project. PowerPoint presentation to United Way of Massachusetts Bay.

Herr, T., & Wagner, S. L. (2007). Beyond barriers to work: A workforce attachment approach that addresses unpredictability, halting progress, and human nature. Chicago, IL: Project Match. Retrieved from http://www.pmatch.org/barriers_feb_ohseven.pdf

Holzer, H. J. (2004). Encouraging job advancement among low-wage workers: A new approach. Brookings Institution Policy Brief. Washington DC: Brookings Institution.

Holzer, H. J., & Martinson, K. (2005). *Can we improve job retention and advancement among low-income working parents?* Discussion Paper No. 1307-05. Madison, WI: Institute for Research on Poverty, University of Wisconsin, Madison.

Iversen, R. R. (2002). *Moving up is a steep climb: Parents' work and children's welfare in the Annie E. Casey Foundation's Jobs Initiative.* Baltimore, MD: Annie E. Casey Foundation. Retrieved from http://www.aecf. org/upload/publicationfiles/moving%20up%20steep%20climb.pdf

Iversen, R. R. (2004). How do workers see advancement? In R. P. Giloth (Ed.), *Workforce intermediaries for the twenty-first century* (pp. 241-262). Philadelphia, PA: Temple University Press.

Iversen, R. R., & Armstrong, A. L. (2006). *Jobs aren't enough: Toward a new economic mobility for low-income families.* Philadelphia, PA: Temple University Press.

Martinson, K., & Hendra, R. (2006). *The Employment Retention and Advancement Project: Results from the Texas ERA site.* New York: MDRC. Retrieved from http://www.mdrc.org/publications/436/full.pdf

Minoff, E., Greenberg, M., & Branosky, N. (2006). Employment retention: Evidence from the UK and the US. In K. Bell et al., *Staying on, stepping up: How can employment retention and advancement policies be made to work for lone parents?* London, UK: One Parent Families.

Mitnik, P. A., & Zeidenberg, M. (2007). *From bad to good jobs? An analysis of the prospects for career ladders in the service industries.* Madison, WI: Center on Wisconsin Strategy. Retrieved from www.cows.org/pdf/rp-bad-good.pdf

Navarro, D., van Dork, M., & Hendra, R. (2007). *The employment retention and advancement project: Results from the Post-Assistance Self-Sufficiency (PASS) program in Riverside, California.* New York: MDRC. Retrieved from http://www.mdrc.org/publications/458/full.pdf

Newman, K. S. (2006). *Chutes and ladders: Navigating the low-wage labor market.* Cambridge, MA: Russell Sage Foundation at Harvard University Press.

Poppe N., Strawn J., & Martinson K. (2003). Whose job is it? Creating opportunities for advancement. In R. P. Giloth (Ed.), *Workforce intermediaries for the twenty-first century* (pp. 31-69). Philadelphia, PA: Temple University Press.

Rangarajan, A., & Novak, T. (1999). *The struggle to sustain employment: The effectiveness of the postemployment services demonstration.* Princeton, NJ: Mathematica Policy Research, Inc.

Strawn, J., & Martinson, K. (2000). *Steady work and better jobs: How to help low-income parents sustain employment and advance in the workforce.* New York: Manpower Demonstration Research Corporation. Retrieved from http://www.mdrc.org/Reports2000/steady_work_guide/SteadyWorkGuide.pdf

Strom, S. (2007, July 27). Foundations find benefits in facing up to failures. *New York Times.*

Tessler, B. L., & Sieth, D. (2007). *From getting by to getting ahead: Navigating career advancement for low-wage workers.* New York, NY: MDRC. Retrieved from http://www.mdrc.org/publications/465/full.pdf

Wagner, S. L., Chang, C., & Herr, T. (2005). *Advancement among Project Match participants: How far? How fast? How frequent?* Chicago, IL: Project Match. Retrieved from http://www.pmatch.org/rp_update_apr_ofive.pdf

Walker, G. (2008). Reflections on the "evaluation revolution." Paper prepared for Hudson Institute's Bradley Center for Philanthropy and Civic Renewal. Retrieved from http://pcr.hudson.org/index.cfm?fuseaction=publication_details&id=5475.

White, G., Nemon, M., & Goldberg, C. (2007). *Baseline evaluation report of the Retention and Advancement Project at the New Careers Program.* Boston, MA: Commonwealth Corporation. Report submitted to United Way of Massachusetts Bay.

---

1   The phrase "quest for certainty" is from John Dewey and his book of that name (Dewey, 1929b).

2   I am grateful to the United Way of Massachusetts Bay and especially its Director of Community Impact, Annie Chin-Louie, for supporting the research that undergirds this paper and for their help in refining the research design.

3   The MDRC researchers interviewed participants and staff to try to discover why the take-up rate was so low. Among the reasons given for not taking the stipend were not working enough hours, not understanding that they were eligible to receive a stipend, problems finding childcare when required monthly workshops were being held, and unwillingness to continue dealing with the welfare bureaucracy (Martinson & Hendra, 2006, pp. 39–40).

4   One of the reviewers of this chapter has suggested that it would be useful to know about the outcomes achieved by members of the program groups who actually took advantage of the services that were offered as opposed to those program group members who did not avail themselves of those services. While this information might, indeed, be suggestive, the evaluation reports do not include such data. In the four random-assignment studies, the evaluations were designed specifically to test whether the differences in outcomes between the program and control groups were statistically significant. Such tests were not performed for subsets of the two groups, owing to both a lack of robustness in the smaller sample sizes and the fact that those who did take advantage of the services constituted a self-selected sample of individuals who were motivated, for whatever reason, to participate at a higher level of intensity. We do not know whether these more motivated individuals achieved more positive retention and advancement outcomes than did those who were less motivated. It would be helpful in future studies to examine such questions more closely; but, unless the evaluation is designed to allow for more robust subsamples, it should be understood that whatever differences in outcomes might be uncovered probably would not hold up under a test of statistical significance.

5   A more practical approach might be to offer case management and other employment supports at One-Stop Career Centers and other central locations and to advertise the availability of those services for people who want them. Other services might include helping people file for the Earned Income Tax Credit (EITC) and helping them gain access to other supports, such as childcare vouchers and tax credits, food stamps, housing assistance, health care benefits, and financing for further education and training. MDRC is now testing such a model at One-Stop Career Centers around the country under the aegis of the

National Work Advancement and Support Center (WASC) Demonstration (Tessler & Seith, 2007).

Underlying WASC is explicit acknowledgement of the fact that many people will continue to do low-wage work for a number of years before taking steps to improve their employment prospects, while many others may never advance beyond low-wage jobs (see also Dresser, 2007; Mitnick & Zeidenberg, 2007). For the great numbers of workers who fall into these categories, an important part of making their employment more sustainable might be to help them take advantage of as complete a package of supplemental supports as possible.

7

In Pursuit of Scale for Nonprofit Organizations: Learning from Constructive Failures

Amy Brown and Kirsten Moy

Introduction

In 2004 and 2005, the Aspen Institute, working under a grant from the Annie E. Casey Foundation, assisted five sites across the country in developing and implementing pilot efforts to test innovative models for achieving scale in Earned Income Tax Credit (EITC) and related asset-building programs. While the pilots showed many positive results, they failed in their fundamental goal; none of the models showed any promise of scalability. Analysis of their mistakes—discussed in more detail later in this chapter—found that:

- Attempts to "borrow" infrastructure, through partnerships with government and the private sector, created challenges to taking the pilots to scale.
- High per-unit costs made scaling up prohibitively expensive; furthermore, the programs did not present a clear value proposition for expected partner contributions.

- None of the community-based agencies managing the pilots had the degree of organizational capacity and sophistication necessary to implement programs at scale.
- The size of the solution must match the size of the problem, and pilots, by their very nature, may never be able to point the way to large-scale implementation.

Among the core lessons learned is that having an idea or innovation—even a successful and seemingly scalable one—is not enough. Innovation must simultaneously develop the infrastructure, standards, efficiencies, and other elements that will allow the idea to make a difference at scale. Based on this and other lessons described in this chapter, the Annie E. Casey Foundation and the Aspen Institute are currently designing and testing a next-generation model for scale.

Background: The Challenge of Scale

Despite all of the important work accomplished by community development organizations over the past decades, scale has remained an elusive goal. This has been true for organizations working in a broad range of areas: affordable housing, community development finance, microenterprise, workforce development, individual development accounts, early childcare, social services, low-income tax preparation, and others with similar anti-poverty missions. The inability to achieve scale—that is, to make a meaningful, sustainable impact by serving large numbers of those in need of assistance—has overshadowed the achievements of individual organizations and the people they serve. This has led to frustration among practitioners, funders, and low-income communities themselves.

For all the valuable work of organizations in the field, current efforts are barely detectable, given the vast needs facing low-income communities. The insignificant impact of the solutions offered by nonprofits threatens to render them irrelevant. Affordable housing provides one example. There has been a steady, annual shortage of about 5.2 million affordable units for low-income renters since at least 1993.

In 2003, 477 community development financial institutions (CDFIs) produced or renovated 44,689 units of affordable housing, or 1 percent of the 5.2 million needed. The story is the same for nearly every area in which the nonprofit sector works.

At the same time, however, there is a growing sense of desperation to finally begin making progress on scale. A set of forces, which includes declining federal support; donors' desire for more impact; a growing interest in learning from for-profit approaches; and increasing penetration by for-profit players in the community economic development and workforce industries, is pushing nonprofits to look for better models that have the potential for scale.

Assumptions and Theories: How the Nonprofit Sector Has Traditionally Thought about Scale and How the Private Sector Does Things Differently

The starting point for approaching this topic is a framework developed by the Aspen Institute (in work done in partnership with the Federal Reserve) to describe how initiatives grow. Figure 7.1 shows a "map" of how the nonprofit sector has traditionally conceptualized growth to scale. Ideas are first tested and refined (often in the context of pilots), then replicated, with additional innovation and refinement as lessons emerge from the early replication. Eventually, best practices are identified, and, at this point, scale is simply expected to happen.

Figure 7.1 How the Nonprofit Sector Has Traditionally Conceptualized Growth to Scale

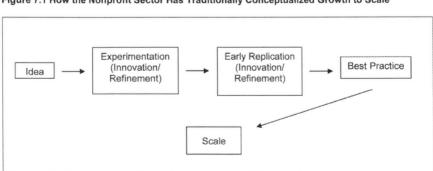

Looking at how the private sector operates provides a starkly different picture. While innovation and testing are key early activities, much more deliberate steps follow the identification of best practices. In particular, as illustrated in Figure 7.2, three additional elements are included in the private sector model: standardization, infrastructure, and roll-out. These elements, described below, are critical steps for moving from best practice to scale.

Figure 7.2 An Alternative (Private Sector) Model for Conceptualizing Growth to Scale

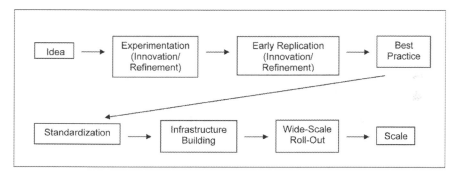

Standardization
Consistently delivering a high-quality product or service that is uniform across customers is one way that corporations deliver products and services in volume. Nonprofit industries, however, have resisted standardization, maintaining that each "solution" must be customized to local conditions and/or individual beneficiaries.

Infrastructure
Infrastructure is made up of widely available systems, products, and services. Infrastructure is based on development of common definitions and standards; standardized procedures, protocols, and methodologies; common databases; technology platforms; and institutional relationships. Together, these enable ideas, products, and programs to spread quickly and efficiently to new areas and expand to meet growing demand.

Roll-Out

Roll-out promotes the widespread adoption of new products and services by actively fostering development of necessary systems and infrastructure. For-profit industries take a deliberate approach to roll-out, while nonprofit organizations generally take a more passive approach, assuming that organizations or communities will copy promising innovations.

Finally, a word about pilots: in the traditional nonprofit pathway to scale, pilots play a central role; they are how new ideas are tested and refined. A lot is riding on these pilots. They must show positive results in a short time and with few resources and small numbers of participants. In contrast, in the for-profit sector, many more new ideas are developed, with more market research, more resources, and more varied on-the-ground testing. At the same time, less is riding on the results, since the vast majority of new ideas are expected to fail. Finally, and perhaps most important, even early testing in the for-profit model is designed with standardization, infrastructure, and roll-out in mind. In other words, scalability is a critical consideration at every stage of innovation, not just at the last ones.

Given the inability of nonprofit industries to achieve their goals for scale, it is worth looking more closely at these differences in how the for-profit sector approaches growth. The EITC pilots offer clues about the importance of standardization, infrastructure, and roll-out and, ultimately, suggest that pilots may be faulty vehicles for identifying scalable innovations.

Lessons from the EITC Pilots

The Annie E. Casey Foundation has long been an active supporter of EITC campaigns across the United States. Building on existing services in their communities, these campaigns provide: (1) education and outreach to promote the EITC and other tax credits for qualified working-poor families; (2) free or low-priced tax preparation services; and (3) links to other programs and services so tax filers can use their refunds to build financial assets.

While the campaigns have helped hundreds of thousands of low-income workers receive tens of millions of dollars in tax refunds, they have been expensive and labor-intensive to operate, and they rely heavily on volunteers. Given the campaigns' ambitious goals and limited resources, there has been increasing interest in identifying alternative models that have greater potential for scale. As the field has developed, the Annie E. Casey Foundation has consistently supported innovation and risk-taking as a way to identify new solutions to common challenges. The pilots are one example of this.

The Pilots: Testing Innovations for Scale

Five programs tested variations of three approaches to scale, involving partnerships with employers, government, and commercial tax preparers. The Aspen Institute documented the design, implementation, and results of each pilot. The mistakes these programs made and the lessons learned from those mistakes expand our understanding of the challenge of scale for the community development field. The pilots are described briefly here.

Chicago

The Chicago innovation sought to expand free tax preparation, financial education, and access to financial services by reaching low-income families through the workplace. Led by the Center for Economic Progress (CEP) and North Side Community Federal Credit Union (NSCFCU), the pilot worked with four employers to expand the role of human resources departments and integrate financial services into employers' benefits packages.

Louisville, Kentucky

The Louisville pilot involved a partnership between the Louisville Asset Building Coalition (LABC)—led by Members First Federal Credit Union—and the local workforce development system. The pilot attempted to increase the scale and impact of LABC activities by providing those services as part of the package of services available to customers of the city's "one-stop" career centers.

Tulsa, Oklahoma

The Community Action Project of Tulsa County (CAPTC) tested the idea of building on the existing capacity of commercial tax preparers. In partnership with H&R Block, CAPTC provided benefits screening for low-income H&R Block customers. The hope was that, rather than provide large-scale tax preparation services itself, it could focus on a narrower constituency of those not served by the for-profit industry, redirecting resources to other anti-poverty and asset-building services.

Atlanta

The Consumer Credit Counseling Service of Greater Atlanta (CCCS) worked with a commercial tax preparer, Liberty Tax Service, to provide tax services to a previously underserved community. The goal was to negotiate a partnership that would benefit Liberty and provide reduced-price services to residents, protecting them from predatory practices and increasing EITC use in the target neighborhood.

Baltimore

To expand its EITC outreach and free tax preparation more efficiently, the Baltimore CASH Campaign had worked with local employers to offer tax preparation services on site at the workplace. A new partnership with Erickson Retirement Communities took the model one step further by offering no-cost quick refunds to participating employees as an alternative to commercial refund anticipation loans.

It is interesting to note, though each of the pilots was developed independently, they all focused primarily on addressing the same barrier to scale: the lack of sufficient infrastructure to significantly expand program operations, one of the three pieces Aspen found to be missing in the traditional nonprofit model. Rather than developing a new infrastructure, however, the pilots attempted to "borrow" or piggyback on existing infrastructure. The Baltimore and Chicago pilots attempted to expand employee benefits programs, and the pilots in Atlanta and Tulsa turned over tax preparation to for-profit firms, while negotiating lower fees or providing add-on services. The Louisville pilot sought to integrate services into the government's one-stop career centers, which serve thousands of low-income clients each week. The pilots saw these institutions as vehicles for reaching a large target audience without developing their own infrastructure.

Things that Went Right: Ways in Which the Pilots Were Successful
To understand the "constructive failure" lessons of the pilots, it is important, first, to give credit where credit is due, because in many ways, the pilots were successful. Low-income workers and families received high-quality services. They received thousands of dollars in tax refunds, opened bank accounts, completed financial education workshops, received credit counseling, and saved money toward homeownership.

Furthermore, each of the pilots was successful in establishing effective partnerships. The new partners—employers, government agencies, and commercial tax firms—were pleased with the programs and willing to continue them. They committed a significant amount of their own resources to the pilots, including planning time, outreach, physical space, and other infrastructure elements. In light of these accomplishments in both process and outcomes, it would be reasonable to write a report praising the efforts and recommending additional investment.

But the goal of the pilots was not just to provide services, it was to identify scalable models, and the results did not suggest that any of the innovations had real potential for scale. Despite their attempts to use existing infrastructure, they were all just as expensive, labor-intensive, and singular as other programs in the field. They all struggled to draw clients and spent a great deal of time engaging partners and maintaining relationships. Their failure was not just in operation or execution, but was due as well to fundamental flaws in design and in the theories and assumptions on which those designs were based. Rather than focus only on their success, the Aspen Institute and the Annie E. Casey Foundation were determined to acknowledge where they failed and learn from it.

Constructive Failure: What the Pilots Didn't Do

So what went wrong? The pilots provide a number of constructive lessons about the issue of scale. Many of those lessons reinforce the ideas presented above—that standardization, infrastructure, and roll-out are critical but missing elements on the path to scale.

Mistake Number 1: Attempts to "borrow" infrastructure, through partnerships with government and the private sector, created challenges to taking the pilots to scale. Developing sufficient infrastructure for scale would require a major investment of resources, which the pilot organizations did not have. As a result, all of the sites sought to attach services onto existing delivery systems. If the need for infrastructure can be met through strategic partnerships, however, then developing and maintaining relationships with partners becomes a primary concern for scale. Indeed, this was a constant challenge across the pilots, taking far more time and effort than anticipated.

In Chicago, turnover and reductions among human resources staff meant that pilot staff were constantly reeducating partners about the project and reestablishing its parameters. In Louisville, the turnover of leadership in three key partners at once may have been bad luck or may be typical of the current landscape. In any case, the pilot was unable to survive the changes.

Furthermore, successful partnerships with government or the private sector require a far greater understanding of those sectors than many in the nonprofit field typically have. For example, the expectation in Chicago was that corporate human resources departments, which already handle payroll and benefits for employees, would be able to add to their role easily. It seemed natural for workers in those departments to talk with employees about the EITC, promote retirement savings, and help with tax-related questions. The reality was far different. All of the human resources departments were already overextended and some were facing staffing cuts. One employer saw its human resources function being consolidated and outsourced as part of a corporate merger. While these experiences reflect industry-wide trends, the pilot failed to anticipate them. And those trends would make large-scale roll-out of employer partnerships (at least in the way the pilot was designed) extremely difficult.

Mistake Number 2: High per-unit costs made scaling up prohibitively expensive; furthermore, the programs did not present a clear value proposition for expected partner contributions. The budgets for the pilot initiatives took into account only direct costs to the nonprofit organizations testing the innovation. For example, the Louisville budget covered a part-time staff person working at the one-stop center and some administrative costs. It did not include any of the contributions by partners, such as costs for space and overhead at the one-stop, recruiting and training the volunteers who prepared tax returns, or staff of the agency that provided credit counseling to participants. A complete understanding of all program costs, both the total and broken down for each potential partner, would be necessary to determine the feasibility of roll-out for any model. And the actual costs in Louisville probably would present a very different, and less impressive, cost-benefit analysis.

Even though the real cost of the pilots was not calculated, the amount of time required by staff members was a common problem. One reason for this, as noted above, is that building and maintaining relationships with partners took far more time than expected. Second, the types of services and the way they were delivered tended to require a large staff commitment. Staff members at all sites were actively engaged in scheduling events, conducting outreach, facilitating workshops, and preparing taxes. That intensive staff commitment makes it unlikely that the programs as designed could be expanded significantly; large-scale roll-out will not be feasible unless per-unit costs can be controlled. And yet, none of the pilots included this consideration in developing their models.

Another key challenge is motivating partners to invest staff and money in community development activities. The nonprofits tended to make assumptions about the inherent value of their contribution, and, as a result, while all five sites found willing partners, the partnerships were founded mostly on goodwill. However, roll-out is not achieved by goodwill alone; partners require a clear value proposition, backed up by data.

The question of value was most critical in Tulsa, where H&R Block had specific goals of its own regarding customer satisfaction and client retention. Even there, the bulk of investment in pilot services came from CAPTC, which provided the software, hired and trained the benefits screeners, and conducted all follow-up with clients. H&R Block's main role was to make clients aware of the benefits screening and refer those who were interested to CAPTC. Despite a positive implementation experience, client feedback suggests that the benefits screening did not improve customer satisfaction or increase customer retention. Given H&R Block's focus on those measures, it seems unlikely that it would continue or expand the project in its current form.

Mistake Number 3: None of the community-based agencies managing the pilots had the degree of organizational capacity and sophistication necessary to implement programs at scale. An issue closely related to infrastructure is organizational capacity. All of the organizations are leaders in their communities, and they include national leaders in EITC outreach, free tax preparation, financial education, and asset development. But while all are good at what they do, none was built to focus on scale.

The lack of operational capacity showed in many ways. In Louisville, a staff member was asked to provide counseling on topics beyond her training. In Baltimore, some services were not implemented until mid-March, after most employees had filed their taxes. In Atlanta, a lack of staff slowed planning, and marketing efforts relied on one-to-one community outreach. Operational capacity affects the ability not only to implement programs, but also to sustain partnerships, especially with private sector businesses that are not used to the slow pace and makeshift methods of the not-for-profit world. To maintain relationships, community-based partners must inspire confidence that they can come through with they have promised in a timely and professional way.

Lack of organizational sophistication also showed in the quality of negotiation and deal-making. The Chicago nonprofits tried for months without success to get employers to put the partnership arrangement in writing. In Tulsa, H&R Block managers came to the table with a clearer idea of what they wanted out of the partnership and were more skilled at getting it. Where the partners had different ideas for the timing and method of outreach, for example, the result went H&R Block's way.

Mistake Number 4: The size of the solution must match the size of the problem, and pilots, by their very nature, may never be able to point the way to large-scale implementation. Finally, the most important lesson to emerge from the pilots may have to do with the inherent limitations of these types of innovations as prototypes for scale. It may be that not all models are scalable—and, in particular, models that begin as small, incremental efforts may never have the potential to grow significantly. Rather, no matter how large or small they are, models must be designed for volume and efficiency from the beginning. As it turned out, the most successful components of the pilots were extremely resource-intensive, making them poor candidates for scale. Research and development (a stage often given short shrift in the pilots) must take scale into account as a primary factor in determining whether to move forward with a new idea.

Furthermore, the size of the solution has to fit the size of the problem. The pilot innovations offer the promise of better targeting, expanded outreach, improved use of resources, and deeper impact. It is not clear, however, whether they could ever be expected to generate more than marginal improvements. One contributor to this problem may be the nature of the community organizations themselves, which are used to thinking and working within with a relatively small geographic and programmatic focus. To achieve their most ambitious goals, nonprofit fields must develop big ideas for big impact. If scale is the goal, then very different models are required, far beyond the innovations tested here.

The question of scale and resources is also something of a chicken-and-egg problem. The pilots were designed to require only minimal investment—with the idea that once they proved their worth, partners would provide the money and staffing necessary to take them to the next level. However, partly because they were built with such a small investment, the pilots never achieved the kind of results that might inspire government or corporations to expand them.

In the traditional context of nonprofit pilot initiatives, the majority of these efforts would be labeled successes. All were based on strong, forward-thinking proposals and most were successfully implemented. The most productive pieces of each will likely continue and even grow. Yet, viewed through the lens of this particular inquiry, the results are less impressive: none of the pilots is a promising candidate for achieving scale.

Conclusion

The inability of the EITC pilots to point the way to scale raises much broader questions about how the nonprofit sector goes about innovation and development. One of the probable reasons scale has been so elusive is because the *process* of innovation has focused on pilots as the primary method for testing new ideas. Because pilots are by nature small-scale interventions, and because so much is resting on their success, the innovations themselves are designed to work on a small scale. This presents a fundamental conflict—exactly what may make them work as pilots may make them unsuitable for scale.

Furthermore, pilots are really only about innovation, a first but only preliminary step on the pathway to achieving scale. Again, largely because of their small scale and intensive focus, pilots do not take into account standardization, infrastructure, and roll-out, the three critical steps to achieving scale. Though they were meant to test innovations for scale, they simply were not designed with scale in mind.

Learning from Failure: Lessons and Questions

These lessons beg a next set of questions for the field: What should we realistically expect pilots to accomplish and to teach us? What types of ideas are most appropriate for pilot-testing? If pilots are not the right vehicle, then what other methods can the field use to test new ideas—with limited early investment, but in a way that prepares for later large-scale growth? If not all ideas are scalable, then what would ideas that are built for scale look like? How can the need for standardization, infrastructure, and roll-out be integrated from the start in the design and testing of new ideas? Can changes in program design anticipate these additional steps and improve the chances for scale? And how can we address—or work around—fundamental limitations in organizational capacity?

We do not have the answers to those questions, but the lessons from the EITC pilots suggest some ideas, if only by inspiring us to think of new alternatives to the traditional nonprofit model of innovation and growth. The following ideas are meant to spark thinking and begin a dialogue about how to move forward.

- Rather than focusing almost exclusively on product and service innovation, we might spend more time developing organizations and larger nonprofit "industries." This means beginning to create national infrastructure and standards as well as building capacity within individual organizations at the local level.

- In addition to identifying and promoting best practices at the local level, we should take a step back and look at broader industry dynamics to identify any existing models or trends that might be scalable. Linking existing programs might be the easiest way to begin to develop infrastructure.

- Public sector and foundation funding streams should increase their large, multiyear, and cross-organizational funding to promote longer-term continuity, stability, and investment in the field. In addition, these funders should invest explicitly in standardization, infrastructure, and roll-out for scale.

- Alternative industry models, such as cooperatives, collaboration, or franchises, may provide structures that can link community-based efforts in a way that preserves their uniqueness while building national infrastructure and core operational standards.

- Research can help us better understand potential partners, the environment in which they operate, and key sectoral trends that affect them. Research can also help identify critical attributes to look for in establishing partnerships and building the data to make a clearer value proposition to potential partners.

- More research should be done on alternative forms of testing new ideas, with an eye toward how the for-profit sector supports research and development (R&D) and investment in scale. This research should also include investigating how corporations use capital, or cash reserves, to support R&D and growth.

- We should also further explore the role technology might play in both supporting expansion to scale and reducing unit costs of operation.

- There may be completely different ways to think about scale. For example, rather than delivering a product or service in larger and larger numbers, we might think in terms of achieving a certain market share—one that is significant enough to change the behavior of other players.

Policy and regulation play critical roles in community development problems and solutions and present another potential route for achieving scale. Policy and regulation can affect far larger numbers of individuals or communities than can direct service delivery.

Despite the formidable challenges, achieving scale remains a central goal for the community economic development field. The failure of the EITC pilots serves as a reality check on how our current models for scale are inadequate for the task. But while the lesson may be harsh, it does offer an opportunity to break from those models and identify a new route to scale.

Platforms for Scale: Testing a New Approach on the Ground

The failures of the EITC pilots, and the lessons learned from their mistakes, have led to a new focus on creating a practical infrastructure for scale. As a result, the next step in the ongoing partnership between the Annie E. Casey Foundation and the Aspen Institute is developing an online "platform" for the field. The idea is to provide a set of high-quality products, services, and supports that increases local capacity in a cost-effective *and scalable* way. Rather than building capacity one organization at a time, the platform is designed to provide a new national infrastructure that supports local mission-focused programs, but at the same time increases standardization across programs and allows best practices to spread quickly.

In advance of the 2008 tax season, the Aspen Institute launched EITCplatform.org, a Web-based platform with a single product: online, self-directed training for tax site Quality Reviewers. Separate research (also supported by the Annie E. Casey Foundation) had identified the Quality Review process as critical to tax preparation accuracy, and the Internal Revenue Service (IRS) requires free tax-preparation sites to include it. By providing online training at no cost to sites, the platform offered an efficient way for sites nationwide to implement the IRS requirement.

In the two years since it was launched, the EITCplatform has proven to be both scalable and valuable to the field. While it does not meet all local program needs, the platform has expanded to include multiple training modules, a data tool, group purchasing of technology, supplies and volunteer management software, and links to asset-building opportunities. More than 2,000 individuals from approximately 500 sites are registered users of the platform. On surveys, users report high levels of satisfaction and say that the platform has increased their programs capacity and quality. An evaluation has confirmed the latter: a review of tax returns prepared during the 2008 tax season found that sites using the online Quality Reviewer training reduced the number of tax return errors by an impressive 75 percent.

The resources on the EITCplatform meet critical needs for local programs. But more than the resources themselves, the main difference between this approach and the earlier EITC pilots is that the former was designed from the beginning with scale in mind. Moving forward, the Aspen Institute is continuing to expand the EITCplatform and is launching a broader platform (AssetPlatform.org) with training, tools, and products for the asset-building field. This new initiative is designed as a second test of the platform model for scale, and we will use it to determine whether that model can work in a much larger, more complex, and more diverse field than do EITC campaigns.

The support of the Annie E. Casey Foundation, along with a willingness by both Casey and the Aspen Institute to acknowledge and learn from failure, has allowed the field to reach this promising point. It is the openness to risk-taking that creates the environment for constructive failures.

References

An informed discussion: Achieving sustainability, scale, and impact in community development finance, a conference summary. (2005, December). *Profitwise News and Views*. Chicago, IL: Federal Reserve Bank of Chicago.

Brown, A. (2005, December). *Innovations for scale and sustainability in EITC campaigns: Lessons for community development from two years of pilots.* Washington, DC: Aspen Institute.

Brown, A. (2008, June). *Quality in EITC campaigns: Results from the 2008 tax season.* Baltimore, MD: The Annie E. Casey Foundation.

Ratliff, G. A., & Moy, K. (2004, December). *New pathways to scale for community development finance. Profitwise News and Views.* Chicago, IL: Federal Reserve Bank of Chicago.

8

Seedco's Community Childcare Assistance Initiative

Neil Kleiman and Emma Oppenheim

Introduction

Over the past 15 years, there has been a noticeable rise in the number of nonprofits attempting to reinvent themselves in the image of for-profit businesses. Inspired by the creativity and enterprising spirit of the dot-com era in the early 1990s, nonprofits by the score began to turn to the business world for answers, sparking a movement that became known as social enterprise.

In many respects, the social enterprise revolution has been a great success. It has fostered an emphasis among nonprofits on achieving measurable results for clients; it has encouraged sound financial planning and fiscal responsibility; and it has made many organizations more dynamic, innovative, efficient, and effective.

Yet nonprofits driven to meet a "double bottom" line for customers and clients far more typically have met with frustration and failure, drawing attention and resources away from the organization's core work, and even the oft-cited success stories are more complicated than they appear.

This chapter begins to reevaluate when and where entrepreneurship can truly enhance and support the work of mission-driven nonprofit organizations—and when nonprofits should be praised and supported simply for doing their vital work and doing it well. There will always be a place, of course, for creative financing, earned income, and outside-the-box thinking in the nonprofit world. Nonprofits have always been entrepreneurial in this sense; they are perhaps the most adept organizations at stretching a dollar or envisioning ways to accomplish their goals on a dime.

We provide an in-depth case study of Seedco's Community Childcare Assistance initiative, a social purpose business whose history reveals some of the major pitfalls of putting such a venture into practice. Overall, the case highlights how nonprofit businesses must carry the most difficult burdens of both nonprofit and for-profit ventures. The Seedco initiative details how the initiative was brought to market as a business, even though it had many of the constraints of a nonprofit: it was undercapitalized at the outset, had immediate and high expectations from philanthropic funders, and Seedco itself attempted to meet multiple social good goals through this one enterprise. The effort also had goals and priorities that did not mirror those of its customers—focusing more on social goals for children and families first rather than on the needs of busy workers and their employers.

Taken together, this case illuminates some of the larger lessons about the limits of social enterprise for nonprofits. The Seedco experiment teaches us that we must ease the pressure on nonprofits to succeed on so many levels at once. This means creating more time for incubation and developing a mixed-revenue financial model. We hope this case study and its lessons will help inform both the expectations and application of nonprofit business ventures in the future.

Background and Context

When the Personal Responsibility and Work Opportunity Reconciliation Act became law in 1996, its supporters heralded it as "the end of welfare as we know it." But as one chapter was officially declared closed, the next was uncharted territory. As more and more people left welfare and entered the workforce, it became clear that these workers had new and different needs.

One of the issues was the need for more childcare. Congress increased funding for childcare by $600 million, or 27 percent, as part of welfare reform, but childcare was not considered an entitlement, and the money often did not meet the new demand for services. Many working parents wound up on waiting lists for subsidized daycare; others simply chose to make their own arrangements. In both cases, however, the arrangements frequently depended on the kindness—and reliability—of relatives, friends, or neighbors.

If there was not enough money to cover the need for primary childcare, there was certainly no money for backup care, yet the problem was preventing otherwise capable people from achieving job stability.

The Idea

Seedco was founded in 1986 with a mandate to bring fresh, innovative ideas to the community development arena. In the late 1990s, Seedco began to expand its focus to include workforce development, and in 1998, it received a large federal welfare-to-work contract to transform a small, locally funded experiment connecting community-based service providers into a major workforce development alliance.

The alliance was an unprecedented attempt to pool the collective strength and competency of community groups to provide workforce services at the exact moment that New York and other cities began a major shift from welfare to work. With more and more services being provided directly by the largest nonprofit or even for-profit companies under massive government contracts, the alliance represented a radically different approach. Rather than providing services itself, Seedco functioned as a central administrative hub for a managed network of local groups that then assisted low-income job seekers coming off welfare. The various community partners in turn offered Seedco immediate feedback on how federal welfare policy changes were playing out on the ground.

It didn't take long for Seedco to notice an unsettling trend among the workers the alliance was helping to train and place. Well over 40 percent of participants reported that their work or training schedule was disrupted because of childcare issues. Seedco learned that absences typically occurred when a family's childcare arrangements fell through at the last minute. In New York City, where there were more workers than jobs at the low end of the economic ladder, a series of absences could easily get an "expendable" employee fired.

It seemed clear that the workers Seedco served through the alliance, and other low-income employees, needed some type of backup or emergency childcare. The question was, how to do it. Seedco knew that workforce-related childcare problems had no quick fixes, so from the outset it looked for a model that would be sustainable over the long term. This was no easy feat given the scarcity of funds for childcare, and the unlikelihood that foundations or government would fund an emergency childcare program beyond its start-up phase.

Seedco settled on a tempting idea: sell backup childcare plans to businesses as an employee benefit that would help reduce absenteeism and promote worker retention. Employers would gain a more stable workforce, the low-wage workers they employed would gain a tool to help them attain job security and stability, and Seedco would create a program that could support itself.

The Program

The Community Childcare Assistance (CCA) initiative was conceived as a creative solution to a welfare-to-work problem, not as a test case for nonprofit social enterprise. The idea was a bold one: Seedco would offer backup childcare through employers, structured as an employee benefit to improve worker stability and productivity. As envisioned, employers would enjoy a more reliable workforce and employees would gain access to needed services, and this would be achieved with far less public or philanthropic subsidization than a traditional social service entitlement.

In practice, however, it didn't work. It would be wrong simply to dismiss CCA as a programmatic misfire. Whatever other factors may have contributed to its struggles, our analysis suggests that the story of CCA reflects some of the significant differences between social purpose ventures and traditional for-profit businesses, as well as the limits of business ventures as a tool for mission-driven nonprofits.

Setup

In 2000, in part with a small grant from the Sirus Foundation, Seedco drafted an internal business plan for what was to become the Community Childcare Assistance initiative. Although Seedco was not a direct childcare provider, it had a deep understanding of the childcare field in New York City, particularly as it affected low-wage workers. Seedco knew that government-run daycare centers had lengthy waiting lists, and that many were contractually unable to take private clients. It also knew that there was significant availability in family-based childcare businesses throughout the city—and this seemed to present a golden opportunity.

Family-based childcare providers are licensed childcare practitioners who typically run small daycare businesses out of their homes. Seedco discovered that, although New York State allows family daycare providers to care for up to six children, those providers typically had an average of two vacant slots, which meant they usually could accommodate additional children at the last minute. A large, decentralized network of providers seemed to offer more convenience for workers than a few scattered daycare centers would. In addition, most of the family daycare providers were women from low-income backgrounds themselves. If Seedco chose to offer backup care through family-based childcare providers, it would be able to leverage the same revenue it was using to assist low-wage employees to support and encourage this group of community-based entrepreneurs as well.

In 2001, MBA students from Columbia Business School conducted a pro bono marketing study to assess CCA's viability as a social purpose business, including a scan of for-profit backup childcare businesses. They found that major employers that offered backup childcare typically did so through one of a handful of large, privately run, national or Manhattan-based companies, and that those companies most frequently provided center-based care. They were also extremely expensive. The business model was to create a high-quality childcare center, but one that only a few employees actually use.

Seedco's vision turned this construct on its head. It wanted to charge as little as possible for each childcare slot and have everyone who was entitled use the service. Its financial paradigm was to eke a small profit from a large number of customers, rather than charging a lot for what, among corporate clients, typically turned out to be very little.

Once it was determined that purchasing slots through commercial daycare centers was simply unaffordable, Seedco explored starting its own stand-alone daycare center or centers, but this required far too much capital investment and financial risk. Other options also proved untenable, and family-based care became the sole focus of Seedco's plan. In addition to the geographic and social advantages of using these providers, Seedco recognized that the extra capacity in family-based care meant that it could establish a pay-as-you-go arrangement with providers rather than purchasing costly daycare slots far in advance, many of which probably would go unused. It also allowed Seedco to guarantee its customers that childcare would be available the same day it was requested—something its competitors in the field could not do.

In March 2001, Seedco finalized its business plan for CCA, using a network of family-based caregivers as its model. Seedco envisioned a small six-month pilot program, tentatively targeted at employers in the Bronx, because that borough had the highest need for emergency childcare among low-income workers, and Seedco had a strong relationship with other local nonprofits there. Once it had succeeded in the Bronx, it would launch CCA in other boroughs.

In May of that year, the Columbia study was completed. It noted some obstacles, but on the whole said that CCA had great potential. The report focused on how CCA should be brought to market, suggesting that the most receptive customers to the CCA model were larger local businesses, businesses that already offered employee benefits, businesses with many entry-level and low-income employees, and businesses with a large number of female workers. It also advised Seedco to focus on quality of care in its marketing campaign to the end user.

Later that year, Seedco received a second series of capitalization grants, totaling $200,000, from a consortium of local childcare funders. As one of the local funders recalled, "I was very impressed with the staff and how well-thought-out the plan was; it seemed plausible. It was a good idea, and if anyone could sell it [to businesses], this staff could."

The Launch

Seedco executives recruited a staff with business and planning backgrounds to bring CCA to market, and officially launched CCA as a pilot program in the Bronx in November 2001. As the Columbia study had recommended, the staff put extensive effort into marketing the program to businesses and to workers. They produced a number of easy-to-understand posters and brochures attesting to the ease of using CCA's backup childcare service and touting its quality. CCA employed a bilingual staff person to canvass the Latino-dominated borough; she went door-to-door to various workplaces trying to sign people up.

Seedco's confidence in the program was reinforced early on when it encountered its ideal client—one that needed the service CCA was offering and believed in the model from the moment it heard about it. The employer was Cooperative Home Care Associates (CHCA), a Bronx-based social enterprise itself. CHCA is a member-owned home health care business that at the time employed 800 women, 55 percent of whom had young children. CHCA administrative staff worked closely with CCA's staff to ensure that it would be easy for workers to use the service, and devised a system under which CHCA would purchase a set number of childcare days in bulk, in advance. CCA's marketing staff person began to show up to talk about the program every Friday when the women collected their paychecks. Eventually, more than 250 were enrolled in the program.

Like Seedco, CHCA was attempting to earn revenue and to address a core social need simultaneously, which made it the right partner for this venture. CHCA's willingness to take the time necessary to understand the model and to be patient with CCA as the service evolved probably was due to the company's unique dedication to its staff and their professional development and, in turn, to the potential social and economic benefits CCA offered.

Unfortunately, CCA's experience with CHCA was not repeated with other employers in the Bronx. In fact, when Seedco called the employers from its initial focus groups, it was surprised to find that none of them was interested in the program.

One reason for the cold reception undoubtedly was the timing of the launch. CCA was brought to market shortly after September 11, 2001, and the economic climate in the city had changed since its business plan had been received so warmly. Seedco concluded that it could not postpone CCA's start date, but the city was in the midst of a recession, and employers were not eager to expand their employee-benefits programs.

In addition, small businesses in the Bronx, many of which employed the workers CCA hoped to reach, were not accustomed to providing any employee benefits and were largely uninterested. Still other businesses found that the specific benefits CCA provided did not meet their needs. For example, family childcare providers could not accommodate parents who worked nights or weekends, or take children who were even mildly sick.

The Struggle

If persuading employers to purchase CCA's services was the initial hurdle the business faced, it was far from the only one. Once they gained access to a pool of workers, CCA staff still had to convince those workers to enroll in the plan and use the service; this was perhaps the most challenging task of all.

Seedco had known that selling the concept of family-based care would take some work, but it was surprised to discover how strongly parents resisted the family care model. Many did not like the formal registration process, which required a doctor's visit for each child being enrolled, or leaving their children in a stranger's home. In addition, many of the family-based childcare providers lived in public housing projects, which was a major deterrent for many parents. And while the childcare networks were spread throughout the Bronx and served many areas, providers were still frequently a mile or more away from a parent's home or workplace.

Although Seedco was following its business plan to the letter, it wasn't generating nearly as much business as it had anticipated. Meanwhile, many of CCA's costs, such as salaries, overhead, and marketing, were fixed, and the business plan depended on CCA's ramping up to serve tens of thousands of users. So the organization began to adjust its approach.

First, to counter the ambivalence of employees, CCA engaged in a labor-intensive customer-service campaign. An outreach worker estimated that she was spending one full day a week coaxing parents to complete the medical paperwork they needed to enroll their children in the program. Frequently, she would visit doctors' offices herself to collect the necessary forms.

Second, CCA tinkered with its pricing and administrative structures, shifting from a traditional employee benefits type of plan, which employers neither understood nor embraced, to a virtual coupon book through which employers could purchase a specific number of slots for the company over a set period and use them as they chose.

Third, although Seedco had always envisioned signing up a large "anchor" client like the New York City Human Resources Administration to help bring the program to scale on its projected timeline, it had to begin exploring other options. Seedco soon learned that it was almost impossible to gain entree with any employer that had a unionized workforce—and most of the larger Bronx-based employers, such as hospitals and universities, were union shops. Although Seedco did make inroads with the Transit Workers Union, its eagerness to provide everything the union wanted led to a proposal that was too murky and complex for the union's leadership to embrace.

Seedco had planned to expand into other boroughs six months after launching the pilot program. This strategy assumed that the pilot program would succeed in establishing a solid client base. Eventually, CCA staff realized that since people who worked in the Bronx didn't necessarily live in the Bronx, CCA would need to expand its offerings to other areas of the city just to make the pilot plan work. In other words, if CCA was going to work at all, it needed to grow sooner rather than later. Seedco considered its options and decided to take the plunge, giving itself six months in 2002 to launch the venture in Brooklyn, Upper Manhattan, and parts of Queens.

By 2004, Seedco and the CCA board concluded that employers were still reluctant to embrace CCA and end users were generally ambivalent, leading Seedco to discontinue the program. In the end, CCA contracted with four employers who used a total of 312 days of care; overall 2,084 children were served.

Case Review and Analysis

The story of CCA is an important one, partly for the specific program challenges its staff faced and for what it tells us about the intricacies of the childcare field, but especially for what it reveals about the pitfalls of nonprofit business ventures in general.

Perhaps the most significant lesson of CCA and the greatest overall caveat it offers is that nonprofit entrepreneurship is a deceptively difficult enterprise, even for the savviest organizations. Succeeding in business is a challenge by itself, but businesses run by nonprofits are subject to pressures and constraints that their for-profit counterparts are not. As CCA amply illustrates, this is doubly true when the business itself is intended to provide a social service, rather than simply to generate earned income to help support the organization's other mission-driven work.

Below we identify some of the areas where, by either choice or necessity, Seedco's business strategy diverged from the traditional for-profit path, analyze the consequences of those differences, and draw some concrete conclusions about the pitfalls of nonprofit social enterprise in general.

The Double Bottom Line

CCA was brought to market as a business with a social purpose, but it was financed and evaluated by its backers as a nonprofit program. Not only was this double standard a major factor in CCA's undoing, it is probably the most glaring shortcoming in the existing social enterprise paradigm overall.

Starting a business costs a great deal of money, often more than most foundations are accustomed to granting nonprofits. Because of this, CCA, like many nonprofit-based businesses, started out undercapitalized.

Unlike businesses, though, nonprofit social programs are not supposed to fail. They may fail to live up to their promise, or require changes in strategy or structure, or prove to be unsustainable, but they are expected to produce something of value with the money foundations and others contribute. Seedco understood from the start that, even if CCA failed as a sustainable business idea, it nonetheless needed to provide a service. It had to show funders that it was achieving measurable social results, on a reasonable timeline, and within a budget.

The pressure to produce social results relatively quickly and with relatively little money makes cutting corners more likely and leads to decisions that may not be in the long-term best interest of the enterprise. While Seedco undoubtedly pleased funders by keeping CCA on a short timeline and tight budget, the result was that it introduced the program in a hostile economic climate, without adequate market research. CCA did not meet the needs of its target market, and CCA's staff had to work hard to persuade its customers that the service was more desirable than it appeared to be.

The Urge to Do More

For most businesses, making money is challenge enough. Social ventures already face a tougher road than do their for-profit peers because, as detailed above, they have obligations and constraints that pure moneymaking enterprises do not.

Not satisfied with just one social purpose, Seedco added additional missions, making its task even more burdensome. Under the heading "objectives," CCA's original business plan specified four goals:

- *First*, it enables low-wage workers to function more effectively and productively in the workplace, thus increasing both job retention and long-term labor outcomes.
- *Second*, it provides affordable, quality care to children through licensed childcare providers.
- *Third*, it supports networks of community-based nonprofit childcare providers to expand their capacity to include emergency childcare and better meet community needs.
- *Finally*, it strengthens community-based providers by enabling them to diversify their sources of revenue and compete more effectively against for-profit providers in emerging childcare markets.

Seedco's impulse to do more with CCA is hardly unique. It is part of the nonprofit mind-set to look for ways to maximize the benefit of its work by reaching as many target groups as possible with one project—and one budget. Yet, every inessential element introduced into a business plan has the potential to detract from the business's main goals.

Customers Are Not Clients

One of CCA's greatest flaws was that the goals and priorities undergirding it did not mirror those of its customers. Seedco assumed that both employers and workers would embrace any decent solution to the problem of unreliable childcare as better than none. Focus group sessions did indicate that workers would welcome backup childcare as an alternative to staying home. On this basis, Seedco set out to design the best service it could, within the given financial and logistical parameters, and then tried to sell it. This proved to be a miscalculation on several fronts.

While the service initially appealed to employers, they almost universally decided that its particulars did not meet their needs well enough to justify the expense. For example, emergency care was not available at night or on weekends, and even mildly sick children could not participate. These limitations significantly reduced CCA's potential value for many employers and workers and made it a far less attractive service.

Additionally, the workers revealed that, contrary to what was said at focus group sessions, they already did have a solution, and that was to stay home from work when they felt they needed to. Seedco had not considered this to be a true solution because CCA's top goal was to help workers stabilize their employment situations. But the workers had different priorities; they were more interested in protecting the health, welfare, and security of their children than they were in keeping their current low-wage jobs.

The difference between serving clients and selling to customers is a significant and demanding one for nonprofits. Organizations accustomed to assessing and fulfilling clients' basic needs must adjust to thinking about what customers desire, and then accept the likelihood that they will have to sacrifice some social goals to produce a marketable product or service. In the best-case scenario, this improves the quality of the service. In the worst-case scenario, it forces an organization to choose between undermining its business model or abandoning its primary social mission.

Realism over Idealism

Although it conceived of CCA as a business, Seedco nonetheless approached the project more like a social program than a for-profit venture. Instead of being direct about what employers and workers really wanted, and then determining whether it could offer those services

148 • *Robert Giloth and Colin Austin*

profitably in a marketable package, its method was to figure out the need first, and then figure out how to make it happen.

While for-profit entrepreneurs may start by envisioning their ideal, they also may be more realistic about whether that vision is practical. Nonprofits rarely have that luxury. Most experienced nonprofits have a sense of the size of grant most foundations will give, and for what types of projects. If they respond to a government RFP, they are frequently being asked to come up with the best proposal they can envision— within a given price range. These economic limitations legitimately breed a tendency to try to work with the tools at hand. Nonprofits survive by maintaining a can-do attitude and enthusiasm for their mission. However, in some cases, that enthusiasm can persuade them to stretch beyond their capacity, and in others, it can preclude nonprofits from seeing potential flaws in their vision.

Conclusion

Far from abandoning the notion of social enterprise, Seedco has incorporated the lessons of CCA to create a better model. First, Seedco no longer suggests that its social ventures will ever be self-sustaining. Instead, these programs are based on a *mixed-revenue financial model.* Second, Seedco now builds in significant *time for incubation.* This is a phased-in gestation period during which a social venture that may have revenue-generating potential is nurtured with heavy subsidies from the public and private sectors. Third, Seedco seeks to *launch new programs in multiple locations* whenever possible. This gives the venture a fair shot of proving itself in a few different environments to determine whether it is a viable model if given the right markets.

Social enterprise continues to be an area very much worth supporting and investing in. As Seedco and many other organizations have shown, there are many unmet market niches and unmet social needs that could be addressed simultaneously. But this must be done with patience, supported by investors willing to allow organizations incubation time, to experiment and determine the optimal market model.

Overall, Seedco embraces social enterprise as much as it ever did. It still is about exploring and using entrepreneurial methods and ideas, but in a way that respects the limits of those methods and the strengths a nonprofit brings to the table.

The story of Seedco's Community Childcare Assistance illuminates some of the significant flaws in the original paradigm for nonprofit social enterprise. Yet, the social entrepreneurship experiment has also broadened the nonprofit mind-set in ways that are well worth retaining. Nonprofits generally now understand the value of having and adhering to a business plan, doing market research, aspiring to fiscal responsibility, and achieving measurable results. They have also been encouraged to think outside the proverbial box, both in terms of pursuing creative solutions to social problems and in envisioning new ways to help support their work financially. Indeed, Seedco itself, far from being put off by its experience with CCA, has embraced the lessons of CCA and incorporated them into its new vision for nonprofit social enterprise—one that has begun to emerge in similar form across the nonprofit community.

Sources and Resources

There is a rich literature dedicated to the field of social enterprise as academics, business writers, media reporters and consultants have issued a growing number of assessments. What follows is a list of documents the authors found most helpful in the development of this paper.

Beinhacker, S. L., & Massarsky, C. W. (2002). *Enterprising nonprofits: Revenue generation in the nonprofit sector.* New Haven, CT: Yale School of Management-The Goldman Sachs Foundation, Partnership on Nonprofit Ventures.

Boschee, J. (2001). *The social enterprise sourcebook—Profiles of social purpose businesses operated by nonprofit organizations.* Minneapolis, MN: Northland Institute.

Bradach, J., & William Foster, W. (2005, February). Should nonprofits seek profits? *Harvard Business Review.* Cambridge, MA: Harvard Business School Publishing Corporation.

Cutler, I. (2005). *The double bottom line: Lessons on social enterprise from Seedco's nonprofit venture network 2001–2004.* New York: Seedco.

Dees, G., & Emerson, J. (2001). *Enterprising nonprofits: A toolkit for social entrepreneurs.* New York: John Wiley.

Dubb, S. (2004, April). *Building wealth: The new asset-based approach to solving social and economic problems.* Washington, DC: Aspen Institute, Nonprofit Sector Research Fund.

Emerson, J. (1998, December). The venture fund initiative: An assessment of current opportunities for social purpose business development and recommendations for advancing the field. San Francisco: The Venture Fund Initiative, REDF.

Grinker, W. J. (2006, April 27). Nonprofit entrepreneurship: Potential and risks. Speech delivered at Baruch College, School of Public Affairs, New York, NY.

Jarvis, O., & Tracey, P. (2006, Spring). An enterprising failure: Why a promising social franchise collapsed. *Stanford Social Innovation Review.*

Kaye, K., & Nightingale, D. S. (2000). The Low wage labor market: Challenges and opportunities for economic self-sufficiency. Washington, DC: The Urban Institute.

Schorr, J. (2006, Summer). Social enterprise 2.0—Moving toward a sustainable model. *Stanford Social Innovation Review.*

Skloot, E. (1999). *Privatization, competition and the future of human services.* New York: Surdna Foundation.

Weisbrod, B. A. (2004, Winter). The pitfalls of profits. *Stanford Social Innovation Review.*

9

The Dangers of Outcome Measures in Workforce Development

Susan Gewirtz

Introduction

The nonprofit world has had an ongoing debate about the importance of results and outcome-based thinking. While most agree that using data, setting targets, and managing for results are critical elements of accountability, continuous improvement, and organizational learning, there are many concerns as well. For example, does a focus on results crowd out innovation, unheard voices, or stories? Where do more qualitative measures fit in this process of assessing program performance and supporting continuous learning? This chapter addresses the constructive mistake of not anticipating the unintended consequences of establishing "robust" indicators of program success. An example from the Annie E. Casey Foundation's Jobs Initiative (JI) illustrates the mistake of setting robust employment retention standards in the absence of a culture of continuous learning and improvement in the workforce development field. Specifically, the Seattle Jobs Initiative's (a high performer among Initiative sites) one-year retention rates compared unfavorably with those *reported* by similar programs in its region, which may have used less rigorous definitions. This example also demonstrates the problem of a national initiative creating workforce measurement standards in isolation without bringing local communities or national stakeholders into the process. This chapter concludes by offering several approaches for policymakers, funders, and workforce practitioners that respond to this type of mistake.

The JI was an eight-year, six-city, $30-million effort to connect low-income, urban communities to good jobs and regional economies. It sought to address the poor performance of much of the employment training field by adopting high standards and evidence-based program models like the Center for Employment Training (CET). The JI was implemented in three phases. Sites began with an 18-month planning period during which they engaged stakeholders, completed labor market research, and did some small "prototyping" to test approaches. All sites produced strategic investment plans that described proposed projects and targets that Annie E. Casey Foundation (AECF) reviewed before sites could move into the operational phase. In the second phase, JI sites executed "jobs projects" that connected lower-skilled workers to good entry-level jobs. The concluding stage focused on "systems reform" and built on the lessons, partnerships, and success of the jobs projects to bring innovations and promising practices to scale. Abt Associates documented and evaluated all phases of the initiative.

Each JI site developed jobs projects to connect lower-skilled job seekers to jobs that paid a minimum of $7.00 an hour, offered health care benefits, and would lead to long-term labor market retention. Sites created more than 40 different jobs projects, resulting in placements of more than 12,000 individuals, with a one-year retention rate for placed participants of more than 54 percent. Abt Associates' evaluation showed an average placement wage of $9.41 (9.5 percent higher than the average wage participants earned from their pre-JI employment). A 36-month follow-up survey showed an average hourly wage increase of nearly 22 percent for individuals who were employed before enrollment in the JI (from $8.23 to $10.03) and an average weekly earnings increase of approximately 29 percent (Abt Associates, Inc., & Metis Associates, 2005).

This chapter describes the growing interest in results accountability in the public and nonprofit sectors, including the workforce development field. It then details why AECF took an investor approach in the JI and how that was used by the foundation and by sites. The chapter then focuses on the constructive mistake of applying highly specialized definitions of success to the JI and the consequences to one site, the Seattle Jobs Initiative, while noting the inherent challenges in comparing performance across programs. It also speculates that, by using somewhat idiosyncratic measures, AECF initiative managers may have inadvertently reduced the Initiative's ability to raise standards in the broader workforce field. Finally, several emerging approaches may offer ways for practitioners, funders, and policymakers to avoid this type of mistake in the future.

The Growing Interest in Accountability

While setting targets and benchmarks is common in the private sector, there is less experience in using this approach in the nonprofit world. Over the past 20 years, the public and nonprofit sectors have begun taking the outcomes frameworks and language from the private sector and applying them to human services programs and funding approaches. This was marked at the beginning by the "Reinventing Government" approach articulated by David Osborne in 1992 and by subsequent attempts to incorporate those strategies in federal and local government programs. Private foundations also began to shift toward outcome thinking and funding, which is reflected in funding decisions and requirements that grantees articulate their intended results. Publications such as *Trying Hard Is Not Good Enough* (Friedman, 2005), *Good Stories Aren't Enough* (Miles, 2006), and the Rensselaerville Institute's *Outcome Funding: A New Approach to Targeted Grantmaking* (Williams, Webb, & Phillips, 1991) all highlight the importance of accountability and identifying the right measures by which to assess program success in the public and nonprofit sectors. The workforce development field also began adopting the principles of results accountability. In the 1980s the federal Job Training Partnership Act required explicit performance measures related to participant outcomes, while most programs still defined performance in terms of process (Barnow & King, 2000).

While the Workforce Investment Act of 1998 (WIA) attempted to address issues of consistency in terms of outcomes and how measures are calculated, it has not resolved the problems of comparable data or how to use data for continuous learning. According to a U.S. Government Accountability Office report, "even when fully implemented, WIA performance measures may still not provide a true picture of WIA-funded program performance largely because data are not comparable across states or timely." The GAO assessment recognized that adequate guidance was not provided on definitions related to enrollment, who should be tracked, and when. The report also found considerable variations among states and localities (U.S. Government Accountability Office [GAO], 2002). In a follow-up report, the GAO found that the Department of Labor's (DOL) additional guidance requiring states to implement common performance measures by July 1, 2005, clarified some key data elements but did not address all of the issues. Furthermore, while DOL had some monitoring processes in place, it lacked a standard monitoring guide to address data quality (GAO, 2005). A 2009 GAO report found that some progress had been made in addressing earlier concerns regarding performance measurement and the accuracy of performance data, but pointed out that more attention needs to be given to understanding what works and for whom (GAO, 2009).

In the absence of common benchmarks and a common approach to measurement, workforce development programs define key measures differently, often based on various funder requirements and by the seat of their pants. Many workforce organizations have ineffective data collection systems and issue reports to community stakeholders and funders in ways that overestimate success and are not comparable to similar programs. For many workforce providers, a significant leap remains between producing data for funders and using data for continuous improvement, and learning that addresses staff and management needs and promotes innovation. Further, as funding for workforce development has been reduced at the federal level, community-based workforce providers feel increasing pressure to demonstrate good results, leaving less room to learn from "failure."

AECF Adopts an Investor Approach to Manage the Jobs Initiative
The designers of the JI decided to take an investor approach to the management of the multiyear initiative for three reasons. First, JI managers believed that using outcomes could be an important tool for creating a framework for continuous improvement and learning, and could enable the foundation and sites to shift funding continuously toward the most successful projects. Second, coming in the wake of the evaluation of JTPA and the perception that workforce programs were ineffective, the foundation knew it would be critical to demonstrate through data and evidence whether and how workforce development efforts can contribute to improved economic outcomes for lower-skilled adults. Finally, the foundation as a whole embraced the importance of using data to improve outcomes for disadvantaged children and families, as evidenced in efforts such as the Kids Count initiative. An investment approach with its attention to targets and common metrics related to job retention and advancement fit well with AECF's Board of Trustees, which included top executives from United Parcel Service.

The JI enlisted the assistance of the Rensselaerville Institute to structure a National Investors Outcome Outline, and a similar one for local sites to complete, that described investor givens, assumptions, strategies, and targets. In 1995 there was no operational consensus on key measures of success for workforce development programs. For example, measures might include any number of indicators, such as family self-sufficiency, job placement rates, short-term job retention, longer-term labor market retention, and wage progression. The National Outcomes

Outline clearly defined AECF's expectations and assumptions. The designers of the Initiative chose measures related to placement, retention, and advancement as the core indicators of success, with particular emphasis on 12-month retention. AECF Initiative managers believed that longer retention in the labor market (not necessarily in the same job) was a critical milestone for individuals to achieve on their journey to becoming steady workers and increasing their income over time. While 12-month retention does not guarantee long-term financial success, it was used in the Jobs Initiative as a proxy measure for employment and income stability. The JI definition of employment retention was more stringent than was commonly used by other funding sources or workforce organizations. For example, the Temporary Assistance for Needy Families (TANF) program required retention follow-up for shorter periods, generally no more than six months, and did not support client tracking beyond that period.

Defining, Measuring, and Reporting Retention in the Jobs Initiative
Beginning in 1997, AECF and the sites formulated the definition of retention that remained in place from 1998 through the conclusion of the Initiative. In summary, the definition for retention had these components:

- Milestones at three, six, nine, and 12 months.
- An individual remains at the same job or moves to a "better" job in a manner that is usually continuous, with only short gaps in between jobs (generally no more than 30 days in any quarter).
- Individuals are credited for retention only if they are in a full-time job that pays at least $7.00 per hour and includes medical benefits.
- The denominator for calculating retention rates is based on the number of placements eligible, based on date of employment.

Table 9.1 demonstrates how all JI sites reported one-year retention information:

Table 9.1 Jobs Initiative One-Year Job Retention Results

Number eligible to reach 12-month retention	Percent reached 12-month retention	Percent did not reach 12-month retention	Percent unknown (unable to reach)
100	55%	30%	15%

AECF created common data definitions within and across the sites as well as a single cross-site database for the purposes of continuous learning and longer-term evaluation. The Foundation also provided substantial technical assistance resources and funding to build the capacity of sites to collect and report on key data. Initiative managers contracted with Metis Associates to build out a common information technology system across sites that could track historic participant-level data so that they conformed to definitions about placement and retention. With assistance from Metis and Abt, some sites were also able to supplement their own tracking capabilities with administrative data gathered from Unemployment Insurance records. Even with considerable resources going toward building data capacity, sites struggled for several years to report and collect data. AECF used performance-based contracts to underscore that data were crucial to the initiative and, in several cases, withheld payments until sites produced quarterly reports with high-quality data.

The Mistake

The JI's mistake was in setting standards and using measures that were highly specific to the initiative and, therefore, not easily comparable to other workforce development programs. While JI focused on continuous improvement that included learning from failure, the six sites operated in the context of local workforce developments systems that were becoming increasingly results-focused as a result of greater competition for limited workforce development funds. Individual JI sites were at a greater disadvantage than other workforce organizations that had lower standards or were less clear about what they were measuring. At the national level, AECF also neglected to connect JI measures and standards to the broader changes that were occurring in workforce development, influenced by the 1996 welfare reform and the 1998 Workforce Investment Act. The JI could have done more to develop common ways to measure results and to engage in dialogue with federal and local agencies while it was operationalizing WIA.

Three years into the operational phase of JI, AECF observed that sites and the evaluation team found it difficult to compare JI results to those of similar programs. Abt Associates had completed a benchmarking effort that compared placement, retention, and costs across JI projects and a select number of similar programs outside of the JI. Abt also tried comparing JI retention results to studies on welfare-to-work participants. As a result of these challenges, AECF commissioned a report to consider how other workforce providers were using and reporting data and to examine the IT systems they were using. A 2001 report completed by Abt Associates with consultation from the Aspen Institute looked at a national sample of workforce development projects to examine data capacity and explore innovative practices (Abt Associates, 2001). While most organizations collected complete employment information for the first job placement, retention information was more inconsistent and frequently missing.

According to the report, retention is often measured during the time participants receive follow-up services, but collection of those data typically ends when services end. The lack of common data and measurement definitions interfered with the ability to conduct analysis across programs and across the workforce field. Some examples of different ways retention was measured include:

- defining retention in terms of whether someone remained employed in the same sector, even if not in the same job;

- tracking employment only in the same job;
- tracking at intervals, regardless of whether employment in the same industry or job; and
- measuring at different time intervals, such as 30 days, three months, nine months, and so forth.

Two additional challenges related to comparing workforce outcomes across programs arose. First, while programs may seem similar at first glance, they may in fact differ in key areas such as the population being served or the level of intensity of the workforce intervention. For example, efforts that are working with TANF recipients should not be compared to efforts that are serving dislocated workers, who have very different employment experience and education and skills. Second, there is the hidden problem in comparing retention across programs, what might be considered the "mystery of the denominator." JI counted individuals as retained based on a denominator of all individuals who were placed and whose date of placement made them eligible for 12-month retention. Typically, workforce development programs do not define the measures used when they report their results, so we are in the dark about denominator. Anecdotally, we know some programs use a denominator that only includes placed individuals who were able to be located or those individuals who were employed for a longer period.

JI's more robust definition did work well within the closed community of the national initiative. At AECF-sponsored learning meetings, sites looked at the retention data and modeled self-assessment; and the cross-site data enabled Abt Associates to complete a benchmarking effort across the Casey projects and a few non-JI programs that looked at results and costs per placement and 12-month retention. But, to support comparability at the community level and expand the influence of JI pertaining to performance measures and continuous improvement, AECF would have had to reach out to more policymakers and public and private investors.

The Seattle Jobs Initiative

In 1995, Seattle was selected as one of the six JI sites to participate in the eight-year effort. The City of Seattle, through its Office of Economic Development (OED), led the Initiative, which was embraced by then-Mayor Norman Rice as a key element in the city's response to the 1996 welfare reform legislation. The Seattle Jobs Initiative (SJI) offered a range of programs, from individualized job placement through community-based organizations for those looking for immediate employment to sector-based training programs delivered in partnership with community colleges. SJI also functioned as a workforce intermediary as it implemented the majority of its work through partnerships with community-based organizations, community colleges, and other employment and training organizations. In January 2003, SJI spun off from the city and established itself as an independent nonprofit with ongoing support from the City of Seattle. SJI's attention to performance management and documenting lessons about its work distinguished it among Jobs Initiative sites. Table 9.2 provides an overview of placement, wages and retention for the SJI.

Table 9.2 Seattle Jobs Initiative Results

Total number of placements (1997-2008):	5,873
Average wage at initial placement (in 2008):	$11.84
One-year retention rate (in 2008):	62%
Cumulative overall wage advancement:	39%

The SJI Dilemma

SJI, among the highest-performing JI sites, had a 12-month retention rate that did not *appear* as strong as those of other similar efforts. SJI, using a definition of 12-month retention that was even more stringent than the standard required by AECF, posted a retention rate of 61 percent in 2006. In contrast, the Web site of the King County Department of Human Services said its own jobs-training program had an 87 percent one-year job retention rate. To count as having reached 12-month retention, SJI had in place the following conditions: the client had to be working on the date on which 12-month retention is checked; had to have work gaps of no more than 90 days during the year; and had to have a job that paid at least $9.00 plus benefits and be working at least 30 hours per week. Table 9.3 shows the one-year retention rate for SJI

Table 9.3 Seattle Jobs Initiative 12-Month Retention Rate, through December 2006*

Number eligible to have reached 12-month retention	% retained for 12 months	% not retained for 12 months	% unknown
4,210	61% (2,575)	22% (942)	17% (693)

*Source: SJI data report, 2007.

That its retention results looked weaker than results for other similar projects was frustrating for SJI, because its leadership had focused on this performance measure since 1998. Because most of SJI's jobs projects did not begin making substantial numbers of employment placements until the summer of 1997, reporting on 12-month retention for placed participants did not occur in earnest until fall 1998. At this early stage, SJI's 12-month retention performance for the reporting period of October through December 1998 was only 43 percent. The OED director concluded that SJI should do considerably better and took a number of steps to improve retention results for SJI participants. First, SJI implemented a multi-faceted, ongoing self-assessment process, with the assistance of researchers from the University of Washington and the Abt evaluation team. Second, SJI restructured its contracts with local providers of workforce development services to place greater emphasis on achieving longer-term retention milestones in determining a provider's level of remuneration. Finally, recognizing the critical role that high-quality case management plays in client outcomes, SJI developed and implemented a training curriculum that emphasized retention supports.

In the year (1999–2000) following OED's decision to focus more attention on retention outcomes, SJI achieved a 12-month retention rate of 58 percent, the highest rate among the six JI sites. The following year, in part reflecting the worsening economy, SJI's 12-month retention rate fell to 50 percent, but it was still the highest rate achieved among the JI sites. By June 2003, SJI's 12-month retention was back up to 58 percent (internal AECF memo, 2004).

The Challenge of Finding Comparable Retention Data

In 2006, at the request of the SJI, Abt Associates began a survey to determine what data other programs in the Seattle area collected and whether they shared any common measures and definitions. As part of this survey, Abt interviewed eight workforce organizations to elicit information about their performance metrics and outcomes and reviewed published data in reports and on Web sites. Abt then selected one workforce program within each organization to obtain more detailed information about programs that were similar to those offered by SJI. For example, Abt looked at programs that included sector training in construction, health care, and manufacturing. The survey showed considerable variation in definitions and measures and prevented Abt from comparing retention results across programs (Abt memo, 2007). Key findings included:

- Organizations use a variety of data collection and performance measurement approaches.
- Definitions of performance measures vary across organizations.

- Performance measurement is motivated largely by funders' requirements.
- The majority of the organizations used performance measures that focused on a program's process or the outputs of the service intervention.
- Only two organizations tracked long-term retention for 12 or 24 months.
- Only three of the eight organizations provided specific definitions of their performance measures.

Conclusion

AECF managers neglected to anticipate the consequences of setting ambitious targets with measures that were highly specific to the JI. The impact of this approach affected high-performing JI sites by making it seem that they were underperforming compared to similar programs in their communities. Further, the JI might have been better positioned to influence the workforce development field if policymakers and other funders had been involved in discussions about definitions, measures, and benchmarks. This could have led to more agreement on measures of workforce success and to more open discussion of the challenges and lessons related to pursuing long-term retention as a key benchmark.

In deconstructing this mistake, AECF came to believe that it was correct in setting ambitious targets with precise and robust measures, but erred by establishing performance measures in isolation from other workforce actors in the JI communities. By recognizing that the low-income earners and job seekers that JI sites would be serving often had work experience but limited continuous attachment, it made sense to push for longer-term labor market attachment. Recent research suggesting that wage progression often involves changing jobs for low-income earners has also affirmed the JI managers' decision to allow for multiple jobs with short gaps in between to be taken into account in retention definition (Andersson, Holzer, & Lane, 2005).

AECF did not take into account sufficiently, however, the competitive environment that workforce development programs operate within locally. The 1990s were particularly eventful years with dramatic changes in funding policy related to welfare and workforce with the passage of the TANF legislation in 1996 and WIA in 1998. Both of these policy shifts had the effect of reducing funding for education and training and signaled an emphasis on work-first strategies. JI sites, while receiving substantial resources from AECF for program support (up to $700,000 a year for seven years), still needed to leverage public funding and foster partnerships, and to do so, they had to demonstrate their comparative effectiveness within their local workforce communities.

If setting ambitious targets was not a mistake, then the question becomes, how can funders avoid repeating AECF's error of requiring measures that left a high-performing program vulnerable in the context of its regional workforce development environment? I propose three approaches.

First, I argue for more openness in sharing definitions and measures across workforce programs. Second, incentives and capacity building are needed to help workforce organizations use performance measurement as a tool for learning and continuous improvement. Third, policymakers, funders, and workforce organizations can work together to create workforce benchmarks that can be adopted more broadly by the workforce field at the program and policy levels.

While the workforce field continues to struggle over data, continuous improvement, and benchmarks, there are examples of the public and nonprofit sectors attempting to address these challenges in new ways. For example, the Department of Labor supported technical assistance, trainings, and online tools to assist local workforce systems to improve their outcomes and achieve performance standards required under WIA. The Performance Enhancement Project (PEP) funded by the U.S. Department of Labor engaged Public/Private Ventures (P/PV) and Social Policy Research Associates to work with 42 states to ensure their understanding of WIA measures and to improve the design and implementation of their programs. This assistance was delivered through workshops, targeted technical assistance, online training courses, and Webinars. DOL also funded the online Federal Research and Evaluation Database (FRED) to make the data it collects from state and local partners more accessible to the training and employment community. FRED enabled analysis of the WIA data related to demographics, services received, and outcomes achieved after clients leave a program.

At a state policy level, the National Governors Association and the State of Washington worked with representatives from a cross-section of workforce development programs in six states to create overarching measures for education and workforce programs. The state teams met several times during 2004 to share experiences, review technical papers, and think through key issues involved in identifying core measures of integrated performance information relevant to policymakers (Wilson, 2005).

Networks of community-based organizations or workforce organizations within a geographic area can also work together to establish common measures, share lessons, and improve program performance. Three examples illustrate how workforce practitioners can become more engaged in continuous improvement. Seedco, a workforce intermediary in New York City, manages a large welfare-to-work contract from the city by subcontracting to a network of community-based organizations through its *Earn*Fair Alliance. Network members use common workforce performance measures and participate in quarterly status meetings where they discuss results and share lessons learned and promising practices. In another example, the Workforce Development Affinity Group of the Association of Baltimore Area Grantmakers has begun an effort to identify a set of common performance measures that their grantees throughout the region could use. These grantmakers believe this approach could strengthen Baltimore's workforce development programs and build knowledge about what is and isn't working to increase access to jobs with family-supporting wages and benefits.

Having learned from the JI mistake of having specialized workforce definitions, JI managers have invested in a benchmarking approach for several years that can be used more broadly by workforce providers, funders, and policymakers. P/PV began exploring this idea to determine whether it was feasible to develop categories related to population demographics and service characteristics as well as definitions pertaining to placement, retention, and advancement that would enable comparisons among similar programs. As of May 2009, the project involved 178 programs and continues to grow. The benchmarking system allows users to post aggregate program information and results on a Web site anonymously. They then receive a report showing how that program compares to similar ones from their region or nationally, for example, programs of similar size, those serving a similar population, or those focused on a particular service strategy such as vocational skills training. This approach also promotes learning for continuous improvement by highlighting programs with the best results and sharing their lessons among participating organizations, as well as providing opportunities for peer learning about using data more effectively as an internal tool. Finally, funders and policymakers could use this information to make better recommendations about appropriate performance goals when supporting and designing workforce strategies and programs.

In 2009, the Workforce Development Funders Group in New York City worked with P/PV to strengthen the capacity of its grantees to use data as a performance management tool by using the benchmarking methodology. P/PV produced individualized reports for each program showing the comparative rankings of their outcomes with the results of other programs sharing similar characteristics. P/PV also held bimonthly learning community forums to discuss trends and common management challenges identified by the group around using data for performance improvement (Public/Private Ventures, 2009).

References

Abt Associates. (2001). *Workforce Development Management Information Systems: An Analysis of Capacity and Use Across a Sample of Workforce Development Projects.* Cambridge, MA

Abt Associates, Inc., & Metis Associates. (2005). *A Jobs Initiative research brief: Approaches to measuring and tracking career advancement.* Cambridge, MA.

Andersson, F., Holzer, H. J., & Lane, J. I. (2005). *Moving up or moving on: Who advances in the low-wage labor market?* New York: Russell Sage Foundation

Barnow, B., & King, C. (2000). *Improving the odds: Increasing the effectiveness of publicly funded training.* Washington, DC: Urban Institute Press

Friedman, M. (2005). *Trying hard is not good enough: How to produce measurable improvements for customers and communities.* Bloomington, IN: Trafford Publishing.

Miles, M. (2006). *Good stories aren't enough: Becoming outcomes-driven in workforce development.* Philadelphia, PA: Public/Private Ventures.

Osborne, D. & Gaebler, T. (1992). *Reinventing Government: How the Entrepreneurial Spirit Is Transforming the Public Sector.* New York: Basic Books.

Public/Private Ventures. (2009). *The Benchmarking Project: Putting data to work in New York City: Year 2 proposal.* New York.

U.S. Government Accountability Office (USGAO). (2002). *Report to Congressional Requesters Workforce Investment Act: Improvements needed in performance measures to a more accurate picture of WIA's effectiveness* (GAO-02-275). Washington, DC: Government Printing Office.

U.S. Government Accountability Office (USGAO). (2005). *Workforce Investment Act: Labor and states have taken actions to improve data quality, but additional steps are needed* (GAO-06-82). Washington, DC: Government Printing Office.

U.S. Government Accountability Office (USGAO). (2009). *Workforce Investment Act: Labor has made progress in addressing areas of concern, but more focus needed on understanding what works and what doesn't* (GAO-09-396T). Washington, DC: Government Printing Office.

Williams, H. S., Webb, A. Y., & Phillips, W. J. (1991). *Outcome funding: A new approach to targeted grantmaking.* Rensselaerville, NY: The Rensselaerville Institute

Wilson, B. (2005). *Integrated performance information for workforce development: A blueprint for states.* Olympia, WA: Washington State Workforce Training and Education Coordinating Board.

$$\boxed{10}$$

Learning the Limits of Project Partnerships

Colin Austin

Introduction

Granting agencies often require communities to organize partnerships, with the notion that local resources can be leveraged and contribute to a better-coordinated and more effective project. Community development practitioners also seek broader impact by having key stakeholders work together. How safe is the assumption that collaboration is a logical and natural approach to change? To what extent can partnerships be expected to produce results, and at what pace? Do the partners themselves understand that the road they are to travel is full of dips and curves?

A growing body of literature and practice identifies reasons why partnerships deliver value, but also points out many of the challenges. This chapter examines the experiences of two recent collaborative-based projects, Connecting People to Jobs and Latino Pathways, both of which chose a partnership model to address large-scale problems in their regions and communities. This examination concludes that the process of mobilizing partners can produce significant results but can also cause unintended and sometimes damaging consequences.

Consider the following scenario: Representatives from a funding agency arrange for a site visit to determine invitees for a new grant program. A meeting is organized with local leaders and relevant institutions to discuss the potential project and test the commitment and readiness of the community to participate. The room is packed. Going around the table, each person talks about the willingness of his or her organization to contribute to a joint endeavor. The event is facilitated by a charismatic executive director of an organization that wants to play a leadership role in the project. The comments of the attendees are honest and the follow-up conversation is serious and hopeful.

Fast-forward two years. A small handful of partners gather to talk about the future of the project. They have not met in months. The organization that was the initial base for the project is in fiscal crisis and the charismatic leader has moved on to other work. The recently hired staff coordinator is unsure about her responsibilities and is frustrated by the lack of guidance. The remaining partners are reluctant to admit defeat, but they are also getting tired and feeling trapped. What started out as an energized collaboration is now a set of stalled program activities.

What went wrong? The components of this scenario are based on real experiences and should be familiar to those working on the ground in community economic development. With the best of intentions, many partnerships fail to achieve desired outcomes and have difficulty functioning.

This chapter describes three principal mistakes of partnership efforts:

- Emphasizing program activities over long-term results.
- Failing to provide clear leadership.
- Expecting too much from community-based partners and project staff.

A set of lessons also suggests that project partners should set their sights on learning and changes in regional workforce systems, with related indicators in place to measure progress. Investors will need to consider the risks and payoffs of the partnership approach and the appropriate timetable for success.

The Case for Partnerships

From the social interdependence of the Settlement House movement to the Federal Community Action Program of the 1960s, social change practitioners have looked to community partnerships to address issues at a broader and more fundamental level (Trattner, 1999). As the field of community economic development grew, the scope of partnerships broadened to include not only service agencies and affected community residents, but also an array of public institutions, businesses, and political leaders. Partnerships can act as a bridge and fill space between traditional institutions and the larger system of the government and community. By their nature, partnerships are also tenuous because they require partners to make joint decisions while retaining their own separate identities and goals (Roberts, 2004). But it is their flexibility and orientation toward risk-taking that make them valuable in many social arenas. This chapter focuses on examples of partnerships that focus on employment and training efforts, sometimes known as "workforce intermediaries," that act as the brokers and integrators that have the potential to produce new methods and ideas (Giloth, 2004).

Through their granting processes, private foundations and government agencies at all levels encourage and reward community programs that are able to bring local actors together. One goal is to maximize the impact of the investment and increase the likelihood of sustainability. Funders may recognize that partnership work is demanding and requires significant levels of cooperation, but the payoff in terms of leverage and results is potentially high (Ford Foundation, 1996).

Nonprofit organizations such as MDC, Inc., have made collaboration a centerpiece of the community change process. In their manual, *Building Community by Design*, MDC authors write, "we use a team-based approach, the goal of which is to build a critical mass of leaders that functions as a support network and an action-oriented team capable of tackling a complex change effort" (Dodson, Thomasson, & Totten, 2002). The partnership team is also a learning group that grows in experience and can make adjustments when contexts change or new opportunities arise.

The move toward collaboration is now common to community economic development practice, but it also has significant and often unexamined assumptions. First, those involved carry an unexamined confidence that they can plan together as a group and collaborate on a shared project. There is an expectation that partners will make joint decisions without acknowledging the disparities in institutional resources and preexisting relationships around a table. Further, there is an assumption that all partners will benefit from the collaborative project and a tendency to take everyone's equal commitment for granted. Often left out are preparations for the messy, nonlinear, and lengthy nature of collaboration (Wheatley, 2004). Examining these assumptions at the front end and sorting through the realities of a partnership take time and trust. Yet, proceeding with unrealistic expectations for partnerships eventually shows up in unnecessary tensions and disappointing results.

Background: Connecting People to Jobs and the Latino Pathways Project

MDC, Inc., is a nonprofit organization that conducts research and manages demonstration projects that often involve building partnerships. In Connecting People to Jobs, and later in Latino Pathways, MDC played the role of convener, facilitator, researcher, and team coach. In both projects MDC worked with new collaborations to break through barriers that were keeping low-wage workers from good jobs.

In 2001 the Mary Reynolds Babcock Foundation became concerned that a "work first" policy was pushing former welfare recipients into low-skilled employment that still left people in poverty. MDC conducted a scan of activity in the South and found that promising job training practices existed but were not well developed. MDC also reported that few grassroots organizations in the South had experience in employment programs, and that work would be needed across institutions to make the system function for disadvantaged job seekers. With additional support from the Annie E. Casey Foundation, the new "Connecting People to Jobs" Initiative was launched in 2002. MDC partnered with coaches and technical-assistance providers from the Center for Community Change. The sites selected for the demonstration were Charleston, West Virginia; Charlottesville, Virginia; and Columbia, South Carolina.

From the beginning, Connecting People to Jobs (CPTJ) focused on building a collaborative that would lead the project. The main partners in CPTJ included grassroots organizations, community colleges, federally funded One Stop Career Centers, and employers. Other community agencies and local leaders were also involved. It was not always clear which partner was best at particular project functions, especially with regard to disadvantaged populations. These roles had to be negotiated and resulted in some partners' being sidelined or left out altogether.

The transition from planning and design to actual project implementation was challenging and required debate regarding hiring staff, setting up an office, developing procedures and protocols, and establishing reporting and oversight mechanisms. The partnerships pursued programmatic opportunities and at the same time dealt with leadership and turf issues that led to conflicts within the group.

The development of the local projects was uneven, but each site eventually launched a program and began operations. The programs developed differently according to the capacities and engagement of the partners at the table. At one site the grassroots organization led the way, achieving high levels of recruitment and job readiness training. At other sites the One Stop Career Center or the community college partners hosted many of the activities, focusing on job attachment or career ladder training. As the local projects moved forward, the partnerships were called on to make strategic decisions about future developments and to provide oversight. The partnership teams also considered their own evolving structure and modes of operation. The CPTJ partners cleared a number of significant hurdles just organizing the work.

Latino Pathways (LP) also proceeded with a partnership model, but with the intention of moving through the planning and design phase even more quickly. Through its ongoing research for *The State of the South*, MDC tracked the growth of the Hispanic population as well as the need for new workers to contribute to the economy (MDC, 2007). With support from the Z. Smith Reynolds Foundation, the Casey Foundation, and the Charles Stewart Mott Foundation, MDC began organizing Latino Pathways in 2003. MDC looked for locations in North Carolina that had the right combination of partners and commitment, eventually choosing Charlotte and Greensboro as the project sites. Local funding agencies in those cities also contributed toward program implementation. Local funding partners in Charlotte included Bank of America, Duke Energy, The Foundation for the Carolinas, and Wachovia. In Greensboro, local funding partners included The Cemala Foundation, The Community Foundation of Greater Greensboro, Duke Energy, The Greensboro-High Point-Guilford County Workforce Development Board, and The Weaver Foundation.

The partnerships faced challenges from the outset. Key partners got sick or injured, priorities or responsibilities changed within their organizations, and in some cases personal commitment waned. But overlaying the individual factors was the general give and take of group formation, of finding the right identity and combination of energy— and the unavoidable decisions about leadership, coordination, and programmatic roles.

In an attempt to focus the work further, MDC introduced sector employment strategies as the primary methodology for Latino Pathways. Instead of preparing participants for a broad range of employment, the partners researched and analyzed particular industry growth sectors that provided career ladders to higher wages. Meetings with employers helped to define the opportunities and skill needs. While these activities were important in establishing relationships with industry, most employers were looking for immediate help filling positions and were not able to take the time needed to participate in program design, recruitment, and, finally, training candidates. In other situations, interested industry supporters simply vanished because of executive changes, or in one case, the relocation of an entire production facility.

In both Connecting People to Jobs and Latino Pathways, MDC's role changed from being an initial convener and strategic planner, to providing technical assistance on workforce programming, and then stepping farther back as learning facilitator and documenter. During this time local program staff gradually took over responsibility for administering the partnership—handling meetings, reports, and other communications. The expectations for these local coordinators were high. These staff members were called on to conduct outreach, manage a caseload of participants, pursue job development opportunities, process data and information, and market the project, all the while supporting and responding to the partnerships.

By the end of project demonstrations, both Connecting People to Jobs and Latino Pathways had produced important results. Hundreds of low-income job seekers enrolled in these projects, and most received some form of career and skills training. Between 50 and 100 individuals at each local site were supported and tracked until they obtained employment. And the partnerships established new ways of working together that created greater access to services and job opportunities.

Despite these successes, the partnerships were unable to sustain their efforts formally. Much of the programmatic work continued, but mostly as a small set of activities within individual organizations. And the partners never reached the level of scale that they hoped for—a strong and ongoing pipeline to good jobs. In short, once the demonstration funds were expended, the partnerships ended.

Analysis of Mistakes
The existing network of local leadership, the history of community engagement, and the direction of the overall economy are factors

that influence, and sometimes determine, eventual outcomes. These macro conditions are largely outside the immediate control of project collaborators who sit around a table. What partners can control are their own actions and decisions regarding project design and strategy. The mistakes and issues that follow represent choices that partners make.

Mistake Number 1: The rush to program. Partnerships often feel pressure to produce near-term outcomes, which usually take the form of actual services to individuals. The partners themselves look for quick victories that build momentum and justify participation in the collaboration. The danger of this mistake is that the partnership becomes program-focused and fails to achieve or even envision systems needed for influencing job advancement, broader-scale career mobility, or changes in labor market policy.

Of course, as a practical matter, funding agencies require outcomes that indicate progress in the short term. It is also important for the partners themselves to see results from the time and effort they are investing. A lack of milestones for achieving unity, consensus, and knowledge creates a frustrating situation for new partnerships that are used to the relatively quick decisions made possible by existing flow charts within institutions.

In Connecting People to Jobs and Latino Pathways, the initial task of the partnership was to gather and analyze data. This process took longer than expected. One reason for the slower pace was that partnership-building efforts occurred simultaneously. It took time for the partners and their MDC coaches to understand the nuances of partner relationships and the unique capacities of each. It also took time for the partners to reconcile differing concepts of the project and conflicting ideas about appropriate institutional roles.

The CPTJ and LP partners knew that they needed to build relationships and introduce changes into the educational and employment systems. These kinds of structural tasks, however, were not framed as goals in and of themselves. Rather, the group was so intent on launching measurable programs that it failed to see the process's intrinsic value.

The MDC coaches attempted to keep the partnerships moving forward through the use of timelines and schedules. These practices were useful for generating discussion and action items among the partners but also proved disheartening when the timeline arrows and deadlines were continually revised and extended. Each of the sites expressed concern that it was falling behind. The work of planning and partnership formation took considerable time and prevented a quick and steady progression toward project activity.

With attention focused on launching a project, the concept of the partnership as a learning team was not fully developed. The emerging information about work conditions and opportunities as well as barriers to training and employment were not recognized as unique and important products. And the partnerships did not perceive themselves as creators or managers of knowledge, which carried over into implementation efforts when the partners were pointed toward short-term programmatic results.

Both the CPTJ and LP partnerships began implementation efforts with mission statements and a set of goals in hand. These guiding statements included broad ideas such as lifelong learning, enhanced job quality, and removing institutional barriers. Correspondingly, many of the early design elements reflected a comprehensive approach to the problem of unemployment and underemployment. It was not long, however, before the partnerships began to focus more narrowly on producing evidence that program activity was underway. Part of the pressure was created by the funding agencies and transmitted through MDC coaches. The partnerships were required to deliver tangible results that included number of people served, trained, and placed in jobs. Outcome charts soon followed, along with a schedule of quarterly reports.

The partners themselves also restricted the program in a number of ways. Larger institutions like the community colleges were used to developing training programs quickly. The colleges wanted to get participants enrolled in existing certificate training. Community organizations wanted to conduct outreach and recruit participants.

The federally funded workforce agencies were willing to make their services available to participants, but they were focused on job-search services and getting people into jobs as soon as possible. In other words, each partner wanted to do what it did best. On the employer side, many industry partners that were looking for help with immediate hiring needs simply walked away from what they perceived as too much talk and too little progress.

Both projects cited systemic and structural change as ultimate deliverables. But the partnerships did not establish specific benchmarks for measuring progress toward desired institutional, structural, and policy change. In part, too much of the partners' time and energy was directed toward simply launching and maintaining even a basic employment and training program. While a great deal of structural work was accomplished, most systems results ended up being reported as anecdotes, essentially as footnotes to the tables outlining numerical outcomes.

Program strategies and delivery models received the most attention and technical assistance. As a result, partners with expertise in the mechanics of workforce development were most highly valued and prominent. Policy efforts and additional information gathering were postponed, and opportunities and connections to the larger development and political agenda of the host cities were lost.

The partnership approach itself made the transition to program work difficult. The changing nature of the partnerships in CPTJ and Latino Pathways contributed to an inability to come to quick decisions and agreement about program design. Actual program management was an even greater hurdle. The maxim that it is hard to run a program by committee proved to be accurate.

Mistake Number 2: To lead or not to lead. Collaborative efforts involve interorganizational negotiation, networking, and accountability. Productive activities beyond planning and coordination are a real challenge. And trying to manage a program through partnerships is unwieldy and full of ongoing complications. Even if relationships are highly structured, with guidelines and agreements, the partners must continually sort through changing personal and institutional dynamics.

Who leads the partnership? Most development efforts recognize the need for a partner that will take responsibility for moving the work forward and knitting together the resources of the other partners. Either a lead partner is identified up front and acts as the convener, or the partners must discuss and analyze the options and come to a joint decision. Choosing the lead partner is a delicate operation that will to a large extent determine the scope of the collaboration's work. As an example, if a public agency or educational institution is the lead partner, then the collaborative will be oriented more toward services and training and less likely to use community organizing or advocacy approaches.

The kinds of institutional representatives at the table also matter. By the time the partnerships in Latino Pathways were ready to move a program forward, they had lost much of their ability to address the larger issues. Many of the executives, political leaders, and policy players withdrew from the partnership, seeing their role as finished. The remaining active partners saw themselves as the worker bees, able to organize program activities but with limited ability to make decisions and commitments, even within their own institutions.

The difficulty of partnership management came to a head on issues of program finances. The partnerships needed to decide early who would be the actual grant recipient and fiscal agent for the group. In both CPTJ and Latino Pathways, a fiscal agent was selected at the beginning of the planning phase. The coaches and technical assistance providers recommended that a community-based organization (CBO) receive the planning grant. They argued that the CBOs were new at the workforce table, and that control of the finances would provide them with an important role and a greater voice among the partners. Underlying that assumption was the belief that efforts to create community change should be grounded at the neighborhood and grassroots level. This perspective did not foresee that an ongoing issue for the community-based organizations was survival and solvency. During the course of the project, the ebbs and flows of funding streams created institutional crises within the CBOs that required cutbacks, staff layoffs, and executive leadership change.

Recurring financial problems often delayed, and in some cases halted, the work on the ground. Each of the CBO fiscal agents experienced times when project funds accounted for more than half of their organizations' operating budgets. This put the CBOs in the difficult situation of having to maintain their organizations and staff while carrying out the objectives of the project. The partners as a group were forced to focus their energy on simply keeping the program functioning.

Mistake Number 3: Too much expected of too few. The CBOs in CPTJ and Latino Pathways were young organizations and relatively small. At the same time their role in the partnerships was large due to their flexibility with regard to operating programs and their ability to cut through bureaucracy to reach special populations. Because they are usually nonprofits driven by a social mission, CBOs have strong ties and commitments to low-income workers and offer a connection to the community that is often missing among educational and workforce providers.

Still, the CBO partners at the local sites were on a learning curve about workforce development and creating job opportunities. The partnerships in these efforts needed to better understand the capacity and potential role of the CBOs. From the CBOs' perspective, they needed support from the partnership and time to do the work. The partnerships thought that the project staff at the CBOs could do it all but did not recognize the internal challenges facing the organization.

The project staff, usually one individual at each project site, was tasked with managing programmatic operations, including outreach, recruitment, and case management of individuals, giving job seekers a single point of contact. As the projects grew, detailed tracking and counseling for hundreds of participants became impossible. The partnerships struggled to find resources for additional staff and to keep job seekers moving through the system. But even after completing assessments and training, most program participants still needed help landing a job. The result in CPTJ and Latino Pathways was that the project staff found themselves initiating contacts with human resources directors and building bridges with industry.

But project staff had difficulty engaging employers. The projects did not have a consistent track record of producing hirable workers. And, in most cases, the project staff had a limited understanding of the culture and language of the industry with which they were working. The partnerships themselves had trouble connecting with employers. Industry representatives tended to be active in the partnership during the planning process but were looking for a quick and dependable pool of job applicants. Without credibility, the partnerships were not able to arrive at a level of industry investment that leads to ongoing feedback and program development and revision (Dworak-Muñoz, 2004).

At the CPTJ site in Columbia, South Carolina, the One Stop Center supported the project staff by providing office space and integrating the project coordinator into the functions of the agency. Over time the CPTJ project developed a good reputation that brought new job seekers to the One Stop and attracted more employers. The One Stop also created spaces for job interviews. This example demonstrates how a partner can support project staff and receive benefits in return. But even in this case, the ability to address job retention and promote actual changes in the workplace was limited by the lack of staff expertise.

On the demand side, the topic of racial and ethnic discrimination was unfamiliar ground for many institutions in CPTJ and Latino Pathways. The project staff and CBOs were expected to be the connection to the populations that they represent and serve. In some cases the CBOs surveyed neighborhoods and held focus groups to determine needs and barriers. But there was no ongoing process of gathering feedback. The partners assumed that, by involving the CBOs, with their proximity to low-income neighborhoods and grassroots leaders, issues of discrimination would be addressed.

Lessons

The mistakes identified in this paper slowed the work down and limited program gains and expansion during implementation. But several valuable lessons can be drawn from the mistakes:

- Partnerships must have a road map that describes the long-term nature of the work and identifies partnership milestones. Partners must see where their efforts are leading and be forewarned about potential setbacks and barriers.

- Project planning and implementation should include goals and indicators for group learning, collaborating, and supporting systems change. Tracking progress along these indicators allows the partnerships to gain credit for hard-earned collaborative results and orient the work beyond the life of a particular project (see Mendel, 2007).

- Project work should be grounded early on in one of the partner institutions, while the partnership should focus on closing gaps in services and addressing policy issues.

- Partners should carefully examine the abilities and strengths of each partner and its appropriate role in moving a project forward, and partners should have credibility in the private sector. Determining the lead partner should include an analysis of fiscal administrative capacity and solvency.

- CBOs provide important grounding and access to disadvantaged populations but require time and partnership support as they experience and learn from projects in development fields.

Conclusion

The great potential of partnerships in community economic development is twofold. First, collaboration can address multi-faceted conditions of job loss and poverty—serious problems that bring various organizations together in common cause. Second, partnerships with wide breadth and scope can respond to future economic challenges and be community resources for ideas and innovation.

A constraining factor is that the dynamics of partnering often go unexamined and are not clearly defined or understood. Direct evaluations of the collaborative process are sporadic, and little is known empirically about their efficacy (Backer, 2003). The experiences of CPTJ and Latino Pathways suggest that partnerships can be an effective tool, but only if they fit the job at hand. In both projects the partnerships focused too much on program activities and lost opportunities for longer-term, structural gains. The community-based partners also struggled with expectations and were given too much responsibility for moving the projects forward.

Several areas stand out for further learning and application. One set of questions involves issues of the collaborative process. Partners need to know more about how to pace the work and about tracking progress—and the potential benefits of a more organic and opportunistic approach. More research is needed on how partnerships collect and manage ideas and information, along with examples of criteria for choosing project leads and deciding partner roles. Also needed are models of systems change indicators that go beyond institutional program activity.

When are partnerships a bad idea? The findings in this chapter suggest that partnerships are an awkward tool if outcomes for individuals are the desired result. If the goal is overall systems reform and alignment of resources, then partnerships make more sense and may ultimately be necessary. Public and private investors should accept that partnerships are often a delicate and risky proposition. The partnership approach will require funding agencies to engage more directly and more often with grantees and work with a different set of measures and timelines.

References

Backer, T. E. (Ed.). (2003). *Evaluating community collaborations.* New York: Springer.

Dodson, D. L., Thomasson, J., & Totten, L. D. (2002). *Building community by design: A resource guide for community change leaders.* Chapel Hill, NC: MDC, Inc.

Dworak-Muñoz, L. (2004). *Building effective employer relations.* Washington DC: The Aspen Institute.

Ford Foundation. (1996). *Perspectives on partnerships.* New York: Author.

Giloth, R. P. (Ed.). (2004). *Workforce intermediaries for the twenty-first century.* Philadelphia, PA: Temple University Press.

MDC, Inc. (2007). *The state of the south 2007.* Chapel Hill, NC: Author.

Mendel, R. (2007). *Expanding economic opportunities for the south's disadvantaged workers: Lessons from connecting people to jobs.* Winston-Salem, NC: Mary Reynolds Babcock Foundation.

Roberts, J. M. (2004). *Alliances, coalitions, and partnerships: Building collaborative organizations.* Gabriola Island, B.C., Canada: New Society Publishers.

Trattner, W. I. (1999). *From poor law to welfare state: A history of social welfare in America.* New York: Free Press.

Wheatley, M. J. (2004). *Finding our way: Leadership for an uncertain time.* San Francisco: Berrett-Koehler Publishers.

11

Mistakes in Place: The Premature Termination of Illinois Workforce Advantage

Richard S. Kordesh

Introduction

Launched by the Illinois governor's office in September 2000, Illinois Workforce Advantage (IWA) was an innovative initiative to strengthen the social fabric and economic base in, first, six, and then, nine, distressed rural and urban communities. By the end of 2002, it had made progress in pursuing this purpose on a number of fronts. IWA was working intensively with a number of anchor projects that it had funded in all of its target areas. Governor's office staff and state agency staff working with IWA had solid working relationships with networks of community leaders in each of the places where it was engaged. The projects it was supporting had taken on a coherent theme that was embraced by partners in the target areas. That theme emphasized family-based and community-based approaches to boost economic development. But, shortly after the next governor's administration took office, IWA was terminated as a state project.

 As the person responsible for leading the initiative during most of the time it was in operation, I consider in this chapter why it did not survive. A firsthand account such as this obviously has its strengths and limitations. My analysis is my own and is colored by the demanding, fascinating, and at times frustrating experience of being IWA's director. Because of the nature of the book of which this chapter is a part, the focus is on the mistakes that were made rather than the good projects that resulted. Those mistakes are important to confront; they helped lead to the premature demise of this creative attempt by a state government to systematically foster place-based community development. Those primary mistakes were twofold. First, despite the fact that it had been created to foster comprehensive, place-based community development, the project was given a name that conflated it with the workforce development system, thereby drawing it unnecessarily into a time-consuming conflict. Second, despite having been given a mission to foster place-based community development, it was not created with a clear guiding model of how many different state agencies were going to coordinate their diverse programs in the targeted places.

Preparations

In early 2000, senior staff in the Illinois governor's office convened a group of high-level agency administrators and governor's office staff to plan the administration's new place-based project. This steering committee met regularly into the summer, reviewing data about communities in Illinois and considering the project's mission and overall approach. With considerable input from the chief of staff, the group dubbed the project, "Illinois Workforce Advantage." Its stated purpose was to make distressed communities in Illinois into good places for parents to raise children. Its overall approach was to identify a group of communities around the state and find opportunities for different state agencies to help them through such resources as grants, loans, technical assistance, and relocated government staff.

I had not yet been hired to direct the project, but I did come to know a number of the staff who had leading roles during this preparatory stage. Many were familiar with the history of place-based policies such as Empowerment Zones and Enterprise Communities.

The literature on policies in the United States that have tried to encourage place-based community development demonstrates two points consistently: (1) despite being difficult, new efforts emerge regularly in states and at the federal level because the idea of place-based community building continues to make sense, and (2) such efforts face enormous obstacles. Often the impediments to success reside in the inherent difficulties in getting very different kinds of programs and agencies—with their widely varying statutory provisions, geographic boundaries, bureaucratic structures, rules, political cultures, and budgets—to mesh together effectively (Baum, 1999; Oakley & Tsao, 2006; O'Conner, 1999; Snow, 1995). It is not always clear how much is learned from such efforts, whether they originate at the state or federal level (Mossberger, 1999). But at the time, those senior staff in the (George) Ryan administration who established IWA were aware of the difficulties generally encountered by place-based policies. Still, they believed that basing a state initiative in a governor's office willing to use its authority to push agencies to collaborate in places had a chance to overcome enough of the existing barriers to make a positive impact.

Led by the governor's senior policy advisor on human services, the steering committee chose six communities to be the target areas: three neighborhoods in Chicago—North Lawndale, Humboldt Park, and Englewood; two small municipalities—Harvey, a suburb south of Chicago, and East St. Louis; and the southernmost seven counties in Illinois—Pope, Hardin, Pulaski, Alexander, Johnson, Union, and Massac. The communities all had high levels of poverty, unemployment, school failure, and other factors. They were also chosen because each one already had some type of significant public project underway or was about to commence one on which IWA's eventual efforts could build.

For example, East St. Louis had already received a significant state investment for a new, mixed-income housing development, and Englewood was soon to benefit from a development effort that would be triggered by the construction of a new community college.

In February 2000, the governor's office included $3 million for IWA in its budget for fiscal year 2001, but the legislature rejected the funding largely because the project was unknown and had little political support.

I was hired in the summer of 2000 to run the project, knowing at the outset that there would be no direct budget allocation with which to work. I sensed correctly that the steering committee had not worked out a rigorous approach for the project to follow. In a three-page implementation plan formulated in March 2000, the steering committee stated that IWA would pursue the following outcomes:

- IWA will create opportunities for community members to be successful in the workplace.
- IWA will improve the health status of its target communities.
- IWA will improve graduation rates.
- IWA will tailor one-stop services to meet the unique needs of each community.
- IWA will institutionalize a sustainable, public/private community development process.
- IWA will support the success of local businesses.

The steering committee summarized the purpose of IWA in the following terms:

> The Illinois Workforce Advantage Initiative (IWA) is a location-based community development program. The ultimate goal is to improve the outcomes for families. The primary strategy for accomplishing this goal is to change the environment in historically distressed communities by creating new or revitalized anchor institutions such as schools, health clinics, human service agencies, and businesses. This IWA targeted initiative in human services infrastructure will ultimately promote

the prevention or amelioration of social problems, more effective treatment interventions for individuals and families, and opportunities for community residents to succeed in the workforce. (Illinois Workforce Advantage Steering Committee, 2000, p. 1)

Very little contact had been made with community organizations in the target areas. Yet, much seemed promising, especially the high level of interest in the project demonstrated by the chief of staff and senior gubernatorial staff. Excited by the steering committee's vision, I took the job and began work in September 2000.

Beginning without a Budget

The first eight months of IWA's operations was a distinctive phase because during that time the project had not yet received its own budget allocation. The steering committee of agency and gubernatorial staff continued to meet and discuss how to proceed in bringing the project to the communities. Most agency representatives were skeptical at the outset, unable to see how a targeted, place-based project could work.

To build a sense of purpose within the steering committee, I crafted concept papers that would be used to introduce IWA to local leaders. One short paper described the "virtual family resource centers" that provide an institutional focus for integrating various agency resources. IWA would seek to learn how communities were using schools, community centers, Workforce Investment Act (WIA) One Stop Centers, or other "anchor institutions" to link diverse programs, possibly colocate some of them, and engage families productively in addressing problems they and their communities faced. IWA would seek to support such efforts with "value-added resources" from the agencies, including grants, loans, tax credits, technical assistance, or, perhaps, repositioning state staff. For example, the concept paper stated that a family resource center could be built into a clinic, a school, a community center, or some other anchor institution locally (Kordesh, 2000).

Another document described how IWA would engage with communities. We would hold workshops jointly with community organizations that enjoyed good standing with local residents and leaders. At such workshops, we would explain IWA's purpose, describe the many state agencies that were involved, and explain how IWA was not prescribing programs, but rather was coming to the communities with a value-adding mind-set. We asked community organizations to present not funding proposals, but profiles of projects that were either underway or in the planning stages that focused on such high-priority issues as job creation, job placement, and improved graduation rates.

Having worked earlier in my career as a community organizer, I wanted to proceed cautiously in introducing IWA to the communities. I first met individually with important community leaders, including some state legislators, in each of the six target areas. Then, after gaining consent from them, IWA held its opening meetings in venues acceptable to the community. The sessions were well attended and well received generally, with the level of acceptance tempered by some leeriness because the project did not put its own budget allocation "on the table."

In the meantime, as the community meetings took place and project profiles were being presented, some of the more committed state agency representatives went to work within their own organizations to find resources. Given that existing statutes and regulations limit the scope of state programs, it was not easy to match up existing grant programs operated by the state agencies with projects being presented in the communities.

Several agencies found funds that could be directed into IWA communities, but only for projects that had not been put forth by participants at the original community meetings. For example, the Illinois Department of Public Health set aside a considerable two-year grant for immunization outreach that it wanted to make available in North Lawndale. The department's data suggested that health and education outcomes would be improved through an intensive immunization effort. We arranged to make the grant to two North

Lawndale agencies that had been very involved in the meetings with us, but had not necessarily been pursuing immunization outreach funds. Nevertheless, they were pleased with the opportunity and the grants were executed.

Another unexpected resource that came available from the state was federal AmeriCorps funds. A colleague in the governor's office persuaded the program director responsible for Illinois's AmeriCorps funds to offer them to IWA for use in the target areas. IWA, with the Illinois Department of Human Services as the actual grant-making agency, was able to make approximately a dozen AmeriCorps positions available to each IWA community to support projects that they were bringing forward at our workshops. Grants went to a university in Chicago and one "downstate" to administer the project and disburse the funds to communities.

A Fiscal Year 2002 Budget Allocation

The goodwill that IWA generated through its community engagement workshops was rewarded when it received a $3.5-million budget allocation in the Department of Human Services' fiscal year 2002 budget.

Fortunately, the funding came from flexible general revenue funds, which allowed IWA to provide funding for the best anchor projects that had been profiled at community meetings. IWA also used its funds to engage universities in community economic development partnerships with community development corporations in the communities. Soon, we were negotiating grants with community leaders to support their versions of "virtual family resource centers." Most of them were school-based or school-linked. One was in a small factory building in East St. Louis that would be rehabilitated as a kind of incubator for family businesses and a base for the expansion of a successful welfare-to-work program, Better Family Life, which was operating in St. Louis. The most unusual anchor project was in North Lawndale—a grant to the newly formed North Lawndale Employment Network for its new, comprehensive ex-offender reentry program.

Having its own budget allocation helped IWA with resources to support projects, but it also raised the project's legitimacy in the eyes of the state agencies and elevated the project's profile with other gubernatorial staff members. Over time, other grants were acquired from state and federal sources. For example, IWA took the lead role in preparing the State of Illinois's application for a $2-million grant from the U.S. Department of Justice for its Going Home ex-offender reentry program. IWA was able to help position North Lawndale to become a target site for the project.

With a number of projects now identified, IWA was moving forward. Reflecting this progress, the legislature granted the project $4 million in the next fiscal year's budget, enabling us to add three more target areas. The project was gaining momentum and acquiring positive recognition in the communities. Most local leaders said they had never before been approached so directly by the governor's office in a flexible, comprehensive community development project, nor had they seen such a regular presence of so many different state agencies in their planning meetings. IWA had come through in funding projects profiled by the communities.

The projects supported by IWA included:

- a family education center in a public school in Harvey;
- a work-readiness center in a remodeled factory building originally reclaimed for community use by an entrepreneurial family in East St. Louis;
- a network of school-based community learning centers in the southern seven counties;
- a school-family network in Englewood educational facilities featuring community organization training for and with families;
- an ex-offender reentry network in North Lawndale;
- a parent education and family leadership development cluster in Little Village;

- a family education center in a Maywood education building; and
- a workforce training initiative in a community center in Rock Island tied to job opportunities in a nearby industrial park.

IWA also invested in a number of community economic development initiatives through university partners. And within the governor's office, progress was being made in building a process for collecting performance indicators from state agencies that matched up with IWA community boundaries

With the good collaborations underway in the communities and an innovative outcome-tracking system being crafted in the governor's offices, pieces were being put together that could be integrated into a more systematic community development approach.

In September 2002 IWA convened a conference at the University of Illinois at Chicago to which it invited community leaders from the nine target areas, state agency representatives, legislators, and governor's staff to review IWA's accomplishments in its first two years (Kordesh, 2002). For the first time, individuals from IWA communities were able to appreciate that they were part of a different kind of statewide initiative. With an election looming, and with the governor already having announced that he would not seek another term, everyone knew that IWA's longevity would depend on its acceptance by the next administration.

IWA had contracted with the Policy Research Action Group (PRAG) at Loyola University to evaluate the project by tracking its progress and pitfalls in three of the target communities. In September 2002, PRAG issued a report that noted that IWA was striving to achieve its mission of supporting place-based development through the efforts of different state agencies:

> What IWA is trying to accomplish is a paradigm shift
> from a problem-based orientation to a place-based

orientation. To move from what one agency representative called a silo mentality to a multi-disciplinary, cross-departmental response to a community's assessment of its needs and priorities. To not just give grants but to engage in a planning and project development process with the communities. (Hellwig, 2002, p. 4)

Based on 80 interviews with community participants, agency staff, and governor's office staff, the PRAG report found mixed results in the communities' capacities to take advantage of the networking and policy opportunities IWA afforded. The PRAG report also identified how progress in two of the three communities studied had been made by building collaborative planning relationships with state agencies:

First of all, on the most basic level, all three IWA communities are enjoying a new level of access to state resources just by being designated as an IWA community. To have a key member of the Governor's staff come out to chat with community leaders in their own conference rooms is new and indicative of the notion that place matters. Some community leaders have had a similar opportunity with their state legislators, but never with the executive branch.

Secondly, the governor's office is listening. Instead of the state, through its various agencies, telling the community that they have a set of grants and programs which the community must wiggle to fit into, they are being asked to set the agenda and write the proposal before the RFP comes out, so to speak. As a result, over a million dollars has flowed into these communities over the last 6 months to fund two major projects in each community . . .

Thirdly, there has been evidence of a new kind of more direct participation of state agencies that

> are joining in the community planning and project
> implementation process. . . . This new approach involves
> agency representatives in creating a winning scenario
> together. (Hellwig, pp. 5–6)

We had hoped that PRAG's progress report would provide some independent legitimacy for IWA, and that the next administration would find a way to embrace it. In short, this acceptance did not occur. Despite some intensive lobbying after the election, which included busloads of community representatives traveling to Springfield to meet with legislators, the next governor's budget eliminated IWA's funding in January 2003. The contracts that had already been set in motion by IWA were in large part executed, but for all practical purposes IWA closed down in early 2003.

The Project's Theory and Brand

Despite the emphasis in its purpose on parents and families, IWA had not begun to demonstrate a consistent, working theory of how its community development efforts would "make communities into good places for parents to raise children" until the second year of the project. This gap then led IWA to begin too late to construct a constituency among the people whom the project was supposed to benefit the most: families, especially parents with children.

What delayed the development of a stable, working theory until late in the second year? Several factors were responsible.

First, the steering committee had not really articulated a theory of change or action model for IWA. For example, some, including the governor himself, seemed to see IWA as a kind of place-based extension of the state's emerging workforce development system. When speaking about IWA, the governor usually emphasized how IWA would create one-stop service centers where people in the communities could access all of the services they needed. He and several others saw the creation of Workforce Investment Act

(WIA) one-stop centers in IWA communities as central to the IWA strategy.

Exacerbated by the project's name, the conflation and confusion regarding IWA and WIA created a significant branding problem for IWA that was painfully apparent. Why, some WIA board presidents asked, would the administration create a parallel project like this when it was trying to build an effective, statewide network of workforce investment boards? IWA was not in fact a parallel project to WIA. Rather, it was a comprehensive community development project in which workforce strategies would play a role. That explanation did not satisfy the WIA leaders and some sought to reallocate future IWA funds into the WIA system.

Others seemed to think that the best way for IWA to have a significant impact would be to concentrate efforts on one or two major building projects in target areas. The approach they advocated would be to find which state agency leases would be expiring, and either build new structures to house them in IWA areas or move them into rehabbed buildings. Some on the steering committee had already carried out preliminary planning for a new state office building that could be built in Harvey. Still others pressed for a comprehensive planning and prevention approach.

Pressed as they were by the chief of staff to get the agencies to support IWA, governor's office staff hunted within the agencies they oversaw for resources that could be targeted for IWA areas. I appreciated these efforts immensely, but collectively they did not add up to a systematic approach for IWA's work in communities.

As noted previously, I had tried to build increased coherence into the IWA model during the first few months of my tenure, with the emphasis on anchor institutions, virtual family resource centers, and community engagement. The steering committee embraced these frameworks, and they did provide loose models within which to work. But at least during 2000 and early 2001, IWA still seemed to be many things to many people.

Little Margin for Strategic Error

IWA was a new and somewhat undefined initiative in 2000. Those of us responsible for it had to work hard to quickly establish its identity and legitimacy to launch it successfully. Perhaps because we were so pressed to launch it quickly and explain it to the communities, we did not think at the outset about the longer-term political sustainability of IWA.

But IWA moved quickly from the trauma of birth to the challenge of survival. It had been conceived in rather precarious political circumstances. It was common knowledge in 2000 that federal prosecutors were investigating several high-level officials and close, longtime associates of the governor for possible criminal violations. The aura of a scandal investigation hung heavily over the administration. Eventually, several associates of the governor and the governor himself were sent to prison.

The visibility of the scandal and anticipated indictments led the governor to choose not to seek a second term. It had become clear that, were IWA to survive beyond 2002, legislators and people in the targeted communities would have to champion it. But, preoccupied as we were with the implementation of new projects, we did not really begin to address these concerns in a concerted effort until the conference in fall 2002.

By that point, with the election less than two months away, senior staff in the governor's office had already been looking toward their next jobs and some had already left. I left my position as director in October 2002, thinking that IWA might better survive with a new administration if staff they associated with the previous administration were no longer attached visibly to the project. It was a painful decision, but I reasoned that I was making the move that a community organizer would make, leaving when the community leaders were ready to own and defend the program.

The conference during fall 2002 seemed to have galvanized the community leaders around the cause of IWA's political sustainability. The statewide network the project had formed had achieved a new level of solidarity. Leaving the project in the hands of my associate director, who had grown up in one of the IWA areas, seemed like a timely and appropriate move. Many at the conference praised me at that point for turning over control to one of the target area's native sons when the project seemed ready to stand on its own.

When the new governor came into office, the incoming administration criticized much of the previous administration's record and touted its own reform agenda. Despite the community representatives' lobbying the new governor's staff, IWA did not survive.

Loss of Valuable Time

The lack of a coherent theory to guide the project at its outset contributed to the lateness of the sustainability efforts. The brand confusion caused me to spend considerable effort fending off efforts to subsume IWA within the WIA system. Without a theory that placed families and parents central in its change strategy, at first there was no concerted programmatic effort across the target areas that focused on them. Thus, time was lost in building a constituency with them.

The lack of funds during the first year also contributed to the problem of programmatic incoherence. Without its own flexible funds, IWA had to rely on the agencies to free up resources from programs whose goals and objectives were already established by previous statutes and regulations. For example, the immunization outreach funds were appreciated at the community level, but did not really crystallize what was unique about the IWA model. Absent its own pool of resources, IWA tended to respond pragmatically to what was available to show the communities that it was working on their behalf, but the diverse nature of the initial grants did not lend itself to a consistent brand.

A coherent theory did begin to emerge as our ideas about anchor institutions took hold and IWA began to concentrate its resources in such projects. With flexible funding, we were more able to align grantmaking around consistent programmatic themes.

Several signature projects emerged in 2002. IWA provided a significant grant to the Sinai Community Institute in North Lawndale to create a new Family Enterprise Institute. That project quickly filled to capacity with families seeking to start their own businesses. IWA also provided funds for projects focused on African American fatherhood and family organizing in schools.

This increasingly consistent focus on productive family involvement in community development, education, and economic development began to build a network of supporters in 2002. I began to refer to this approach as "family-based community development" (Kordesh, 2006).

Lessons and Discussion

Two interrelated lessons emerge that can be applied to helping policy innovations survive what can be perilous political transitions: (1) be attentive to the brand and symbols chosen to represent the project, and (2) craft and implement rigorously a strategy based on a model and theory of change that reflects the brand. In addition, be prepared to complete both tasks in time to communicate to representatives of an incoming administration what the project's value is and why it would be in the new governor's interest to continue it.

Starting early on sustainability depends on the existence of a clear and stable theory of change. The theory not only should specify how outcomes will be achieved, but also who will benefit and what their roles will be. The beneficiaries will be important to sustaining a project like IWA, especially when the administration that launched it loses its political capital as a result of a crisis situation.

IWA's steering committee had not involved the community leaders or families in the initial planning of the project. Before I was hired, the planning had taken place mostly among the state agency representatives and governor's office staff. I would argue that, had they involved community leaders and parents in the planning from the beginning, it would have become more apparent how vitally important they would be in building support for the project in the legislature. They also would have asked questions about how the initiative would work that would have sharpened the committee's implementation model.

That the administration had chosen a brand for its place-based project that was so similar to WIA puzzled me when I was hired, and it puzzles me now. My sense was that it was meant to couple the project symbolically to the WIA agenda without diluting the project's unique comprehensiveness and place-based focus. WIA had broad support across party lines and geographic areas; everyone could rally around government-industry partnerships that fostered job creation and training. On the other hand, empowerment zones and other place-based initiatives in the recent past had become somewhat discredited due to their perceived ineffectiveness. Thus, perhaps the term "IWA" rather than "Illinois Community Investments" or some similar name might have seemed politically more acceptable. However, its similarity to WIA symbolically opened the door to an aggressive attempt by the state workforce board leadership to capture IWA's funds and subsume the project.

One might ask whether we might have cultivated local government leaders more effectively as supporters of IWA's continuation. We approached mayors and their senior staff in each locality. What the mayors typically wanted were large capital grants. When we explained the emphasis of the project was on community engagement, community development, and a mix of human services with economic development, they tended to lose interest. For example, after hearing our presentation, the mayor of Cairo told us that we ought to work with the regional Empowerment Zone, rather than with his city government.

Announcing the capital projects at the "roll-out" event in Harvey might have created the impression that such initiatives would characterize all of IWA's efforts. That was certainly the impression of the planning director in that municipality. She expressed extreme disappointment when no subsequent capital funds would be immediately forthcoming and became so negative that we shifted our focus, with very successful results, to working with Harvey's superintendent of schools.

IWA probably would have garnered more support from mayors had it continued for another year or two, since several of its planning efforts likely would have led to more substantial capital projects. IWA was on the right track, but had not had the time to mount the major building or infrastructure initiatives that might have made it more central to the interests of the mayors with whom we met.

With another year or two for planning projects to move into development, IWA might have solidified its ties with city officials. Had the administration launched IWA during the first year of its term, rather than in the third, IWA would have had time to mature into a broader community development project.

Then, of course, there is the matter of communicating with the representatives of the candidates seeking to become the next governor. The case of IWA's sustainability is limited as an illustrative case in this respect. Because of the corruption scandal, I do not believe that conditions were present in the late summer and fall of 2002 to encourage IWA's continuation directly from the governor's office. Governor Ryan's reputation was so tainted that other candidates were essentially running away from him.

However, there were discussions among community supporters of IWA with legislators and the transition team of the incoming governor, Rod Blagojevich, about renaming the project and enabling the new administration to take credit for transforming and improving it. It is not clear to me how high in the new administration this conversation went. A new place-based initiative, Team Illinois, did emerge eventually, but it was not based in the governor's office, it targeted mostly very small communities, and it was not allocated its own funding. Perhaps this was the new IWA; perhaps not.

Despite the above difficulties, the administration and the steering committee, especially a few of the senior staff most devoted to the project, deserve considerable credit for having launched such an innovative project. They pulled together 18 different state agencies for a place-based community development project. They approached the target communities with a personalized, flexible outreach that community leaders said they had never seen from a governor's office before. And that flexibility allowed for unexpected opportunities to emerge, such as the AmeriCorps initiative and others.

Even had IWA begun with a clear consensus on its theory of change and appropriate name, and even had it mounted political sustainability efforts early, it still would have faced tough going during the transition. The incoming administration aggressively exploited the scandal that engulfed the governor and some of his associates, which cast almost every policy tied to the outgoing governor in a negative light. But, this situation was foreseeable, even in 2001, and a strong network of community leaders, parents, mayors, legislators, and state agency leaders might have been able to help IWA weather the political storm and survive, if not in name, at least as a stable initiative.

References

Baum, H. S. (1999). Education and the empowerment zone: Ad hoc development of an interorganizational domain. *Journal of Urban Affairs, 21*(3), 289–308.

Hellwig, M. (2002). *Illinois Workforce Advantage: An experiment in place-based government/community partnerships.* Chicago, IL: Policy Research Action Group, Loyola University.

Illinois Workforce Advantage Steering Committee. (2000, March). *IWA implementation plan.* Chicago, IL: Office of the Governor, State of Illinois.

Kordesh, R. S. (2000, Fall). *Family resource centers: A centerpiece of Illinois Workforce Advantage.* Chicago, IL: Office of the Governor, State of Illinois.

Kordesh, R. S. (2002, September). *Illinois Workforce Advantage: State of Illinois' place-based community development initiative.* Chicago, IL: Office of the Governor, State of Illinois.

Kordesh, R. S. (2006). *Restoring power to parents and places: The case for family-based community development.* New York: iUniverse.

Mossberger, K. (1999, Summer). State-federal diffusion and policy learning: From enterprise zones to empowerment zones. *Publius: The Journal of Federalism, 29*(3), 31–50.

Oakley, D., & and Tsao, H-S. (2006). A new way of revitalizing distressed urban communities? Assessing the impact of the Federal Empowerment Zone Program. *Journal of Urban Affairs, 28*(5), 443–471

O'Conner, A. (1999). Swimming against the tide: A brief history of federal policy in poor communities. In R. F. Ferguson & W. T. Dickens (Eds.), *Urban problems and community development* (pp. 77–137). Washington, DC: Brookings Institution.

Snow, L. (1995). Economic development breaks the mold: Community-building, place-targeting, and empowerment zones. *Economic Development Quarterly, 9*(2), 185–198.

12

Drive to Succeed

Carolyn D. Hayden

Introduction

While the average American family may be able to easily access products and services they need to build economic security for their children's futures, low-wage working families often have poor access to these same resources because they lack a car and, in many cases, are paying more for the same products and services others take for granted. A lack of transportation options severely limits a family's ability to seek and obtain employment, health care, childcare, and the competitively priced goods and services available to others. Public transportation is an option, but for most low-wage working families (and the general population), a car provides the most mobility and flexibility to seek and/or improve their employment opportunities and take care of their families' needs.

Low-wage working families often have few choices in the automobile retail market because many have low credit scores. They are often forced to purchase overpriced vehicles with extraordinarily high interest rates from local vehicle retailers, often so-called Buy Here Pay Here (BHPH) lots or other used car dealers. The poor end up paying higher prices and interest rates for older, lower-quality cars, leading to higher debt and hurting their ability to advance financially, as demonstrated in Table 12.1. Low-wage workers also use a higher portion of their budgets to own and operate a vehicle than do other workers[1], which leaves them with fewer opportunities to build assets and gain mobility.

Table 12.1 Interest Rates Are a Key Factor in Affordability

The amount of interest charged for a used car loan is a critical factor in the vehicle's overall affordability. The difference between 6 percent and 24 percent (the highest rate generally charged by Buy Here Pay Here lots in states without caps), totals an additional charge to the client of more than $2,000 over the life of a three-year loan.

Loan Period	Interest Rate	Total Interest Paid	Total Monthly Payment
3 years	6 %	666.33	212.95
	8 %	896.76	219.35
	10%	1,131.33	225.87
	15%	1,735.66	242.66
	20%	2,365.22	260.15
	24%	2,886.68	274.63
4 years	6%	890.97	164.40
	8%	1,202.74	170.89
	10%	1,521.83	177.54
	15%	2,351.13	194.82
	20%	3,224.60	213.01
	24%	3,954.22	228.21

In 2003, a team of three people interested in helping low-wage working families obtain reliable private transportation joined to create the

Driven to Succeed program pilot. This team was responding to a pressing social problem: millions of low-wage working Americans had to find and keep a job, care for children, and do errands each day with limited transportation options. For those living in rural or central urban areas far from jobs, the problem was even more pronounced. The team recognized that the nation's major automobile manufacturers were not involved in a comprehensive effort to address this issue, but it thought manufacturers could play a significant role in alleviating the problem. The key was gaining access to the existing vehicle distribution system manufacturers used to move millions of used cars across the country, and using this system to provide high-quality, affordable used vehicles to the families that needed them most. Automobile manufacturers, their franchised dealers, and the national automobile auctions already had networks in place to distribute used vehicles quickly and efficiently, and the team hoped to use this network to implement the Driven to Succeed pilot.

Three key factors influence the affordability of car ownership: vehicle pricing, vehicle financing, and insurance, in addition to other factors such as driver's licensing and vehicle maintenance. With the understanding that incorporating all three factors into this project was too ambitious, the team chose to focus on vehicle pricing. Its goal was to determine all of the price markup points of a vehicle at every phase of a used car's distribution process and minimize them, so that the vehicle's final selling price would be affordable to low-wage working families.

For the pilot to work, the team needed the cooperation of a Big Three automobile manufacturer, collaboration within the manufacturer's system, the services of vehicle auction partners, and a lender, which in this case was a nonprofit car ownership program. Despite the challenges involved in bringing so many organizations together, the team was able to do it and create a functioning network.

The initiators of this plan were the author of this chapter, Carolyn Hayden, who at the time this project was implemented was vice president of a national nonprofit intermediary organization, and two recently retired senior executives from the automotive manufacturing sector who were committed to the idea that major manufacturers could play a role in helping low-wage working families acquire affordable automobiles. While car dealers, automobile auctions, and lenders all have roles in delivering vehicles to consumers, the concept of bringing these entities together to work toward a targeted common social benefits goal was a novel one. The team hoped that Driven to Succeed would result in matching many deserving families with reliable automobiles and a strong positive image for the corporate partners that participated. While the program was successful in accessing vehicles through the manufacturer's national distribution system, a number of factors, some foreseeable and some not, created an environment that did not allow the successful launch of the pilot on the ground. The following is an overview of Driven to Succeed as well as an analysis of the mistakes and possible alternate paths that could have led to completing the distribution circle and providing cars to families that needed them.

Mistakes

While the concept of the pilot program was sound, several unexpected issues arose, which the team struggled to respond to quickly. In hindsight, the lack of ability to respond to these changes was a key mistake, but several other mistakes along the way also impeded overall progress. They include:

- not selecting all of the right criteria for site assessment;
- inadequate understanding of each player's needs and limitations;
- poor launch timing;
- having an extended planning and processing time;
- lacking the ability to adjust to a rapidly changing environment;
- unanticipated market factors;
- lack of bottom-line incentives for dealers (limited profit margin);

- underestimating the capacity needed to implement a program that was both national and local; and
- having no "plan B."

Each of these mistakes is explored in full, following an in-depth look at the program's details below.

Program Background

Driven to Succeed was intended to influence the thinking of major automobile manufacturers, financial institutions, automobile dealers, and others by illustrating that low-wage working consumers represented a viable new market for their mainstream products, and that these same products could be made available at discounted, competitive prices without excessive risk to the provider. Ultimately, the pilot was intended to demonstrate that a major automobile manufacturer could help provide a solution to transportation problems for low-wage working families by using its existing national vehicle distribution systems.

In many cases, a car is the second-largest single purchase for low-wage working families, after their home. The Driven to Succeed team's work in the field of car ownership indicated that a growing field of nonprofit car ownership programs focused on increasing access to private vehicles for low-income families, and that these efforts had resulted in important positive outcomes for the families they served. Unfortunately, limitations in funding, resources, local supplies of donated cars, and other factors make it impossible for these programs to have broad reach for low-wage consumers.

At the same time, some large-scale vehicle distribution systems have the resources and the supply to serve a significantly larger number of customers; this realization prompted the development of Driven to Succeed. The program's primary goal was to distribute good-quality, price-controlled used vehicles to low-wage working families by bringing together an automobile manufacturer, a vehicle auction partner, and the critical resources provided by the members of Opportunity Cars, a network of more than 130 nonprofit car ownership programs operating in 35 states. According to the most recent available data, Opportunity Cars programs have made more than 50,000 vehicles available to low-wage working families. These programs promote increased mobility, economic well-being, and employment stability and security by using one of the following three primary approaches:

1. Selling or leasing vehicles to low-wage working families at significantly subsidized prices or giving them away to families who are at the first tier of the economic ladder.
2. Making low-interest loans for car purchases, the type of program that participated in the Driven to Succeed pilot.
3. Facilitating matched savings to be used for car down payments and/or purchases.

Opportunity Cars programs do more than provide the tangible means for families to own a car. They understand that the price of the car, along with the cost and terms of financing and insurance, preclude many struggling families from owning one. To address these barriers, the majority of Opportunity Cars programs provide budgeting assistance, car maintenance workshops, and help with insurance and repairs, as well as other services either directly or through local partners. External studies conducted on car ownership programs within the Opportunity Cars network report that, after receiving cars, program clients were able to get a job, retain their current job or find a better one, receive higher wages or work more hours, and spend more time with their families. Findings also point to the importance of education and training in achieving positive outcomes, such as financial literacy training and credit counseling. Most car ownership programs report that access to quality and affordable vehicles is a constant issue, so the prospect of including them in the pilot would help address one of their major program challenges.

The proposed pilot, which had significant potential for serving a large number of low-wage consumers, involved five key strategic alliance partners. They were:

1. *Manufacturer Captive Finance Company.* The "captive" is the primary financing source for the manufacturer's franchise dealers. For the purposes of this phase of the project, the captive holds the title for many of the vehicles customers return to local dealers at the end of their lease period. Because the captive remains the titled owner until a dealer purchases the vehicle, the project team had to get its buy-in to the program, which it did.

2. *Manufacturer Vehicle Remarketing System (MVRS).* MVRS is authorized by its customer (in this case, the captive) to act as its wholesale agent to dispose of used vehicles. On behalf of its customers, MVRS makes the final decision on how vehicles will be wholesaled. MVRS controls the redistribution of manufacturer vehicles through the national automobile auction system where they are purchased through a bidding process, and directly, through dealers, when they purchase vehicles electronically through the MVRS electronic auction database. MVRS agreed to support Driven to Succeed by validating the process for selecting cars from the supply stream and by providing an extra vehicle inspection to facilitate selection of vehicles for the program (that is, ones that would not require additional repairs). MVRS also agreed to add selected vehicles to the electronic auction format at the targeted auctions.

3. *National Vehicle Auction.* The nation's two largest automobile auctions sell used vehicles consigned by automobile manufacturers, captive finance companies, automobile dealers, banks, and others, to licensed new and used vehicle dealers. The auction supported the program by providing an

additional inspection of purchased vehicles and transporting the vehicles to a dealer at cost or at a reduced price. It also provided a program contact to serve as a liaison between Driven to Succeed and the auction.

4. *Local Manufacturer Franchise Dealers.* Local dealers agreed to participate in Driven to Succeed and supported it by working with the assigned nonprofit partner, working closely with a national automobile auction in close geographic proximity, assigning a point of contact for the program, and doing the following:

   - purchasing selected vehicles from the auction;
   - inspecting vehicles for certification and reconditioning the vehicle, if necessary, to meet certification standards;
   - certifying the vehicle so it could be sold as "Manufacturer Certified";
   - completing delivery to the customer, including handling washing, prep, documentation, tax, title and license, and demonstration; and
   - providing a service representative consultation.

5. *Car Ownership Loan Program.* The car ownership loan program, which was a community development financial institution (CDFI), provided low-interest loans for the car buyers. It identified, screened, and prepared low-wage clients to take ownership of the vehicles. It also worked with local dealer partners to coordinate vehicle delivery to their clients and to provide a number of support services to promote successful and sustained vehicle ownership. Finally, it was the direct link between the consumer and the dealer.

The *Driven to Succeed* program was designed to work as follows:

- Leased vehicles are returned to dealers at the end of the lease term.

- The manufacturer enters the vehicle into its database of vehicles available for sale and notifies the local auction partner.
- The auction partner picks up the vehicle from the dealer.
- The auction partner enters the vehicle into its database and conducts an inspection.
- MVRS inspects the vehicle at the auction and authorizes needed repairs.
- The auction partner sells the vehicle to a dealer.
- Eligible customers are screened and selected by the CDFI.
- The dealer sells certified used cars with a warranty to customers.

For the system to work, the program had to address three primary issues:

Issue 1: Accessing Existing National Vehicle Distribution Systems. The pilot program needed access to the manufacturer's robust national distribution system to have a large supply of used cars. The operational components of this pilot were implemented within the normal wholesale distribution system, as described above.

Issue 2: Reducing High Markups in the Price of the Car. Price markups occur on cars throughout the distribution system. The strategic alliance partners agreed to hold the price of the cars selected for this program at the wholesale level and to add on only *negotiated* products and services at or near cost, thereby holding the price of newer (three- to four-year-old) vehicles that were returned at lease termination as close to actual wholesale cost as feasible. See Table 12.2 for pricing specifics.

Table 12.2 Vehicle Pricing Model

Wholesale prices fluctuate daily and are defined by supply and demand in the market. The basis for establishing the wholesale price of any vehicle is the sale price of thousands of like makes and models sold daily through the national auction system. The goal of this project was to sell vehicles at or near wholesale prices to low-income customers by minimizing value-added service costs that occur through the distribution chain. Assuming that we are working UP from wholesale, the following key add-on costs represent profit at different stages of the distribution and wholesale system:

Items	Cost
2001 4-door compact car, 35,000–40,000 miles arrives at dealer	
(Estimated wholesale price, rounded)	$5,400
Manufacturer Extended Service Plan plus warranty (60,000 miles/6 yrs from original in service date)	
Dealer cost and subsidized by manufacturer	$600
Subtotal	**$6,000**
Dealer-certified inspection	$100
Average reconditioning at dealership	$200
Buyer's fee (rounded up from $82.50)	$100
Subtotal	**$6,400**
Tags, tax, & licenses (TTL) fee +	
6% sales tax & licensing fees	$600
Total Vehicle Cost (without financing)	**$7,000***

*Costs for routine maintenance programs may be added to this total.

Typical used car dealers (including BHPH dealers) significantly mark up vehicles of questionable quality to maximize their profits.

The Driven to Succeed program had a goal of providing solid-quality vehicles to buyers at low prices and with fair credit terms. Table 12.3 illustrates the significant cost and quality differentials that buyers typically experienced among BHPH dealers, traditional retail outlets (dealerships), and the Driven to Succeed program.

Table 12.3 Comparison of Costs and Quality Among Three Car-Purchase Options

Category	Buy Here Pay Here	Traditional Retail	Driven to Succeed
Price Range	$2,500–$3,500	$6,000	$6,000 + (wholesale)
Profit Margin	50% +	30%	5%
Pricing Decision	Dealer-controlled	Dealer-controlled	Program-controlled
Type of Car	7–10 years old 100,000+ miles No specific vehicle type	5 years or less 40,000–60,000 miles New vehicle trade-ins	3–4 years 35,000–60,000 miles Lease-end designated auction units
Ownership History	3–4 previous owners	1–3 previous owners	1 previous owner
Service History	Unknown	Inconsistent regularly scheduled maintenance	Generally regularly scheduled maintenance

Issue 3: Addressing the High Cost of Financing. The pilot made allowances for financing costs to be added to the purchase price of all financed vehicles. At this stage in the model, a primary role of the CDFI was to provide access to below-market or market-rate financing. The team developed a financing analysis that illustrated a sample range of financing costs for a vehicle priced at $7,000. All rates assumed 12 monthly payments per year. The amount of interest charged for a used car loan is a critical factor in the vehicle's overall affordability. Ii is easy to see in Table 12.1 the difference in payments with a 6 percent interest rate, compared to a 24 percent interest rate (the highest rate BHPH dealers generally charge in states without caps). The higher interest rate results in an additional charge to the client of more than $2,000 over the life of a three-year loan. The CDFI-provided loans were capped at 8 percent for a three-year period, making the loan more affordable for low-wage working families.

The team determined that the ideal vehicle for the pilot would be a 2001 model year compact car, priced at no more than $7,000 (including dealer add-ons, such as inspection), with good fuel efficiency. Cars that were three to four years old would have relatively low mileage —usually between 38,000 and 50,000—and would offer buyers good performance for many years. Finally, Driven to Succeed's primary desired outcomes were to:

1. Gain access to the established systems that identify and distribute wholesale used vehicles for sale to the general public.
2. Identify the key stakeholders and negotiate reduced price markups with them to keep the final retail sales price close to the wholesale cost (stakeholders would have to agree to a reduced profit margin).
3. Provide 50 to 75 cars to low-wage clients at each of two pilot sites.

Analysis of Mistakes

The first pilot launch was attempted in fall 2004 in Michigan. The team wanted a high-profile site that allowed the dealer, the auction partner, and the car ownership loan program to be in close proximity to one another. This launch attempt did not achieve the desired result because of a number of factors.

At the time, Detroit had the highest overall cost for car ownership in the nation because of its high insurance rates, and potential buyers were increasingly priced out of qualifying for a loan. The cost constraint illustrates the result of (1) *not selecting all of the right criteria for site assessment.* The team should have incorporated all costs of vehicle ownership when selecting pilot sites. Additionally, the car program at this location lacked the infrastructure to implement the pilot, due in part to internal problems with issuing loans, selecting clients, and marketing to attract clients. This information only became apparent when we attempted implementation. The team did not do enough independent due diligence before choosing its car program partner; we made assumptions about the partner's capacity and failed to document whether the partner had the capability to implement the program on site. This demonstrates that there was (2) *inadequate understanding of each player's needs and limitations* among the team. Finally, the rising wholesale price of the selected compact car meant that the final sales price would exceed $7,000. However, the highest loan the car program was able to offer in the pilot program was $7,000, so it was no longer feasible to use that program as a lending partner. By the time the team came to this realization, it was too late to find a new nonprofit lender.

The program also faced (3) *poor launch timing* in Detroit. Every fall, used cars are often at their highest price point for the year because of the cyclical nature of the market. Although other circumstances surrounding the pilot forced a fall launch, the team should have factored this market information into its timing decision and expected outcome.

In June 2005, a second pilot was launched in Ohio. A key mistake this time was (4) *having an extended planning and processing time.* Involved conversations to establish program details with all stakeholders/strategic alliance partners (in an effort to remedy mistakes made in Detroit) took more time than anticipated. Meanwhile, market conditions were changing and team members did not notice their impact on the program. This oversight illustrates the mistake of (5) *lacking the ability to adjust to a rapidly changing environment.* If the team had additional members responsible for monitoring market conditions while it worked on creating the strategic alliance and establishing plan logistics, it could have been more flexible and better able to respond to rising market challenges.

The changing market conditions included the increasing wholesale prices on compact vehicles, due in part to natural disasters during the summer months of 2005 as well as a scarcity of vehicles on the market because of a reduction in leased vehicle returns, lower rental car sales, and fewer fleet sales. Dealers were also choosing to retain more termed-lease cars rather than sending them to auction because of their current profitability. Moreover, the increase in gas prices increased the demand for compact, fuel-efficient cars, which in turn raised their price. Natural disasters and all of the consequences described comprise the (6) *unanticipated market factors* mistake.

Another challenge in Ohio was synchronizing the timing of matching a qualifying vehicle with a qualifying buyer. Nonprofit organizations and for-profit corporations often have very different perspectives on the best pace for reaching a desired result. No one accounted for this cultural divide when pulling the pilot together, and the team took it for granted that the car ownership loan program and the dealer would be in sync with regard to timing and pacing. This was not the case, however, since the dealer expected the car program to refer clients quickly, while the car program had an intensive loan review process that made client referrals a relatively slower process. There was an obvious disparity in views on client handling; the team underestimated its impact, and it became a significant problem. Purchasing increasingly popular compact cars at wholesale prices became more difficult; timing it so a car was secured at the same time the car program identified a qualified buyer was even harder. These problems fall into the previously described category of having an *inadequate understanding of each player's needs and limitations.* In the end, this pilot succeeded in matching one client with a vehicle.

In August 2005, a third and final pilot launch was attempted in Buffalo, New York. This site was also plagued with the vehicle/customer identification timing problem. The August timing also worked against this pilot since natural disasters over the summer months had affected used car prices and availability, and the high price point months (September and October) were just ahead.

While more flexibility from the dealers may have helped the program's progress, dealers had little incentive to do more than they already were because they (7) *lacked bottom-line incentives.* The team did an excellent job in negotiating markups to keep prices low, but it may have done its job too well. Its efforts helped consumers, but relied on the dealer's desire to have social goodwill in the community, rather than a fair profit, as motivation.

In the end, the team realized that Driven to Succeed needed a two-level approach. First, the team needed to implement the national framework of the program. Without such a framework, the local partners (dealers and local auction staff) would not have the authority to make decisions and succeed. The team was successful, after much hard work, in pulling together the national level of the program as described. However, instead of trying to do the local network building themselves, they should have added local contacts to the team to make the process smoother and have a better chance of success. There were simply too many details to handle in separate markets for three people to manage everything. This large factor falls under the mistake of (8) *underestimating the capacity needed to implement a program that was both national and local.*

In addition to the issue of adequate capacity, we wondered whether the allocated resources were adequate to support the work. All partners dedicated more personal time to the effort than there were resources to cover. To add more local partners would have required more financial resources, time, and management. In retrospect, the absence of an on-the-ground partner was a critical factor in our inability to address timing and coordination issues. Of course, this all ties into the issue of the availability of cars in the first place.

Every step within the pilots indicated that (9) *having no "plan B"* was a mistake. This may have been the mistake that provided the most valuable learning experience of the Driven to Succeed program.

Lessons Learned and Successes

Ultimately, the mistakes made in implementing Driven to Succeed led to some key lessons that can be very helpful in a renewed attempt or in implementing any other large change initiatives. These are the team's primary lessons learned:

1. *Planning took too long and was too narrowly focused.* The program's model was well planned and should have been functional, but the team did not factor external market factors into the planning as well as it should have, which led to the lack of program implementation on the ground. This leads us to ask, which of the market forces that affected our work could have been predicted? Obviously, we could have anticipated seasonal price swings, but not the hurricane and its impact on the market.

2. *Getting partners' buy-in is not enough.* It is extremely important to carefully examine each partner's abilities, strengths, and weaknesses, and their impact on the overall process. Should we have explored other lender partners, whose lending limits would not have been capped, thus allowing more flexibility when the price swings occurred?

3. *Always have a "plan B."* Unforeseen circumstances such as illness or changes in a partner's program capacity can completely derail even the smoothest process.

4. *Be more nimble in the implementation phase.* Building the cross-sector collaboration needed to make the program components work smoothly on site was more challenging

than anticipated because of a number of factors, including the internal processes the car ownership program required; the culture of the dealer, which was to move quickly and efficiently; and the time-intensive involvement required of the team in every step of the process.

5. *Establish a local implementation team to manage the program details and process.* This resource would have freed the team to manage the program's national structure and be better able to respond to market changes and manage internal issues.

6. *Be flexible with the program's design and communicate the need for flexibility to all partners.* When car availability declined, the team reluctantly decided that noncertified used cars would be acceptable for the program. However, this change made the dealers hesitant to participate in the program. Without the certification component, the dealers may have faced additional requests for repairs after the sale. They were also concerned that it could damage their reputation in the community.

7. *Balance social benefits with balance sheet benefits.* In this pilot, profit margins were very slim for the dealers (5 percent versus an estimated retail profit margin of 30 percent). They did not have a big incentive to take part unless they were driven by social mission. In hindsight, profit margins should have been higher for the dealers so they could achieve profits at acceptable levels while keeping customers in the mainstream retail market and out of the sub-prime, predatory market.

8. *Incorporate external expert assistance where necessary.* The team would have benefitted from investing in a formal business planning process to incorporate the right assumptions into its planning and have the right components in place to have a higher probability of success.

The Driven to Succeed program was created to be a win-win for all stakeholders. While much of the for-profit sector engages in corporate social responsibility in a number of forms, this sector is driven primarily by the financial success of its brand. Building brand loyalty is a major goal for all auto manufacturers, especially if they are able to identify new markets and expand their customer base. Many of the families that could have benefited from this program would have been driving a newer, reliable car for the first time. That experience had the potential to create a future base of customers who would return to purchase another vehicle. Participating dealerships would have had an opportunity to improve their competitive position in their community as a "dealer of choice" and build their service, parts, and sales department business. Financial institutions would have had the opportunity to serve a new customer segment and the potential to earn Community Reinvestment Act credits with their loans. Most important, low-wage families would have benefited through increased mobility, stronger credit scores, and forging relationships with mainstream institutions.

Despite its mistakes, Driven to Succeed did experience some significant success. Industry partners agreed to reduce their profits significantly and support the pilot. The team successfully accessed sources of used cars through existing national distribution systems, and the car ownership program secured its board's approval to increase the amount and terms of the loans to accommodate the pilot. Additionally, retired executives from a major automobile manufacturer contributed their time and efforts at no or reduced cost to support this work.

Driven to Succeed was an ambitious and challenging model. Bringing unlikely national corporate partners to the table, teaching them to realize the value of the program, and securing their agreement to forgo profit for the benefit of low-wage working customers were significant successes. Although the program did not fulfill its full potential, the concept was sound, and if tried again, it has the potential to benefit thousands of deserving families across the nation.

---

1   Roberto, E. (2008, February). Commuting to opportunity: The working poor and commuting in the United States. Transportation Reform Series for the Metropolitan Policy Program at Brookings. Washington, DC: The Brookings Institution.

13

CDC Management Lessons: Insights from the Demise of Eastside Community Investments, Inc.

Robert O. Zdenek and Carla J. Robinson

Over the past 40 years, the community economic development (CED) field has paid relatively little attention to organizational management. Community development corporations (CDCs) tend to focus on developing programs and projects that meet the needs of the communities and residents they serve. Funders frequently emphasize project outcomes and results in their work with the CDCs they support financially. It is ironic that researchers point to effective management procedures and strong leadership as key factors in CDC effectiveness, suggesting that project outcomes tend to be compromised when organizations are not managed well.

Concern about the excessive focus on production numbers rather than methods and process surfaced at a 1998 meeting the Local Initiatives Support Corporation (LISC) sponsored to assess threats to the health of CDCs. According to the meeting summary, many of the participants believed "'high performance' in community development has become virtually synonymous with rapid, large-scale production" (Local Initiatives Support Corporation [LISC], 1998, p. 7). The unintentional consequences of both CDCs' and funders' focusing on outputs is that we neglect critical strategic, governance, administrative, and process challenges.

Even when CED leaders address matters such as sustainability and effectiveness, quite often they end up treating them from the vantage point of questions about resources, strategy, and other aspects of production and output. What typically gets lost is the role of effective management practices in enabling CDCs to operate successfully and enhance their chances for long-term viability. A few studies of CDC effectiveness have explored the importance of intentionality in management. Perhaps the most notable is the 2003 study in which Rohe, Bratt, and Biswas examined CDC failures, downsizings, and mergers. The authors concluded that "internal management problems" contributed to all three types of organizational change, and they found problems with project management and property management to be particular factors in organizational failure. The demise of Eastside Community Investments, Inc. (ECI), once a well-known and multi-faceted Indianapolis CDC, offers an instructive example of how a large, well-resourced CDC can quickly collapse. The combination of ECI's visibility and the research done on the demise of the organization makes ECI a compelling example for exploring leadership and management failures in the community economic development field. Founded in 1976, ECI became a multi-million-dollar operation with a staff of more than 80 by the late 1990s. ECI enjoyed a reputation as a leader and innovator in the CED field, but, in 1997, it could no longer meet its payroll. It transferred many of its economic development initiatives and programs to other organizations and eliminated others altogether. ECI ceased operations in 2001; several leadership and management mistakes contributed to the organization's demise:

- *Failure to "connect the boxes."* Organizational charts typically use boxes and lines to depict the structure of and relationships among departments and functions. Effective organizations clearly specify departmental functions and ensure that departments receive the human, technical, and financial resources they need to succeed. This requires a shared policy perspective and vision among the board of directors, executive staff, program staff, and volunteers. Toward the end, ECI lacked both a cohesive vision and a sound policy framework capable of guiding the implementation of sophisticated development initiatives.

- *Failure to consider options and risk.* Community-based economic development is a risky undertaking, for example, attempting to create shopping centers from vacant lots and housing from boarded-up buildings. Effective CDCs know how to manage and mitigate risk to avoid threatening their overall viability, and these CDCs are able to spread risk and/ or determine the point beyond which those risks are likely to prove detrimental or even fatal. ECI failed to anticipate and manage risks associated with its strategies and ventures.

- *Failure to build and maintain a foundation for growth.* CDC boards and staff need to assess their core competencies carefully and think strategically about whether to add new ones based on additional opportunities or to find partners with the expertise needed. During its first decade, ECI focused on refurbishing rental and owner-occupied homes, opening an industrial park, and financing small businesses. The board and staff later expanded the focus to include "quality of life" initiatives in areas where ECI had limited competencies. The explosion of new activities in diverse fields contributed in part to the organization's downfall.

- *Failure to assemble and organize the needed resources.* Many CDCs face the challenge of making the transition from start-up or real-estate-driven entities to more enduring and comprehensive organizations. ECI transformed itself from a traditional CDC into an organization at the cutting edge of human development, youth initiatives, small-business support, special-needs housing, and family-based childcare support. The organization faced challenges in hiring staff to meet these diverse needs and employing senior managers who could provide leadership for such innovative and complex initiatives.

- *Failure to manage information.* CDC leaders need timely and accurate financial and programmatic data on the organization's performance to make informed decisions. ECI relied on outmoded data and information systems. Until 1996, the organization used an information system that had been developed in the late 1980s. The lack of a suitable information system left the organization with no diagnostic early-warning mechanism.

- *Failure of external funders to provide ECI with in-depth scrutiny and feedback.* During a period of rapid growth and programmatic expansion, ECI received limited scrutiny and feedback from its constellation of funders. Many of these funders were attracted to ECI because of its innovative and comprehensive work, which generated many positive articles in the media. It was not until 1997 that several core funders of ECI commissioned a financial audit of ECI activities, which was released several weeks after Dennis West's (ECI president) departure in 1997 and showed that the vast majority of ECI initiatives were losing money. A full-blown crisis and virtual "fire sale" of ECI programs followed, permanently crippling the organization. If funders had required the independent financial audit earlier, the result may have been quite different for ECI.

The CED field is undergoing major changes that include the departure of many CDCs' founding directors, population shifts accompanied by the arrival of new constituencies, and increased emphasis in the field on scale and sustainability. These challenges make it more important than ever for practitioners to clarify their objectives and the best methods to achieve them. In this chapter we offer lessons from the ECI experience that might help practitioners meet these challenges. We first provide background information about ECI, then analyze the organization's mistakes and failures, and, finally, offer lessons in the form of indicators of success for CDCs, funders, intermediaries, government officials, and policymakers who support CDCs.

Eastside Community Investments

ECI grew out of the efforts of the Near Eastside Community Organization (NESCO) of Indianapolis, a grassroots organization created to represent the community's interests in a range of issues, including economic development. After forming ECI to plan and implement CED projects, NESCO secured a planning grant from the Urban-Rural Special Impact Program (SIP) of the U.S. Community Services Administration (CSA). ECI named a board of directors of 16 residents and six outside professionals, assembled a five-person staff, and completed an Overall Economic Development Plan (OEDP). The OEDP focused on improving the existing housing stock, identifying new industrial opportunities, supporting the expansion of existing small businesses, and creating jobs for local residents. On completing the OEDP, ECI received a two-year operating and equity grant from CSA. During the first eight years of its existence, ECI established an impressive record of accomplishments. It started a Fix Up/Paint Up program that provided financing and materials to refurbish 500 homes in two years. The organization created a $1-million loan pool to offer low-interest, fixed-rate mortgages to homebuyers in the area. It also acquired land adjacent to an interstate highway and developed an industrial park.

Following the loss of federal CSA dollars in 1981, ECI received a three-year grant from the locally based Lilly Endowment, which stabilized ECI, albeit with a smaller staff. By 1984, the organization had completed several buildings in the industrial park and eventually leased more than 100,000 square feet of space in the park to a variety of tenants that employed more than 1,000 workers.

ECI Expands Its Focus

Tom Creasser, the founding president of ECI, resigned in 1983, and in the spring of 1984, the ECI board selected Dennis West, an urban planner and an ECI board member, to become the new president. West and the board and staff immediately pursued new initiatives that offered financial stabilization and led to eight years of sustained growth. Using real estate syndication and a limited partnership structure, ECI converted a former school into 24 units of low-income rental housing and developed its first major rental housing project, Whittier Place Apartments. ECI also created a for-profit, real estate management firm, the HCJ Corporation, to manage this project. By 1986, ECI had built a reputation as a real estate developer and business lender.

ECI's expertise in housing development and its understanding of real estate syndications and the tax code positioned it to take advantage of the Low-Income Housing Tax Credit, which Congress created in 1986. Between 1987 and 1994, ECI formed 11 limited partnerships that spurred the development of 10 major rental projects, leading to the production of 484 affordable housing units. Between its founding in 1984 and 1992, ECI's property management division (the HCJ Corporation) grew from two to 17 staff members.

In 1987, the ECI board and staff revisited the organization's mission and completed a long-range strategic plan. In an effort to provide more opportunities for residents to become self-sufficient, they expanded the mission from job creation and housing to improving the quality of life for residents. By the early 1990s, many in the community economic development field regarded ECI as one of the nation's leading comprehensive CDCs. Early in the expansion process, ECI established the Eastside Day Care Homes Cooperative to help home-based childcare providers obtain financing, housing, licensing, training, and peer support.

ECI next turned its attention to the issue of domestic violence, creating the Basta program to provide 10 units of housing, along with social supports, for abused women transitioning to independent living with their children. In addition, ECI formed the Youth Investment Program (YIP) to offer construction and childcare training and employment for young parents between the ages of 16 and 22 who had dropped out of school. ECI continued to expand its industrial and business development initiatives in the late 1980s and early 1990s. By 1992, 30 businesses had located in the industrial park, offering a diverse array of products and services that employed 1,500 individuals.

A New Mission: Investing in People, Buildings, Land, and Industry

In 1993, the ECI board revised its mission statement to emphasize investing in people, buildings, land, and industry. Investments in people promoted the development of economic opportunities and skills and served as the centerpiece of the strategy. These investments required careful integration of ECI's initiatives in education, training, job creation, transitional housing, and special supports. In identifying projects, ECI looked for businesses that offered opportunities to combine training with employment and supportive services.

An example of the new business approach was Shelter Systems LLC, created in 1994 as a wholly owned subsidiary that manufactured roof trusses and wall panels. ECI intended for Shelter Systems to provide community residents, particularly disadvantaged youth, with training and job opportunities in the construction trades. In its first year, the company employed 16 full-time and five part-time workers and had sales of $479,399. It encountered difficulty in generating sufficient revenue to cover the costs of trainees and employees, losing $800,000 in its first 18 months of operation. In 1997, ECI sold the business to a lumber company, which leased space in the ECI industrial park and retained many of the company's jobs.

ECI also created the Opportunity Factory, another ambitious effort to combine workforce development (education, training, placement, childcare, and transportation) and economic development (job creation and real estate development). The Opportunity Factory planned to offer classes in basic education and career skills development for disadvantaged older youths and adults. Although it operated the program in partnership with an array of other organizations, ECI assumed all of the risk associated with the project. By early 1997, the Opportunity Factory had outstripped ECI's fiscal and administrative capacity, generating a loss of $1 million, and was shut down.

Organizational Decline and Demise

ECI experienced enormous organizational growth between 1984 and 1995, expanding from seven employees in 1984 to more than 80 by 1994. The organization's budget grew from $859,184 in 1986 to more than $8.5 million in 1994, and revenues grew from $2 million in 1991 to $8 million in 1994. In their article on the rise and fall of ECI, Reingold and Johnson (2003) point out that the organization's "construction revenue was very volatile in the mid-1980s through the mid-1990s" (p. 536); it dropped from a high of nearly $3.5 million to "virtually zero" (p. 536) in 1996. As ECI encountered increasing competition from other developers for tax credits, it secured fewer of them. Changes in federal regulations that reduced the fees developers could receive from tax credit projects also adversely affected ECI's revenue stream. Development fees received by ECI reached a high of $1.2 million in 1996, accounting for 25 percent of the organization's total revenue. In 1997, these figures fell dramatically, to $400,000 and 10 percent, respectively (p. 537). Between 1990 and 1996, ECI poured more than $8 million in cash into its real estate investments, but it received a return on those investments only in 1991 and 1994. The organization's debt burden grew from $3.5 million in 1994 to $8 million in 1996, when it accounted for 80 percent of revenues. Dennis West, who was aware of the mounting problems at ECI, resigned as president at the end of August 1997. ECI turned to Phil Thom, a former board chair, and Jim Higgs, a consultant who had led ECI's housing initiatives in the 1980s, to put the organization back on track.

Both Thom and Higgs agreed to serve in an interim capacity, intending to hand responsibility for the organization to new leadership. Within a few weeks of West's departure, several local funders, including LISC and the Lilly Endowment, received the audit they had commissioned, which reported that the vast majority of ECI's initiatives were losing money. In an attempt to salvage the organization's viable programs, LISC, the Lilly Endowment, and ECI's other core funders required ECI to transfer its programs to other community-based organizations and private businesses and to transfer or eliminate the related staff positions. ECI tried to rebound and, in 1998, hired additional staff. Unable to reverse its dramatic collapse, the organization closed its doors in 2001.

Analysis of ECI's Leadership and Management Failures

Several major factors contributed to ECI's demise: the organization's rapid and uncontrolled growth; its dependence on revenue generated by development fees from federal tax credit projects, which turned out to be an unstable proposition given the increased competition for tax credits and changes in public policy; and its decision to encompass social as well as economic objectives. These factors can be traced in turn to a set of leadership and management failures. In analyzing sources of failure, Cohen and Gooch (1990) note "the temptation to focus on any particular component to the exclusion of the rest, or to seek universal causes of failure" (p. 233). They observe: "It is in the deficiencies of particular organizations confronted with particular tasks that the embryo of misfortune develops" (p. 233). CDC failures are similarly complex in that they frequently involve multiple components. But although the circumstances of particular CDCs matter, those circumstances can best be examined in the context of a set of organizational failures that pose threats to all CDCs. Our analysis of the ECI case identifies six such failures.

Failure to "Connect the Boxes"

Organizational structures, policies, and procedures are designed to enable the organization and its departments to integrate their activities—in other words, to connect the boxes typically pictured on organizational charts. In the case of a nonprofit organization, one of the important boxes on its organizational chart represents the board of directors. Several studies have identified a well-functioning board as one of the essential features of successful CDCs (Gittell & Wilder, 1999; Glickman & Servon, 1998; Rohe, Bratt, & Biswas, 2003; Vidal, 1997). Board members offer a wealth of knowledge and experience that is invaluable for setting a strategic direction for a CDC. An effective board provides an objective perspective that serves as a critical counterpoint when a CDC deviates from its designated course of action or takes major financial risks that jeopardize the organization's viability.

The ability of the ECI board to function effectively appears to have been limited. In interviews conducted in 1997, ECI president Dennis West, the board chair at the time, and a former chair all indicated that the board tended to participate more actively in making and analyzing decisions when the organization had strong board chairs. However, as the organization's work expanded and became more complex, board meetings became more technical. Few members possessed the requisite skills to assess ECI's various initiatives. Consequently, they acted more as supporters of Dennis West's vision than as knowledgeable guides who could make objective and informed strategic decisions, monitor progress, and identify potential problems.

As nonprofits increasingly recognize the importance of funders and other supporters, they include boxes representing those entities on organizational charts that more broadly depict the organizations' operating environments. CDCs serve and work with a variety of stakeholders, including other community organizations, businesses, government agencies, and nonprofits. They need to develop effective vehicles that allow them to build relationships with these entities and communicate information about their activities and accomplishments. They must also be able to mobilize stakeholders to work collaboratively to improve conditions in the community. ECI did not always provide key stakeholders with information about its challenges, nor did it attempt to draw from their expertise as it adopted more comprehensive strategies. Better collaboration and communication with other organizations might have enabled ECI to address some of its problems more successfully.

Improved relationships with funders and intermediaries might have been particularly helpful for ECI. This topic arose at the 1998 meeting LISC organized to examine six CDCs that had recently closed or scaled back significantly. Many of the participants felt that "early, preventive measures" by funders and other outside stakeholders "were either lacking or inadequate in most cases" (LISC, 1998, p. 14). The lesson is that funders need to be vigilant in assessing the financial condition and performance of their major grantees. They can ask tough questions that other stakeholders may be uncomfortable asking.

Failure to Consider Options and Manage Risk
Although CDCs should never violate the principles that are dear to them, occasionally they must challenge their beliefs and assumptions when weighing strategic options. Changes in community circumstances and community development orthodoxies trigger new approaches. This has prompted more and more CDCs to reorient their work, for example, by expanding their geographic areas, working with diverse new constituents, and working in different ways with private entities.

In 1994, ECI hired ShoreBank Advisory Services (SAS) to help the board and staff identify new strategic directions. One of the three strategic options SAS presented to the board involved expanding ECI's housing and lending activity throughout Indianapolis. The board chose not to pursue this option, believing that ECI should limit its operations to the Near Eastside, even if additional opportunities existed elsewhere in the city. Instead, the board selected the riskiest option presented by SAS and decided to start a business (Shelter Systems) manufacturing roof trusses and wall panels. The board's inability to help assess the risks associated with these alternative strategic investments probably contributed to the rapid decline of ECI in 1996 and 1997.

All innovative organizations and initiatives involve risk. Effective CDCs know how to manage risk and mitigate it so it does not threaten their overall viability. A seasoned board and outside consultants can help an organization analyze the risks associated with particular endeavors and determine the point beyond which those risks are likely to prove detrimental or even fatal. ECI failed to anticipate and manage the risks associated with its strategies and ventures. There was no guarantee that using for-profit ventures like Shelter Systems to finance nonprofit programs would generate sufficient revenue to sustain the programs' operations.

Failure to Build a Foundation for Growth

CDC boards and staff need to assess their core competencies carefully and to think strategically about whether to add new ones, since new programs may compromise a CDC's ability to be effective in its core areas. Vidal (1997) found that most successful CDCs identify a high-priority area of work and stay with it for a sustained period. ECI's failure to stick to its core competencies or to acquire the competencies needed to operate in the new arenas contributed to the organization's downfall. The lesson here is that CDCs must assess their competencies carefully to determine which community needs they should attempt to meet themselves and which they should address by working in partnership with other entities.

Participants in the 1998 LISC meeting on CDC closures and downsizings identified rapid growth that outpaces a CDC's resources as a signal of impending danger. "In many cases, a clear sign of approaching trouble was a period of explosive growth, unmatched by commensurate expansion in the organization's management capacity. In such cases, the growth soon became impossible for organizations to manage well" (LISC, 1998, p. 10).

Failure to Assemble and Organize the Needed Resources

Many CDCs face the challenge of making the transition from a start-up to a more enduring organization. Dominant leaders who are visionary and tenacious serve fledgling organizations well, but they can present impediments as organizations grow and become more complex. As CDCs start implementing numerous projects, they need to disperse decision making and develop leadership structures that are more horizontal.

CDCs need staff members who have knowledge of and connections to the community, as well as staff members who have technical skills in finance, management, information systems, and other areas. The need for access to technical skills increases as CDCs' initiatives become more complex. CDCs can acquire technical expertise by hiring additional staff, contracting with consultants, or partnering with organizations that have the needed skills. Staff turnover can also pose a huge problem, since hiring and training new staff is both time-consuming and costly. Several studies point to the effects of staff capacity and turnover on CDC performance (Cowan, Rohe, & Baku, 1999; Gittell & Wilder, 1999; Glickman & Servon, 1998). During periods of rapid growth and/or high turnover, CDC leaders, along with funders and intermediaries, need "to look with redoubled care at the CDC's mounting workload, the pressures on its leadership, and the organization's ability to pay for enough growth to manage more and more projects" (LISC, 1998, p. 10).

As ECI became more complex, it failed to shift its staffing mix to incorporate people and organizations with the expertise required to manage and staff the new initiatives. This resulted in the misalignment of the organization's vision and capacity and contributed to program and financial difficulties. ECI hired staff for virtually all of these new endeavors, which required both staff with program-specific expertise and staff with general management skills who could coordinate the various initiatives. In some cases, ECI started these activities before hiring the complete staff, causing existing staff to be stretched thin and leading to low morale and high turnover. CDCs that either become more comprehensive or attempt to significantly expand their production capacity and/or service areas need to address staffing and organizational capacity in their strategic-planning and expansion processes.

Failure to Receive In-Depth Scrutiny and Feedback from External Funders
CDCs are complex institutions with multiple objectives and initiatives that can be difficult to assess. ECI operated at a much higher level of complexity than most CDCs, especially when its mission evolved by the early 1990s into advancing "quality of life" in the Near Eastside. ECI rapidly launched an array of new initiatives focused on daycare, domestic violence, youth development, and sheltered work enterprises.

As ECI became more innovative and exciting, funders began to shift from being "stewards" of resources for ECI to being "cheerleaders" of growth for ECI. The changing perspective of ECI funders, at the height of ECI's influence, is not unique. Funders, stakeholders, and the community want to see success, and when they perceive it growing, they tend to celebrate and promote it. This usually leads to more funding for the organization. The balancing act for external funders in this scenario involves maintaining a supportive stance with organizations while also frankly assessing whether the organizations have the requisite financial, administrative, and organizational capacity to sustain growth. Knowledgeable funders can ask questions about liquidity, management, risk analysis, market analysis, expertise, and management. Core funders are among the few stakeholders who can influence a visionary CDC to strengthen its organizational capacity.

The 1997 financial and programmatic audit of ECI was conducted too late for the organization to take corrective action, forcing the funders and ECI to "off-load" salvageable programs and initiatives to other organizations. Today's environment is different from the 1990s' when ECI operated. CDCs have access to high-quality financial software packages, and there is increased emphasis on greater transparency and accountability due in part to the Sarbanes-Oxley financial regulation legislation. Still, external funders need to scrutinize the financial condition and organizational effectiveness of their core CDC grantees regularly.

Failure to Manage Information

A core element of a CDC's management system is its ability to collect, store, and access information about the organization's financial, programmatic, personnel, and other operations. At the 1998 LISC conference on CDC closures and downsizings, participants agreed that "alarms should go off when financial information is either too skimpy or too dense, or is too irregular or infrequent, for principals to make informed plans and decisions" (LISC, 1998, p. 11).

ECI's rapid growth after 1985 placed considerable stress on the organization's outmoded data and information systems. Until 1996, the organization used a Lotus software system developed in the late 1980s. It failed to develop adequate processes for tracking, analyzing, and reporting organizational and project performance, and it invested $1.5 million in Shelter Systems before gaining an understanding of the financial outflow associated with the enterprise. A 1997 program and financial assessment revealed in several instances funds allocated for special initiatives had been spent elsewhere, leading a major funder to question ECI's credibility. By the time the board members learned of the organization's financial problems, they could do little to rectify the situation. CDCs must ensure they have the staffing and/or contract support needed to track and analyze information about their performance. A number of CDCs receive funding from large intermediaries (LISC, NeighborWorks America, Enterprise Community Partners, etc.) that provide assistance with sophisticated data and management systems and software.

Lessons for Community Economic Development

ECI had a significant and positive impact on the Near Eastside of Indianapolis for more than 20 years and was rightly viewed as a national model for community economic development. Despite its record of impressive achievements, the organization encountered leadership and management problems that eventually led to its demise. The analysis of ECI's failures suggests that CDCs and their supporters should pay attention to six indicators of success that emerge from the ECI case.

Strategic Thinking

The complex internal and external environments of sophisticated CDCs mandate that their leaders place a high priority on strategic thinking and decision making. This is especially important in today's environment of rapid change and heightened competition. CDCs need to be clear about their strengths and how they can build capacity and deploy resources. One of the hallmarks of an organization that focuses on strategic thinking is board and senior staff devoting sufficient time and attention to planning and strategy development. A number of entities now offer leadership and management assistance to CDCs. NeighborWorks America formally certifies its NeighborWorks Organization (NWO) affiliates and requires that member NWOs establish leadership and management benchmarks in such areas as board development, management systems, and leadership development.

Board Leadership

Successful CDCs rely heavily on experienced board members. Organizations are more likely to make effective strategic decisions if they have informed board members who draw from their collective knowledge and wisdom in setting organizational directions. Boards need members who represent both continuity and change and who understand how the organization evolved and what made it effective. They also need other newer members who bring energy, ideas, skills, networks, and resources that can help their organizations thrive in the future. Reach CDC in Portland, Oregon, uses a grid to help recruit and retain board members. The grid includes information about the skills the board needs, as well as information about where current board members live, the organizations or interests they represent, and how they contribute to the organization.

Risk Management

One of ECI's most obvious failures was the organization's extremely high tolerance for risk. CDCs must be able to assess the risk associated with potential projects. Quite often, funders, intermediaries, and other partners can help CDCs access the expertise they need to conduct these analyses. They can begin to manage risk by asking a series of questions when considering major new initiatives that include: How will the initiative be financed? Which partners can help reduce the risk of the CDC? What will those partners want in return?

All parties involved need to have the discipline not to proceed with popular projects when the assessments indicate unacceptably high levels of risk. CDCs should avoid assuming all of the financial liability associated with projects and, instead, carefully spread it among investors, partners, and other funders.

Alignment

CDCs need to assemble sufficient leadership, staff, and management structures before expanding the scale or scope of their activities. They and their funding partners need to understand the importance of both investing in the organizations' capacity and spending the time required to align their organizations for new opportunities and directions. Alignment does not imply that CDCs should stop being entrepreneurial organizations. However, they need to determine the extent to which they can undertake new initiatives, and then adapt their capacity accordingly. They and their supporters must temper the desire to grow with careful analyses of resource and organizational requirements. The extent to which ECI relied on such analyses remains unclear. Did ECI perform these analyses? If so, what did they reveal? How accurate were the findings? How did ECI use the findings to determine how to proceed? Answers to such questions may shed additional light on the reasons for ECI's demise.

Information Tracking and Analysis

One of ECI's major failures was its inability to collect and report timely financial information about the organization's projects and overall performance. Routinely providing performance information to board members, funders, intermediaries, and other partners can identify problems early before they become crises. Having diverse stakeholders receive and be able to use timely information is crucial for effective decision making and efficient resource deployment.

Communication and Collaboration with Key Stakeholders

One of the major changes within the community economic development field during the past decade is the increased importance of partnerships and collaboration involving CDCs and other organizations with similar missions. Traditionally, CDCs tended to be entrepreneurial organizations that only occasionally joined forces with other organizations. They now serve and work with a variety of stakeholders, including other community organizations, businesses, government agencies, charter schools, childcare centers, workforce development institutions, and other nonprofit organizations. They need to develop effective communication channels that allow them to share information about their activities and accomplishments. They must also be able to mobilize stakeholders to work collaboratively to improve conditions in the community. ECI did not always inform key stakeholders about its challenges, nor did it attempt to draw from their expertise as it adopted more comprehensive strategies. Better communication and collaboration with other organizations might have enabled ECI to be more successful in addressing some of its problems and spreading its financial risk.

The ECI case demonstrates that leadership and management failures can undermine the potential of organizations that, on the surface, appear to be quite promising. In its early years, ECI established an impressive record of accomplishment in real estate development and business lending. It faltered, however, as it sought to build on that record by implementing a wide array of new initiatives that required new and different program and management skills. ECI did not seek appropriate partner organizations with the requisite skills and resources to manage the new initiatives and opted, instead, to incorporate them into its own organizational structure. Although it effectively identified community needs and initiated an expanded set of innovative programs to respond to them, for a variety of reasons, ECI never established the organizational stability or financial viability required to sustain those efforts. The story of ECI is a cautionary tale that all CDCs looking to develop new initiatives or become more comprehensive should heed.

References

Cohen, E. A., & Gooch, J. (1990). *Military misfortunes: The anatomy of failure in war.* New York: The Free Press.

Cowan, S. M., Rohe, W., & Baku, E. (1999). Factors influencing the performance of community development corporations. *Journal of Urban Affairs, 21*, 325–340.

Gittell, R., & Wilder, M. (1999). Community development corporations: Critical factors that influence success. *Journal of Urban Affairs, 21*, 341–362.

Glickman, N. J., & Servon, L. J. (1998). More than bricks and sticks: Five components of community development capacity. *Housing Policy Debate, 9*, 497–539.

Local Initiatives Support Corporation (LISC). (1998). *Building durable CDCs: A summary of the proceedings of a conference organized by the Local Initiatives Support Corporation.* Retrieved from http://liscstage.forumone.com/content/publications/detail/824

Reingold, D. A., & Johnson, C. L. (2003). The rise and fall of Eastside Community Investments, Inc.: The life of an extraordinary community development corporation. *Journal of Urban Affairs, 25*, 527–549.

Rohe, W. M., Bratt, R. G., & Biswas, P. (2003). *Evolving challenges for community development corporations: The causes and impacts of failures, downsizings, and mergers.* Chapel Hill, NC: The University of North Carolina at Chapel Hill, Center for Urban and Regional Studies.

Vidal, A. C. (1997). Can community development re-invent itself? *Journal of the American Planning Association, 63*, 429–438.

14

Mistakes to Success: Learning and Adapting When Things Go Wrong

Robert Giloth and Colin Austin

On a gusty day in 1903, Wilbur and Orville Wright achieved what many at the time thought was impossible—controlled, self-propelled flight. Their accomplishment sparked immense innovation and an entirely new mode of transportation. To realize this breakthrough, the Wright brothers relied on experimentation and a series of constructive mistakes. Year after year the Wright brothers tested kites and gliders on the sand dunes of the Outer Banks in North Carolina. Most of these efforts resulted in crashes and failures, even when they followed promising models of the time. But the Wright brothers carefully took notes and found ways to understand the dynamics of air pressure, balance, and lift. Their major success was not building the motorized glider that flew at Kitty Hawk. The Wright brothers' most significant contribution was the learning process that placed high value on understanding why things went wrong. As one Wright biographer writes, Wilbur was "the perfect engineer—isolating a basic problem, defining it in the most precise terms, and identifying the missing information that would enable him to solve it" (Crouch, 1989, p. 165).

Before the Wright brothers, most aeronautical enthusiasts sketched out ideas built around a vision for success. The results usually ranged from disappointment to severe injury, and there were few attempts to learn from mistakes and many reasons to cover up failures.

In a similar fashion, nonprofit practitioners and investors still line up to jump off hills aboard the latest model project, but without knowing the problems they will surely encounter or good guidance about how to experiment and control their flight.

On two occasions the authors of *Mistakes to Success* chapters convened at the Annie E. Casey Foundation in Baltimore to exchange stories, findings, and lessons. Mistakes and lessons were discussed critically in an open atmosphere. This search-and-discovery exercise was enjoyable and enlightening—especially since project failure is typically not a topic for polite conversation in the nonprofit sector. The group admitted that when "failure" is mentioned, faces drop and participants often substitute euphemisms such as "challenges" or "delays." At the same time, learning from mistakes is critical for solving complex problems and practitioners must not be bound by taboos.

The Case for Considering Failures

While not a comprehensive overview of failures in community economic development (CED), these chapters represent enough examples of common mistakes to draw lessons for the field and begin to outline a process for more intentional learning from mistakes. The chapters are grounded in actual project activity, mostly described by authors with firsthand knowledge. Their perspectives illuminate the subtle and not-so-subtle underlying issues. As the authors sort through analysis and implications, the conversation about mistakes moves toward innovation.

Why do nonprofits have trouble learning from mistakes when they are so common? A lack of critical analysis and evidence leads nonprofits to rely on success stories, called "best practices," as a major resource for program design. The conceptual value behind the best practices approach is that someone else has already hit on an idea that seems to produce results. As noted in Chapter 1, best practices in community economic development provide a set of preselected answers to very complicated problems. Karen Chapple writes in her chapter that so-called best practices are frequently the models that are "in the air," or attractive when the issues are broad and there are few clear solutions.

In addition to programmatic complexity, the chapters in this book describe shifting configurations of organizations that carry out the work. Many of these new partnerships are looking for help in understanding roles and strategies to guide organizational interplay and partnership building. Aligning new systems and recasting organizational responsibilities due to political and economic change present opportunities for innovation (Melendez, 2004). Yet, project partners on the ground often struggle with defining their roles and may overemphasize basic program operations rather than reflection and testing.

The result is that best practices are used to justify launching projects, but they regularly fail when adjustments to time and place are required as projects evolve. Even when best practices fit initially, local practitioners' lack of understanding about the actual dynamics of models leaves them grasping for modifications when contexts inevitably change. As the chapters here demonstrate, changing economic, political, leadership, and financial trends are inevitable.

A more useful approach to defining model practices may be to assign weights or gradations to specific practices. A "promising" practice would be a new idea based on clear logic but with little evidence to prove its worth. A "good" practice would have a track record of experiences at a single location that produce a set of outcomes. A "best" practice would be one that grows in several different contexts and uses data and more rigorous research designs to demonstrate some degree of causation. This final level of model practice could be certified according to a list of criteria developed by a national organization or government agency. Differentiation in the language of model practices will allow practitioners to select strategies with greater knowledge of their probable effects.

Permission to Be Wrong

There are good reasons to hide project failures. Practitioners and nonprofit implementers by necessity are highly sensitive to funding relationships. Without a "safe" space for examining project failures, nonprofit grantees will continue to sugarcoat results and keep real problems hidden. Another deterrent is that nonprofits operate in communities with many players and partners where public relations and reputations are critical. Exposing mistakes may upset relationships and damage the organization's operating environment. Even during the course of the *Mistakes to Success* project, several authors eventually withdrew their chapters because executive management of their organizations perceived too high a risk in going public with their problems.

The authors noted that philanthropy is uniquely positioned to help nonprofit organizations shine a light on mistakes. Investments from private foundations can be more flexible than public funding and cover a longer period. Foundations and their staff can also serve as reservoirs of knowledge gained through multiple grant cycles and comparative work across regions or neighborhoods. Yet, the dangers of recognizing failure still loom when philanthropic trustees demand clean outcomes and program officers feel obligated to put the best face on projects under their stewardship.

Looking hard at mistakes involves taking risks. But associated with those risks are potentially higher gains or even breakthroughs. In the business world this is often the domain of venture capital, where investors look for good ideas but also people and companies that evaluate results critically and make changes. When nonprofit organizations have no space for working with mistakes, they invariably fall back on standardized strategies and loose performance measures.

Part of the problem for nonprofit organizations is setting inappropriate expectations for the life cycle of a project. Several of the authors here recount pressures to take project activity to a higher and broader level. "Going to scale" is often the ultimate objective. At the same time, nonprofits rarely if ever have the resources necessary for the prototyping and market testing outlined by Amy Brown and Kirsten Moy in their chapter on scaling. Nonprofits end up fighting a losing battle for which they are poorly equipped in the pursuit of higher numbers and greater impact.

Several chapters in this book provide lessons about the tendency to overreach to create greater or more comprehensive change. Social entrepreneurism is an example of nonprofits' desire to engage a marketplace for which they are often poorly equipped. Neil Kleiman and Emma Oppenheim write about having a social enterprise rise and fall relatively quickly as a nonprofit takes on too much business development activity and eventually fails.

The chapters also teach about the central role of leadership in responding to mistakes. Robert Brehm writes of executive leadership that recognizes failure and reimagines a project based on cash flow realities and feedback from participants. Robert Zdenek and Carla Robinson relate the importance of organizational self-management, including executives and nonprofit boards that must align to keep projects moving forward. And, ultimately, they establish mechanisms for responding to the inevitable problems that arise.

A Methodology for Learning from Mistakes

How do we prepare for, reflect on, and adapt to mistakes? The authors of *Mistakes to Success* point to the need for a learning methodology or a framework for how and when project failures should be acknowledged and addressed. While an integrated approach has yet to be defined, elements of a methodology are emerging.

Anticipating mistakes as decisions are made before project work begins is an important first step. Examples include clarifying project goals, defining and selecting project sites, designing models, and setting appropriate outcome measures. With hindsight, the faulty assumptions at this stage stand out, but can we identify potential mistakes with any certainty when making innovative investments? After projects take flight, the mistakes in planning can be hard to correct or rewire and may require shutting down work and starting over.

When do CED projects and investments take on too much? A part of the problem is not recognizing all the dimensions of complex problems, environments, and solutions; another part is not having a handle on the "drivers of change" required to address complexity successfully, whether they are power, information, relationships, or resources. Often it seems like a badge of courage or commitment to take on the impossible as if being "right" ensures success. Unfortunately, complexity more frequently defeats good intentions.

One method for anticipating what can go wrong involves allocating time and resources for unbiased feasibility studies. A number of these chapters recount the failure of "in-house" feasibility studies to offer useful critique and, when needed, appropriate warning. As Robert Giloth recommends in his chapter on site selection, a set of more rigorous standards should guide these pre-project evaluations. A peer review process could also provide critical insights into program design, especially during project formation before resources are committed. Tools such as *pre-mortems* can help develop organizational skills to identify risks in advance and test key design and environmental assumptions.

Mistakes often grow out of an inability to see problems clearly when a project is underway. It is also at this stage that original plans must be altered and crisis situations require attention. Here it is important to distinguish mistakes related to simple human error from constructive failures. One can address human shortcomings; constructive failures require rethinking project strategy and expose significant gaps in knowledge.

Adaptation occurs when projects attempt mid-course corrections. As suggested in Chapter 1, the best kinds of mistakes stimulate corrective actions that address problems in design and consequently produce better results. Examples from this stage include changing strategies, altering program design, and redefining organizational roles. Successful adaptation asks difficult questions: Why did we fail and collapse? What did we do wrong? While reflecting on these questions helps to isolate problems and potential improvements, in nonprofit settings they may be swept under the rug as an embarrassment and a sign of weakness. Unusual leadership is needed to correct course in midstream, especially when expectations for mission outcomes remain the same.

Unfortunately, sometimes we can confront mistakes only when projects are ended and some time has passed. Project autopsies can reveal important malfunctions and contributors to failure. Yet we often shy away from taking a hard look at problems that could have been overcome with proper attention and just move on.

The Terrain of Success

At the outset of *Mistakes to Success*, we hoped that our diverse set of mistakes stories would yield important hypotheses about CED practice. What we have found instead is a set of dilemmas about social innovation that are relevant to a wide array of nonprofits as well as for-profit and public sector investors. Being successful and avoiding failure is not reducible to a set of unambiguous rules or guidelines. There are many lessons for dealing with mistakes, as these chapters illustrate, but applying these lessons and under what circumstances remains a challenge.

We have already discussed several key dilemmas—questions about best or promising practices and complexity. Scale represents another dilemma. If we just pursue pilot projects without thinking about scaling requirements, our efforts may remain small and inconsequential; however, going to scale without a good theory of change and adequate resources may result in few results and many frustrations. We have also seen that entrepreneurial, risk-taking leadership is necessary to get innovative projects, policies, and organizations off the ground. Yet this same leadership can be blind to political, market, and organizational realities, sometimes leading innovators and their organizations off the cliff. Picking good sites can make a difference, but even good sites will founder if the timing is wrong or the environment shifts. Finally, gathering adequate evidence itself is more problematic than many social researchers acknowledge. Can we do evidence-based innovation? And what if the evidence changes?

What this means for practitioners and investors is that we need to get even smarter and more realistic about the innovation and replication business. This will not guarantee success, but it will increase the probability that our future mistakes are more constructive and hence contribute more to our overall social learning about CED and other social policy endeavors.

Recommendations

A key finding from these mistakes stories is that no one organization bears all of the responsibility for preventing or learning from mistakes. Indeed, we have found it to be a mistake in CED when organizations and projects are not supported and held accountable by a web of stakeholders and investors. We offer recommendations for nonprofit practitioners, private and public investors, and policymakers.

For Practitioners

Document and analyze mistakes. Nonprofit practitioners are familiar with tracking program participants and producing reports on outcomes, but they rarely record tactical decisions, unexpected pressures, or unexpected activities. Actual problems are often mentioned briefly only as part of an overall success narrative. At the same time, practitioners are often aware through their on-the-ground experience of important influences that are not easily addressed by a grant or a logic model. Learning can spread through an organization, although usually for only a limited time due to changes and staff turnover. Most of the knowledge generated by constructive failures in community economic development rests with individuals, whether they are executive management, project coordinators, or community members. A careful documentation process is needed to capture these stories and can suggest a great deal about how to address design flaws, constraints, and capacity needs.

For Philanthropic Investors
Design outcome measures that capture learning about failed strategies and evidence of innovation. Grantmaking can be an important source of social venture capital that takes risks and demonstrates new ideas. One implication of a mistakes-focused approach is that privately funded CED projects should focus on gaps in knowledge and practice, instead of attempting to achieve high-level results through comprehensive and complicated initiatives. The temptation for philanthropy is to solve large-scale problems like poverty and inequity without attention to the smaller, Wright Brothers–type details of adjustment, curvature, and control. Much about learning from mistakes is engineering work, but it can ultimately lead to big breakthroughs.

For Public Investors at the Federal, State, and Local Level
Introduce mistakes reflection in funded services and carry innovations to larger delivery networks. Public funding agencies can play a larger role in generating knowledge derived from failure and at the same time encourage the spread of effective new ideas. Failure to transmit knowledge effectively remains a problem as we try to ensure that promising practices are more than "in the air." All investors, both public and private, can make room for funded projects to examine their actions and results honestly and help to educate the broader field about mistakes and lessons.

For Policymakers
Build a bank or clearinghouse of projects that allows for comparison and analysis of attempts and recoveries. Academics and business leaders rely on a wealth of information in books, journals, and professional associations. In contrast, nonprofit practitioners have few resources to

draw on. Literature about nonprofit operations exists but only in broad organizational terms, without the detail necessary for designing and testing particular projects. Trade publications and membership groups are rare, and a learning methodology can only go so far without these forms of knowledge resources.

The Way Forward

A first step is to collect and share relevant failure stories from our own field. The great need in the United States for solutions to poverty, job loss, and educational deficits calls into question the cycle of hidden mistakes that are repeated over and over. As practitioners and investors, we can no longer afford to soothe our consciences with good intentions and isolated examples of promising activity. Yet now we face a new policy environment that supports innovation and replication without fully acknowledging our legacy of constructive and nonconstructive mistakes.

Conversations about mistakes must continue. The *Mistakes to Success* meetings demonstrated that such candid discussions can occur among practitioners with encouragement and in a safe setting. Other potential forums include conference presentations and panels, Web-based networking sites, and ongoing seminars that combine thinking and doing. Many of the authors in this book are beginning to introduce more language about mistakes into their own communications and presentations to their colleagues.

Competition focused on innovation may also raise the profile of project failures as practitioners seek to understand what went wrong with their own projects and those being tried elsewhere. The prize in this case might be professional recognition, an organizational award, or a special grants program.

Even with incentives, telling stories about mistakes will not be easy. Engaging practitioners in self-disclosure will require "choice architecture" to alter behavior in the field (Thaler & Sunstein, 2008). Media used for talking about project failures should be secure and easy to use. Very few practitioners will be able to take the time to write a research article. Many more will be able to write about experiences on a blog or respond to a survey with a list of options, especially if project investors encourage them to do so. Defaults can also be set that continue to involve practitioners in forums for relating mistakes.

As mistakes are analyzed, we can delineate a more demanding set of questions and hypotheses for the community economic development field. At present there is no structure for doing this. One disheartening observation from these stories is the blurry line between constructive and nonconstructive mistakes, and how often matters of poor judgment and bad leadership prevent even a test flight. We should not ignore the importance of solid decision making and prudent leadership.

Pursuing a *Mistakes to Success* approach involves building a culture that values ongoing learning and testing. At the outset this will require gathering enough evidence of the corrective power of mistakes to influence the development and implementation of high-profile community economic development projects. But the challenge also falls to individuals. Learning more from mistakes will require support for a dedicated group of experimenters currently in the field and a training process for the next generation of investors and practitioners.

References

Crouch, T. D. (1989). *The bishop's boys: A life of Wilbur and Orville Wright*. New York: Norton.

Melendez, E. (2004). *Communities and workforce development*. Kalamazoo, MI: Upjohn Institute.

Thaler, R. H., & Sunstein. C. R. (2008). *Nudge: Improving decisions about health, wealth, and happiness*. New York: Penguin Books.

About the Authors

Colin Austin directs workforce development programs at MDC, Inc., in Chapel Hill, North Carolina, where he designs and manages projects related to career advancement for low-wage workers. He also conducts research on the changing Southern economy and workforce readiness, with a particular focus on immigrant labor.

Bob Brehm, executive director of Bickerdike Redevelopment Corporation from 1978 through 1994, has taught practitioners in community and organizational development and consulted for community groups.

Amy Brown, a senior consultant with the Aspen Institute's Economic Opportunities Program, currently focuses on asset development, scalability, and behavioral economics.

Karen Chapple is an associate professor of city and regional planning at the University of California, Berkeley, where she specializes in community and economic development, metropolitan planning, and poverty.

Susan Gewirtz is a senior associate at the Annie E. Casey Foundation. Her work focuses on economic advancement and family self-sufficiency. She participated in the implementation of Casey's Jobs Initiative and now directs a related effort, called the Center for Working Families.

Robert Giloth is vice president, Center for Family Economic Success, at the Annie E. Casey Foundation in Baltimore, Maryland. He has directed community development corporations in Baltimore and Chicago, served as a deputy commissioner of economic development with the City of Chicago, and written widely about community economic development. He also designed and managed the Casey Jobs Initiative and was site team leader for the start-up of five Making Connections sites.

Charles N. Goldberg is a senior analyst for the Commonwealth Corporation in Boston, Massachusetts. His most recent work includes evaluation studies of career path training, prisoner re-entry programs, and job retention and advancement projects.

Carolyn D. Hayden, president and founder of One World Consulting Group, LLC, has more than 25 years of executive experience in the nonprofit and for-profit sectors, and has provided strategic consulting services to foundations, nonprofits, and Fortune 500 companies. Her work focuses on documenting and building fields of practice, conducting research, strengthening organizational effectiveness, and creating cross-sector partnerships to address social and business needs. She also manages Opportunity Cars, a national network of more than 120 nonprofit organizations that promotes car ownership for working families as a strategy for improving employment and quality-of-life outcomes.

Neil Kleiman is director of policy and research at Living Cities. He was formerly vice president for policy and communications at Seedco and was the director of the Center for an Urban Future, a nonprofit public policy institute working on economic and workforce development issues in New York City.

Richard S. Kordesh is a fellow at the Great Cities Institute, University of Illinois at Chicago, and codirector of Illinois ResourceNet, a statewide capacity-building project focusing on nonprofit organizations and local governments. He also directed Illinois Workforce Advantage, an innovative, place-based community development project working with nine rural and urban communities, and maintains a lifelong career focus on public policy design and its impact on community development.

Kirsten Moy is director of the Economic Opportunities Program at the Aspen Institute, which promotes learning about highly promising poverty alleviation, self-employment, and employment strategies.

Emma Oppenheim is manager of workforce development policy initiatives at the National Council of La Raza, and previously was policy and research associate with Seedco.

Carla J. Robinson is an independent consultant. She previously served as a visiting fellow at the Lincoln Institute of Land Policy and has held positions at the National Housing Institute, the Center for the Study of Social Policy, and the United Way of Metropolitan Atlanta.

Robert O. Zdenek is an independent consultant in community development and cofounder of Common Bond LLP, which facilitates organizational partnerships. He has held a number of leadership positions in community development, including president of the National Congress for Community Economic Development, executive director of the Alliance for Healthy Homes, vice president of community building at United Way of America, and interim director of the National Housing Institute. In addition, he has taught community development at New School University for nearly a decade.